RUSKIN AND ST. MARK'S

1 The northwest angle of St. Mark's (reversed image), daguerreotype, probably 1852

JOHN UNRAU

Ruskin and St. Mark's

With 166 illustrations, 38 in color

THAMES AND HUDSON

For Olive, Cathleen, and John Ivan

© 1984 John Unrau

First published in the USA in 1984 by Thames and Hudson Inc.,
500 Fifth Avenue, New York, New York 10110

Library of Congress Catalog Card Number 83-72971

Typeset by August Filmsetting, Haydock, Merseyside.
Printed and bound in Great Britain by Balding & Mansell Ltd, Wisbech.

CONTENTS

Preface   7

1 TRUTH IN MOSAIC   9
   St Mark's and *The Stones of Venice*

2 THE GREAT CADENCE   51
   West front: large-scale considerations

3 BOUND WITH ALABASTER   61
   The west front: horizontally continuous
   or repeated features
   Plinths and associated mouldings   61
   Capitals   66
   Dentilled arches   71
   Carvings in low relief   72

4 A CONFUSION OF DELIGHT   75
   Porticoes and porches of the west front
   The northwest portico   75
   The first porch   84
   The second porch   90
   The wall piers at both sides of the third
   (central) porch   94
   The third porch   94
   The fourth porch   107
   The fifth porch   110
   The southwest portico   114

5 PEACOCK'S FEATHERS IN THE SUN   121
   The north and south sides

6 CHAPTERS TO BE WRITTEN   128
   The interior

7 ONE GREEK SCHOOL   171
   Studies of 1876–77: the mosaics

8 SERVILE AND HORRIBLE RIGIDITY 191
  The campaign against rebuilding

9 CONCLUSION 206

  Notes 212

  Bibliography 227

  List of illustrations 231

  Index 237

REFERENCES

Throughout this work, reference will be made to the Library Edition of *The Works of John Ruskin*, ed E.T. Cook and A. Wedderburn in 39 vols (1903–12). This edition will be referred to by volume and page number, thus (23.164).

The following abbreviations will be used for other published and unpublished works:

D.   *The Diaries of John Ruskin*, 3 vols, ed J. Evans and J.H. Whitehouse (Oxford, 1956–59).

RI.   *Ruskin in Italy: Letters to His Parents: 1845*, ed H.I. Shapiro (Oxford, 1972).

LV.   *Ruskin's Letters from Venice: 1851–52*, ed J.L. Bradley (New Haven, 1955).

BD.   *The Brantwood Diary of John Ruskin*, ed H.G. Viljoen (New Haven, 1971).

SMB. *St. M. Book* (Ruskin Galleries, Bembridge).

WS.   Ruskin's numbered architectural worksheets (mainly at Ruskin Galleries, Bembridge).

M.   Diary/Notebook for 1849–50 (Ruskin Galleries, Bembridge).

M2.   Diary/Notebook for 1849–50 (Beinecke Library, Yale University).

Add. Manuscripts described as 'Ruskin. Stones of Venice II. Chapter 4. Additional' (Pierpont Morgan Library, New York). Ruskin's pagination is followed.

Illustration references: monochrome in *italic*, colour in ROMAN.

PREFACE

ST. MARK'S is one of the world's great buildings, John Ruskin among the most visually acute of its admirers. Much of his description, depiction and analysis has remained unpublished, and the wide diffusion of the published references and drawings limits their usefulness for visitors to Venice. This book attempts a concise gathering of studies which maintain visual focus on the building. Here is a difficult and demanding Ruskin, with a unique gift for what Arthur Helps[1] described in 1874 as 'looking hard at things, and seeing more in them at once than the rest of us do' (BD.457–58). Nobody absorbing these analyses and drawings – if only to question his interpretations – could subsequently look at St. Mark's or any other building without new respect for the complexity of visual experience.

St. Mark's suffered extensive, indeed criminal, rebuilding in the nineteenth century. Ruskin's studies make it possible to document many of the alterations – especially to the fifth western porch and southwest portico – with accuracy. The survival of the remainder of the old west front can be credited largely to his inspiration, and verbal and financial backing, of protests which in the late 1870s halted the rebuilding that had irreversibly altered the north and south sides. Pollution continues the destruction left unfinished by nineteenth-century engineers. The photographs and catalogue entries in Wolfgang Wolters' *Skulpturen von San Marco in Venedig* (1979) show that the external sculpture had by the mid-1970s lost much of its surface articulation. In 1982 the west front was partially hidden behind a gigantic hoarding. Excellent though the latest campaign of preservation may prove to be, it would be optimistic to think that the church of St. Mark can withstand much longer the corrosive flatulence of 'St. Petroleum' (24.262). Ruskin's study of the façade in the mid-nineteenth century may – simply as archaeological documentation – prove a great legacy to admirers of the building.

There has been considerable and sometimes rather confident talk recently about 'taking Ruskin whole'. At a time when many manuscripts and letters and the majority of the drawings remain unpublished – often not even located – attempts at such feats of ingestion are surely somewhat premature. Though this book limits itself to a small segment of Ruskin's architectural study, important items – including even some drawings of St. Mark's listed in the Library Edition's fragmentary catalogue – have eluded all efforts at location.

7

Illustrations are provided where possible by Ruskin's drawings, and daguerreotypes and photographs known to have been in his collection. The external colour of St. Mark's has been greatly modified by restoration and pollution, and drawings by Ruskin, J.W. Bunney and H.R. Newman reproduced here can merely hint at what has been lost. Ruskin made few attempts to capture the interior colour on paper. Since that colour is in some respects finer now than in his day, when lighting arrangements produced a film of lampblack on the marbles and mosaics, it seemed appropriate to illustrate in colour a number of views which received his attention. Transparencies used for this purpose were taken in February 1982 under natural light such as that which illuminated Ruskin's studies during the winters of 1849–50, 1851–52 and 1876–77.

I have been helped at every stage of my work by James Dearden, Curator of the Ruskin Galleries. Jean Caslin, Jeanne Clegg and Brian Whittaker were generous with their time and expertise. For various help and encouragement I would also like to thank Kent Ahrens, David Alston, David Brown, Dinah Birch, David Blythe, Dorothy Bosomworth, Van Akin Burd, Herbert Cahoon, Andrea Carruthers, Richard Dellamora, Stuart Feld, Joan Fitzgerald, Kenneth Garlick, Bruce Hanson, John Hayman, Robert Hewison, Wolfgang Kemp, Joseph G. Links, Betty McAndrew, Eleanor Nicholes, John D. Rosenberg, Wilbur Ross, Harold Shapiro, Ian Sowton, Noli Swatman, Rachel Trickett, Marcus Whiffen, Catherine Wragge-Morley and Marjorie Wynne. Staff at the British and North American libraries listed in the bibliography, and the Biblioteca Marciana and Museo Civico Correr in Venice, were all most helpful. The pleasure of working at St. Mark's was increased by the unfailing courtesy of its custodians. For research grants which supported my studies, I am deeply indebted to the Social Sciences and Humanities Research Council of Canada and the Gladys K. Delmas Foundation. The colour reproductions were made possible by the generosity of the Delmas Foundation, as well as grants from the Office of the Dean and the Council of Atkinson College of York University in Toronto. I am grateful to all owners of Ruskin manuscripts for permitting me to quote previously unpublished passages, as well as to the Ruskin Literary Trustees, owners of the copyright in these materials, and their publishers, George Allen and Unwin Ltd., for kindly consenting to their publication. I wish to thank all owners of Ruskin drawings for allowing me to reproduce the works illustrated in this book. Finally, special thanks are due to Rachel Sharp, Susan Foley, Harold Brodie and my mother for their constant support.

I TRUTH IN MOSAIC
St Mark's and *The Stones of Venice*

Ruskin's introduction of St. Mark's in *The Stones of Venice* (1851–53) is one of the great moments in literature. A walk through dark, constricted lanes has led the traveller with mounting impatience, past modernized shop-fronts and lounging tourists,

into the shadow of the pillars at the end of the 'Bocca di Piazza,' and then we forget them all; for between those pillars there opens a great light, and, in the midst of it, as we advance slowly, the vast tower of St. Mark seems to lift itself visibly forth from the level field of chequered stones; and, on each side, the countless arches prolong themselves into ranged symmetry, as if the rugged and irregular houses that pressed together above us in the dark alley had been struck back into sudden obedience and lovely order, and all their rude casements and broken walls had been transformed into arches charged with goodly sculpture, and fluted shafts of delicate stone.

And well may they fall back, for beyond those troops of ordered arches there rises a vision out of the earth, and all the great square seems to have opened from it in a kind of awe, that we may see it far away; – a multitude of pillars and white domes, clustered into a long low pyramid of coloured light; a treasure-heap, it seems, partly of gold, and partly of opal and mother-of-pearl, hollowed beneath into five great vaulted porches, ceiled with fair mosaic, and beset with sculpture of alabaster, clear as amber and delicate as ivory, – sculpture fantastic and involved, of palm leaves and lilies, and grapes and pomegranates, and birds clinging and fluttering among the branches, all twined together into an endless network of buds and plumes; and in the midst of it, the solemn forms of angels, sceptred, and robed to the feet, and leaning to each other across the gates, their figures indistinct among the gleaming of the golden ground through the leaves beside them, interrupted and dim, like the morning light as it faded back among the branches of Eden, when first its gates were angel-guarded long ago. And round the walls of the porches there are set pillars of variegated stones, jasper and porphyry, and deep-green serpentine spotted with flakes of snow, and marbles, that half refuse and half yield to the sunshine, Cleopatra-like, 'their bluest veins to kiss' – the shadow, as it steals back from them, revealing line after line of azure undulation, as a receding tide leaves the waved sand; their capitals rich with interwoven tracery, rooted knots of herbage, and drifting leaves of acanthus and vine, and mystical signs, all beginning and ending in the Cross; and above them, in the broad archivolts, a continuous chain of language and of life – angels, and the signs of heaven, and the labours of men, each in its appointed season upon the earth; and above these, another range of glittering pinnacles, mixed with white arches edged with scarlet flowers, – a confusion of delight, amidst

2 St. Mark's from the west during the rebuilding of the north side, 1860–64

which the breasts of the Greek horses are seen blazing in their breadth of golden strength, and the St. Mark's lion, lifted on a blue field covered with stars, until at last, as if in ecstasy, the crests of the arches break into a marble foam, and toss themselves far into the blue sky in flashes and wreaths of sculptured spray, as if the breakers on the Lido shore had been frost-bound before they fell, and the sea-nymphs had inlaid them with coral and amethyst. (10.82–83)

2, XI This passage is almost as exciting as one's first glimpse of St. Mark's, evoking not only an uncanny sense of the spectator's movement toward the building, but a feeling that the stones of the Piazza are themselves charged with stirring life. Thus the Campanile, which is merely seen to 'rise higher & higher still' in Ruskin's first draft for the passage,[1] now 'seems to lift itself visibly forth', and throughout the rest of the description architectural features are presented as active entities. The dimension of depth, the shifting viewpoint, are captured with cinematic effect. Ruskin had first described the upper *3* 'arches that seem fringed with foam' immediately after his introduction of the 'long, low, pyramid of coloured light'.[2] Now these

3 Sculpture of the upper arches on the north side of St. Mark's

4 Central doorway of St. Mark's

5 Two of the horses of St. Mark's, *c.* 1880

2, 4
5, xxxvii carvings are singled out only at the end of his eastward movement and seen, not against the domes as they would be if viewed from the end of the square, but tossed 'far into the blue sky' of an upward perspective. Similarly, the bronze horses, standing before the bottom of the upper central arch in distant view, have moved up into lines of sight that range them against the 'arches edged with scarlet flowers' and 'glittering pinnacles'. A subtler coincident motion is that of the sun, implied in the shadow's 'stealing back' from the pillars. It is afternoon, and the viewer is now near enough to see the veins of the Proconnesian marble of many of the face shafts.[3] The predominantly horizontal striation of these marbles – which Ruskin, following a venerable tradition that will be adhered to in this book, usually refers to as alabaster[4] – must indeed in the early 1850s still have revealed the 'line after line of azure undulation' now clearly seen only in some columns of the atrium and interior (but see VII, lower left, and XXXIII, lower right, for a suggestion of the effect he describes).

Triumphant as an architectural evocation, the passage actually serves to undermine one of Ruskin's chief aims in writing *The Stones*

12

of Venice: the striking of 'effectual blows' at the 'pestilent art of the Renaissance' (9.47). His words here emphasize the role of the Renaissance arcades flanking the Piazza as visual frames for St. **2** Mark's. Their 'ranged symmetry', 'lovely order', and 'goodly sculpture' seem anything but pestilential in this context, while their optical subordination to the church ('struck back into sudden obedience') is as effective a reply as could be imagined to his harangue on Renaissance 'Pride' in the third volume of the *Stones*. The porches are 'ceiled with fair mosaic' — yet elsewhere the **XI** 'Renaissance' mosaics of four of them, and of all the upper storey, are furiously denounced. Finally, the sculpture surmounting the upper arches, repeatedly rebuked as corrupt Gothic yielding to Renaissance **3** contagion (9.44; 11.12–13), becomes in that final cadence the visual consummation of the entire façade. Ruskin's eloquence is such, however, that he and his readers remain unaware of such anomalies.

The fact is that while *The Stones of Venice* is one of the most brilliant, it is at the same time one of the silliest, books ever written about architecture. Invariably perceptive while maintaining visual focus on its subject, it lapses repeatedly into absurdity as Ruskin turns from the buildings to pontificate about the ethical attributes of the individuals and societies that created them.[5] Passages expressing architectural insight are so widely scattered — and then either enmeshed in grandiloquent generalization or relegated to quiet backwaters or appendices of the book — that the reader with architectural interests is apt to abandon it in frustration. Otto Demus, Ruskin's greatest successor in study of St. Mark's, does not even mention the *Stones* in the huge bibliography of his *Church of San Marco in Venice* (1960). Yet it is the reader intent on grasping the optical reality of buildings who loses most by ignoring Ruskin. His insights are too acute to deserve entombment in a comfortably 'Ruskinian' approach — Ruskin himself was deeply offended by it — which concentrates on the Master's sensitivity, complexity, style, 'genius': everything, in short, except those things external to Ruskin to which he wished to direct attention.

Even readers of the whole of the *Stones* might suppose that Ruskin's famous word-paintings of the façade and interior are based **pp. 9, 128** on inspired but rapid viewing of St. Mark's. They are in fact distilled from months of painstaking study, much of which has remained unpublished. Such drawings as survive confirm the care for accuracy apparent in the measurements and diagrams of the notebooks and worksheets.

Ruskin's powers of analytical viewing and precise draughtsman-ship were not easily gained. A tiny engraving represents what may **6**

6 *The west front of St. Mark's* (detail of engraving in Samuel Rogers' *Italy*) *c.* 1830

7 John Ruskin *St. Mark's from the southwest* 1835

well have been his first impression of the façade of St. Mark's. This travesty of Gentile Bellini's *Procession in St. Mark's Square*, engraved in Samuel Rogers' *Italy* (1830 ed.), came under Ruskin's magnifying glass sometime between his eleventh and fourteenth years.[6] In its distortion of every form – especially in that bustle of impossibly inflated domes – it is an apt accompaniment to Rogers' swollen verses, which were still bumbling through Ruskin's head when, at sixteen, he first visited Venice in 1835.[7] The city presents itself to the young devotee of Byron and Rogers as 'a monument, a tomb. / . . . . Along the moonlit pavement of St. Mark / The restless dead seem flitting through the gloom' (2.440). Profound thoughts about the 'Fall' of Venice – which were later to help 'carry off the dead weight' of the architectural analysis of the *Stones* (LV.81) – are already drearily eloquent in the sixteen-year-old's reflections on that 'shade of melancholy' upon Venice's beauty 'which is rapidly increasing, and will increase, until the waves which have been the ministers of her majesty become her sepulchre' (1.544). Though the colours of the doomed city attract him, the young Ruskin's descriptions are visually imprecise, and often ludicrous, as when he writes of 'columns of the richest material, variegated with innumerable colours, and their bases ornamented with mosaics of verd-antique and lapis lazuli' (1.545).

During this first visit he made a number of pencil sketches of Venetian scenes, later worked up into pen drawings of hard outline and fanciful perspective. One such pair shows St. Mark's from the southwest. The sketch is marginally preferable to its derivative, which exhibits every vice Ruskin came to loathe in architectural illustration. Aside from numerous distortions of form (note Ruskin's perky little dome, already too slim in the sketch; the emaciated columns; the taper given the so-called Pillars of Acre), the pen

14

8 John Ruskin *St. Mark's from the southwest* 1835

9 St. Mark's from the southwest, 1982

15

drawing is misleading in its rendering of texture and ornament. There is little indication of the incrustation of the façades; and the delicate inlaying of the upper Treasury wall, hinted at in the sketch, becomes a heavy coffering. The capitals could as easily be cabbages. Ruskin's attack in 1851 on a plate in H.G. Knight's *Ecclesiastical Architecture of Italy* (1842–44) applies perfectly to these drawings: 'every bit of the ornament . . . *is drawn out of the artist's head*' (9.431).[8]

The uncertainty of the youth's grasp of visual fact is still glaringly evident the following year in his defence of Turner's *Juliet and Her Nurse* against a critic's charge that 'the scene is a composition as from models of different parts of Venice, thrown higgledy-piggledy together' (3.636n). Ruskin retorts:

> The view is accurate in every particular, even to the number of divisions in the Gothic of the Doge's palace. (3.637)

Turner, who tactfully advised against publication of Ruskin's letter, must have been tickled by this line of defence. For, judged in the sense intended by Ruskin, the picture – even if we ignore the church of the Redentore, magnificently adrift on the left horizon some miles east of northeast of its present position – is astonishingly inaccurate. The west wing of the Doge's Palace, for example, which is considerably longer than the façade of St. Mark's, is in Turner's rendering scarcely half as long. Liberties taken with St. Mark's itself – notably in the proportions of the portals, placement of the upper arches, and shapes of the domes – are equally extreme. Small wonder that Ruskin later recalled his state of mind during this period as one of 'majestic imbecility' (35.182).

10 After J. M. W. Turner (engraved by G. Hollis) *St. Mark's Place, Venice – Juliet and her nurse* (detail) 1842

16

11 John Ruskin *Courtyard of the Doge's Palace* 1841

His second visit took place in 1841. Entranced by Venetian 'stage effect', he singles out the 'outline of St. Mark's against the twilight' (D1.184) and spends

a delicious afternoon . . . in St. Mark's [Square] – trying to get the local colour of the church. It was such a pleasure to have one's eye kept on those beautiful and strange details with the quiet sketching attention (D1.185).

Two days later he records: 'utterly spoiled my St. Mark's . . . . my eyes are bad, and I have got a headache with vexation' (D1.187). In *Praeterita* he says of the 1841 drawings:

they could not have been much better done. I knew absolutely nothing of architecture proper . . . but . . . was entirely certain and delicate in pencil-touch; and drew with an acuteness of delight in the thing as it actually stood, which makes the sketch living and like, from corner to corner. (35.296)

Another Venetian drawing of 1841, the *Courtyard of the Doge's Palace*, 11 justifies such praise. The delicacy with which it renders two of the domes makes one wish more had survived to tell of the visual pleasure he took in St. Mark's during this visit.

12 Southwest portico of St. Mark's from the west, daguerreotype, 1845–52

18

More rigorous studies begin in 1845. Planning the second volume of *Modern Painters*, and intending a fortnight's study in Venice of Titian and the Bellinis, he stays five weeks. One reason for lingering is his discovery of Tintoretto, the other his absorption in architecture, intensified by the restoration evident all over Venice. Though expecting before arrival to draw 'little architecture, if any, at Venice' (RI.197), he is soon so alarmed that he 'must stay a week more than I intended, to get a few of the more precious details before they are lost for ever' (RI.200).

I am but barely in time to see the last of dear old St. Mark's. They . . . are *scraping* St. Mark's clean. Off go all the glorious old weather stains, the rich hues of the marble which nature . . . has taken ten centuries to bestow – and already the noble corner farthest from the sea . . . is reduced to the colour of magnesia, the old marbles displaced & torn down (RI.201–2).[9]

In fact, the incrustation of the west front had been partially restored early in the eighteenth century (the green wall marbles of the central porch, favourites of Ruskin's, were placed in position in 1716),[10] and the thousand years' weathering had been modified as recently as the 1780s during a cleaning of the façade.[11] Nonetheless, many capitals were 'either scraped down, or cleaned with an acid' at this time (RI.203), and, on parts of the exterior, missing marbles were replaced by 'painted stucco' imitating alabaster (RI.224).[12] Despite a justified concern about such practices, there is something faintly amusing about the drama with which Ruskin invests his activities during this visit: 'I cannot draw here for the tears'; 'Venice *itself* is now nothing'; 'I must do what I can to save a little' (RI.200; 207; 208).

This notion of himself as last recorder of a doomed beauty hastens a new development in his drawing. A desire to analyse and grasp mentally what he records – henceforth Ruskin's distinctive strength as a draughtsman – appears for the first time. 'I am dreadfully particular about my details now', he writes, and 'have no pleasure in architecture at all unless I have all the designs of it' (RI.197). An architectural drawing 'is no use to me unless I have it right out & know all about it' (RI.207). This hunger for visual understanding brings both distress and increased pleasure. 'St Mark's . . . sets me aghast every time I go near it – since I have been studying architecture carefully, I see things about five times as beautiful as I used to do' (RI.218). On his twenty-fifth day in Venice Ruskin finally produces 'what I consider a good & useful drawing of part of the outside of St Mark's';[13] even so,

I fail 3 times out of four, I suppose from trying to do too much, & yet it is just this too much that I want, for as to taking common loose sketches in a hackneyed place like Venice, it is utter folly. (RI.219)

By 'too much' he means all the details of form and colour visible from a particular position, and, inevitably, he is soon 'reduced to knocking my fists together and moaning' (RI.218). Within a few days, however, he discovers an ally in

some most beautiful, though small, Daguerreotypes of the palaces I have been trying to draw – and certainly Daguerreotypes taken by this vivid sunlight are glorious things. . . . every chip of stone & stain is there – and of course, there is no mistake about *proportions*. (RI.220)

12, 13 The daguerreotype will allow him to 'regularly do the Venetians, book them in spite of their te[et]h' (RI.220). Among 'pet bits' specially taken for him were a number showing St. Mark's. Two days after leaving Venice, Ruskin writes from Padua:

I have been walking all over St Mark's place today, and found a lot of things in the Daguerreotype that I never had noticed in the place itself. It is such a happy thing to be able to depend on *everything* – to be sure not only that the painter is perfectly honest, but that he *can't* make a mistake. I have . . . booked St Mark's up, down, and round about. (RI.225)[14]

But the daguerreotype cannot capture the qualities that move him most deeply, 'the glorious old weather stains, the rich hues of the marble' (RI.201), and Ruskin complains: 'Venice has never yet been painted as she should, never', cursing 'That foul son of a deal board, Canaletti – to have lived in the middle of it all & left us *nothing*' (RI.209).

IV Problems encountered in his 1845 drawings result in new passages on architectural illustration in the third edition of *Modern Painters I* (1846). Bellini's *Procession* is 'the best Church of St. Mark's that has ever been painted' (3.210), providing 'faithful' evidence for 'conjecturing the former beauty of those few desecrated fragments, the last of which are now being rapidly swept away by the idiocy of modern Venetians' (3.209). While anticipating later writers in use of Bellini's painting as historical evidence,[15] Ruskin finds such works flawed as 'architectural drawing'. There is

little light and shade . . . so that, in rendering the character of the relieved parts, their solidity, depth, or gloom, the representation fails altogether, and it is moreover lifeless from its very completion, both the signs of age and the effects of use and habitation being utterly rejected (3.209).

This was written about the time of a fortnight's visit to Venice in May 1846, and he now asserts that though 'the reconciliation of true aërial perspective and chiaroscuro with the splendour and dignity obtained by the real gilding and elaborate detail, is a problem yet to be accomplished', with 'the help of the daguerreotype, and the

13 South wall of the Treasury of St. Mark's (reversed image), daguerreotype, 1845–52

lessons of colour given by the later Venetians, we ought now to be able to accomplish it' (3.210).

While Bellini and the daguerreotype give positive examples, Canaletto's

> miserable, virtueless, heartless mechanism . . . is . . . among the most striking signs of the lost sensation and deadened intellect of the nation at that time . . . . Professing the most servile and mindless imitation, it imitates nothing but the blackness of the shadows; it gives no single architectural ornament, however near, so much form as might enable us even to guess at its actual one (3.214–15).

A Canaletto in the Royal Collection shows the southwest portico at close range. For the actual capitals – the lower two lilies and upper four zigzags of the south face – Canaletto substitutes masses that look like bunches of long hair in pin-curlers. The columns of the portico are badly misproportioned.[16] But it is Canaletto's arbitrary colouring – or better, discolouring – in rendering the marbles that offends Ruskin most deeply.[17]

The brief 1846 visit exhibits an increasingly detailed approach to St. Mark's. A watercolour of the south side is preoccupied with

88, VIII

14

II

21

14 Antonio
Canaletto *Piazza
San Marco from the
Piazzetta* (detail)
1726–28

selected details rather than picturesque effect.[18] Numbers inscribed
on the drawing refer to supplementary sketches. At top right in the
drawing shown here is a 'Quadrant of the inner dark part of the 15
uppermost circle under the arch', its carving 'Entirely open: but
looks more like iron work than stone'. The other discs are 'plain
marble, but all surrounded by the usual Venetian moulding' (the
dentil, whose visual effect is carefully rendered in parts of the
watercolour, and analysed later in some detail). Ruskin's fig. 4 gives p. 71
the horizontal decorative band beneath the corresponding number,
and fig. 3 the disc seen in shadow a little lower, in the watercolour. A
diary entry concentrates on this latter disc:

In the details drawn in yellow paper book . . . in the circle marked three, III
the brown bands should be so shaped and so thick that the blue, green and
central yellow spaces should be nearly perfect circles, while the red and
outer yellow spaces should be rather pear shaped, the stalks inwards.
(DI.340)

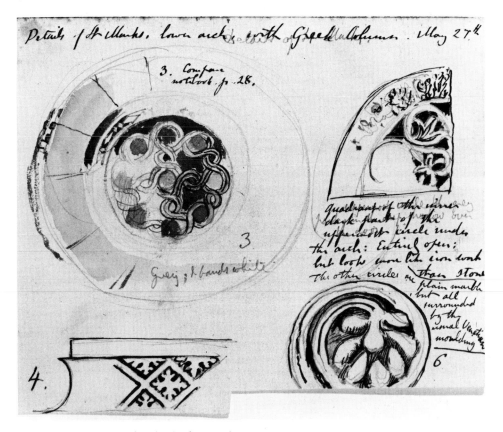

15 John Ruskin *Details of south side of St. Mark's* 1846

16 Southwest portico of St. Mark's from the loggia of the Doge's Palace (reversed image), daguerreotype, 1845–49

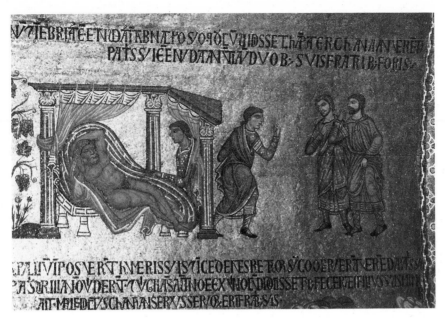

17 Mosaic of the Drunkenness of Noah in the atrium of St. Mark's

These new methods of study troubled John James Ruskin, who complained that his son, though 'drawing perpetually', was producing

no drawing such as in former days you or I might compliment in the usual way by saying it deserved a frame; but fragments of everything from a Cupola to a Cart-wheel, but in such bits that it is to the common eye a mass of Hieroglyphics – all true – truth itself, but Truth in mosaic. (8.xxiii)

Ruskin explains in *Praeterita* that while it would have been easy to persist in increasingly refined outline drawings of 'grand buildings and sublime scenes', he had become obsessed with 'learning more, and teaching what truth I knew'. Hence the 'now constant habit of making little patches and scratches of the sections and fractions of things in a notebook which used to live in my waistcoat pocket' (35.419).

The visual 'truth' Ruskin now investigates is not limited to colour and fine details. A searching look at the composition of the west front, accompanied by crude attempts at measurement, is recorded in the 1846 diary.[19] The porticoes of the northwest and southwest angles are also scrutinized, and with his daguerreotypes under his lens Ruskin taunts contemporary architects: 'There is more mind poured out in turning a single angle' of St. Mark's 'than would serve to build

p. 51, 52
16

25

a modern cathedral' (4.307). The diary also records a first response to the mosaics. Ruskin's interest in narrative and representation fixes inevitably on the Old Testament cycle in the atrium. The dreams of Pharaoh are 'quaintly told', while the Drunkenness of Noah is, in his splendid phrase, 'securely but vulgarly told' (D1.339).[20] His longest comment concerns the mosaic of the Flood, impressive in its treatment of

the ark seen through the rain; the rain is in close blue and white stripes, but through the blue the form of the ark is shown in brown; and because this, from its darkness, would escape notice, the square window of the ark is given in bright gold, which shows in vivid light with black and white border, between the stripes, having exactly the effect of a window lighted by reflected sunshine. The ponderousness of the rain, and the real existence of the object, though thus slightly hinted, are thus more impressively suggested than in any other instance I know. (D1.339)

Ruskin does not yet show any awareness that the mosaics may be part of a greater architectural or iconographical whole.

He did not return to Venice until 1849, but St. Mark's remained in his thoughts. In the spring of 1847 he read Lord Lindsay's *Sketches of the History of Christian Art* (1847), which contains a long section on Byzantine art and architecture, as well as the popular image of a morally 'fallen' Venice soon to be regurgitated in *The Stones of Venice* ('the widowed flag-staffs and the unpeopled piazza tell of a glory that has passed away, – there you are lost in a moral solitude').[21] In an article for the *Quarterly Review* (June 1847) Ruskin passes over the book's Byzantine section in silence, but his disagreement with the author's preference for northern over Italian buildings anticipates important aspects of his visual analysis of St. Mark's. Lord Lindsay, he says, underrates the influence of materials and lighting on design:

The accessibility of marble throughout North Italy . . . modified the aim of all design . . . . a marble surface receives in its age hues of continually increasing glow and grandeur; its stains are never foul nor dim; its undecomposing surface preserves a soft, fruit-like polish for ever, slowly flushed by the maturing suns of centuries. Hence, while in the Northern Gothic the effort of the architect was always so to diffuse his ornament as to prevent the eye from permanently resting on the blank material, the Italian fearlessly left fallow large fields of uncarved surface, and concentrated the labour of the chisel on detached portions, in which the eye, being rather directed to them by their isolation than attracted by their salience, required perfect finish and pure design rather than force of shade or breadth of parts; and further, the intensity of Italian sunshine articulated by perfect gradations, and defined by sharp shadows at the edge, such inner anatomy and minuteness of outline as would have been utterly vain and valueless under the gloom of a northern sky (12.197–8).

Memories of the veined marbles of St. Mark's are evident, too, in his xii, xv remark that it is a 'necessity in all fine harmonies of colour that many tints should merge imperceptibly into their following or succeeding ones' (12.239).

Ruskin's architectural reading,[22] and three months' intensive study of mediaeval buildings in Normandy in the autumn of 1848,[23] culminated in *The Seven Lamps of Architecture*, written and illustrated between November 1848 and April 1849. The 'Lamps' – a heterogeneous collection of nouns with positive associations, 'Sacrifice', 'Truth', 'Life', etc. – are related, often on the strength of Ruskin's eloquence alone, to descriptions and analyses of specific buildings and their details. Though the proportion of thought to verbiage in the book is rather low – long stretches are, in Ruskin's phrase of 1880, 'a mere mist of fine words' (8.17n) – its visual commentary shows him nearing the height of his analytical capacity.

In 'The Lamp of Power' the sculptured ornament of St. Mark's is praised for its subordination of detail to optically dominant forms. Because the dome had become the leading element in large-scale Byzantine design,

The decorative masses were thenceforward managed with reference to, and in sympathy with, the chief feature of the building. Hence arose, among the Byzantine architects, a system of ornament, entirely restrained within the superficies of curvilinear masses, on which the light fell with as unbroken gradation as on a dome or column, while the illumined surface was nevertheless cut into details of singular and most ingenious intricacy. (8.119–20)

Drawing analogies with thunder clouds, mountains, and trees – all of which gather multitudinous subdivisions of form into clearly defined masses – Ruskin insists upon 'that diffusion of light for which the Byzantine ornaments were designed' (8.120).[24] This anticipates his later and more detailed analysis of both Byzantine design and the superb sculpture of the central porch of St. Mark's which was so largely inspired by Byzantine traditions. The stone ball from this p. 105 porch which he etches to illustrate his argument is 'singularly 18, 70 beautiful in its unity of lightness, and delicacy of detail, with breadth of light' (8.121).

In 'The Lamp of Life', a celebration of irregularity in mediaeval design, Ruskin reproduces part of the panel under the main pulpit of 19 St. Mark's (the original, reversed in his etching, is at the north end of the west face of the panel):

a most singular instance both of rude execution and defied symmetry . . . . The imperfection (not merely simplicity, but actual rudeness and ugliness) of the leaf ornament will strike the eye at once: this is general in works of

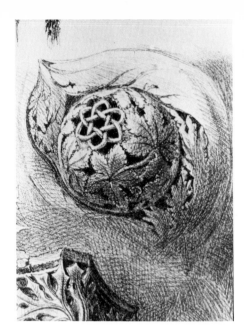

18 John Ruskin *Sculptured ball from the face of the outer central arch of St. Mark's* (*Seven Lamps*, 1849)

19 John Ruskin *Spandrel from a panel under the pulpit of St. Mark's* (reversed image; *Seven Lamps*, 1849)

the time, but it is not so common to find a capital which has been so carelessly cut; its imperfect volutes being pushed up one side far higher than on the other, and contracted on that side, an additional drill hole being put in to fill the space; besides this, the member *a* of the moulding, is a roll where it follows the arch, and a flat fillet at *a*; the one being slurred into the other at the angle *b*, and finally stopped short altogether at the other side by the most uncourteous and remorseless interference of the outer moulding: and in spite of all this, the grace, proportion, and feeling of the whole arrangement are so great, that, in its place, it leaves nothing to be desired; all the science and symmetry in the world could not beat it. (8.199–200)

p. 52 Such defiance of symmetry is not confined at St. Mark's to small details. A lengthy passage in the same chapter emphasizes the roles of asymmetry and irregularity in drawing the west front together visually. This analysis was based in part on his diary of 1846, but relied heavily on study of daguerreotypes, possibly including one surviving but damaged view of the whole façade.[25] He regrets that he 'cannot state the actual measures' of the great arches as he 'gave up the taking them upon the spot' in 1846, owing to 'their excessive complexity, and the embarrassment caused by the yielding and subsidence of the arches' (8.209).

Ruskin remedied such deficiencies in his visual documentation of

St. Mark's during a visit to Venice between November 1849 and March 1850. The progress of his study of the building – perhaps a third of that devoted to architecture during this stay – cannot be traced here in detail,[26] but a few glimpses provided by his wife Effie indicate the intensity of his concentration. On 27 November she finds him 'stretched all his length on the ground drawing one of a series of exquisite Alabaster columns surrounded by an admiring audience of idlers'.[27] The hundred-odd pages of diagrams, sketches, measurements and descriptions of the west front in the *St. M. Book*, cross-referenced to large worksheets, are begun in February 1850.[28] This work involved much awkward climbing – with Ruskin supplying his own ladders and a remarkable head for heights[29] – and moved Effie to comment on 24 February:

85, 86

84

John excites the liveliest astonishment to all and sundry in Venice and I do not think they have made up their minds yet whether he is very mad or very wise. Nothing interrupts him and whether the Square is crowded or empty he is either seen with a black cloth over his head taking Daguerrotypes or climbing about the capitals covered with dust, or else with cobwebs exactly as if he had just arrived from taking a voyage with the old woman on her broomstick. Then when he comes down he stands very meekly to be brushed down by Domenico quite regardless of the scores of idlers who cannot understand him at all.[30]

20 The west front of St. Mark's, daguerreotype, 1845 or 1852

The diagrams and measurements made during this study are so detailed that they can be used to pinpoint changes made to the façade after 1850 (see Chapter 4). Yet Ruskin makes surprisingly little use of them in either the chapter on St. Mark's in *Stones II* (first draft written in Venice, Nov. 1851 – early spring 1852; published 1853) or in his folio *Examples of the Architecture of Venice* (3 vols, issued between May and Nov. 1851).[31] Similarly, a number of careful worksheets studying details of the interior, and a scattering of manuscript text analysing the visual effect of the nave arcades, leave no echo in the *Stones*, though Ruskin prepared a ground plan[32] and several careful drawings keyed to these fragments. Though three huge plates in *Examples* give details of the exterior, another, probably engraved in 1851–52, was abandoned; two large companion drawings and a series of plans of the porches, intended for a volume of *Examples* to be devoted to the west front, were never published.[33]

Why did Ruskin abandon so much carefully gathered visual information? Editorial influence by his father played an important role. Neither the first volume of the *Stones* (1851) nor the three numbers of *Examples* were selling well, and John James Ruskin rightly concluded that the British public was no more excited than he by the intelligent introduction to structure and ornament provided by the former, or the detailed architectural plates of the latter. More rhetorical colour and spiritual uplift were clearly needed, and Ruskin, responding to parental concern, found himself 'continually forced to abridge and simplify my designs' for the *Stones* (LV.50) in attempting to 'really make this second volume as popular as I can' (LV.81). Consequently, the chapter on St. Mark's, though a magnificent piece of writing, fails to do justice to his visual study of the building. Furthermore, his rash attempt – on the basis of an acquaintance with Venetian examples alone – to enunciate general 'laws' for Byzantine architecture (paragraphs 23–47), while containing splendid insights, is also notable for errors and contradictions of the kind he falls into so often when he takes his eye off his subject. Ruskin yielded only grudgingly to John James's popularizing impulse, however, convinced that in doing so he was evading a duty he was uniquely qualified to fulfil.[34]

Another reason for the change of emphasis was Ruskin's frustration in attempting to provide illustrations which were worthy of his descriptions and analyses. He undertook extraordinary labours not only in preparing drawings, but in supervising his engravers. The gigantic plates in *Examples* required 'two new drawings to be made of every subject; one a carefully penned outline for the etcher, and then a finished drawing upon the etching' (9.9), and Ruskin was

21

XXIII, *108*

45, 64, 88

82

V, VIII

43, 57, 60, 78

p. *149*

St Marks.

In the Nave: there are three great shafts on each side carrying stilted arches. Of these the bases are remarkable first for the appearance of a band a ring about the bottom of the shaft: so completely resembling an addition for protection that I at first supposed it so: it is a – b in section: projecting more or less: in one or two of the shafts hardly ¼ an inch, in others an inch. It is a separate slab put under the shaft – the section is confused both at a and b by the mortar: it is decidedly ungraceful.

The fillet c d seems to have been intended for a contrast – but it slopes outwards more or less: sometimes considerably.

The lores . b c . & h . are very flattened and rude semicircles. perhaps from wear . h i . k l are two simple square slabs which bear the circular upper members: The section is of course through the side . h g . becoming long at the angle.

In the third, that next the central dome, on the right hand as one enters, there angles are occupied by heart-shaped poupées, the germs of those of the Doges palace as shown above at B. – but entirely without decoration – heavy . blunt pointed . and reminding one a little of a shoe sole. The measures of the entire base are very various – but on an average are

One side of sq. of lower slab . at l . or k .	3	"	2.
—— ——— —— upper —— – i or h .	2	"	10
Circumference at f		7	"	8½
Breadth of the root of each of four leaves out of that circumference on the 3rd shaft . —		"	10
Height . l k . from ground; red verona marble.		——	6 . vary to 8.
—— i h : white sugary marble . From . i . all is worked in a block up to b.		——	5 . vary to 7 – 6½
Height h b . approximately . ——		"	11
Roll . g f . ——		.	6½
Concave . c d : Note the descent from c . —		"	5
Roll . c b . ——		"	4
Circumference of shaft at a ——	6	"	vary to 6 . 2.
Fillets . c f . c d . both about . ——		"	1
Fillet a b . ——		"	4
Interval between main shafts at level a	8	"	10

No 20. St Marks.   Pillars of Nave.
Nov. 20th 1849

21 John Ruskin *Study of bases in the nave of St. Mark's* (Worksheet 20) 1849

dissatisfied with the results. Some plates turned out 'too black' (LV.270), and a drawing for the ambitious plate of the southwest portico of St. Mark's was 'spoiled by cross shadows and very vile' (38.298). Even the small plates for *Stones I* caused 'a great deal of worry with engravers' (LV.170), such worry becoming acrimonious at times in his assessment of work by England's finest engravers on the second and third volumes. R.P. Cuff, for example, receives a stinging letter about a proof for the fourth plate in volume II. After a withering reference to Cuff's slowness, Ruskin says the plate is 'much improved' over an earlier version

and will do very well – but please in future recollect never to execute any plate for *me* in the same way again. You have taken great pains and displayed much wonderful mechanical skill – the imitation of the piece of marble in the middle is wonderful – but mind in future never to make your textures in the shadows Sandy . . . .

Ruskin then provides sketches of magnified engravers' strokes showing how Cuff's shadows 'ought to have been' executed. Enclosing four Turner engravings containing 'textures I like', Ruskin warns: 'Do not let me have to explain this to you any more'.[35] Cuff must have hearkened, for in March 1852 Ruskin praises his work on a later plate (possibly the twelfth in *Stones II*):

Cuff's experiment most excellent: you [JJR] rightly find fault with the want of the little refinements in distribution of shades – but these things can never be expected in a copy – If these refinements *were* perceived and followed – Cuff would cease to be Cuff – and become Ruskin – All that can be hoped for is the diligent *try* to follow, and the care in measurements and other such mechanical points, as well as delicacy in execution, all which this engraving has in a high degree . . . .

Nevertheless, it will have to be done over again (LV.221).

Even the great J.H. Le Keux (1812–96) receives criticism of a proof for plate 2 of *Stones II*: 'I took pains with this drawing – & I must have it facsimiled'.[36] Subsequently, Ruskin orders a number of new plates (including 8, 10, and 11 of *Stones II*), while rejecting a proof of the famous lily capital:

it would take both me and you a vast amount of trouble to get it to what I want. and I cannot now afford the time. It is, to my eye, rather coarse & hard – not free – it is very good – but this capital was to be the subject of great praise – and unless it came very beautiful – I cannot use it.

Ruskin explains that 'many of the *curves* are wrong for one thing', and finds Le Keux's stylized depiction of shadow in 'a recess in white marble' no substitute for 'the most delicate tints of which the graver is capable'. Recognizing that he is making unprecedented visual

Continued on p. 49

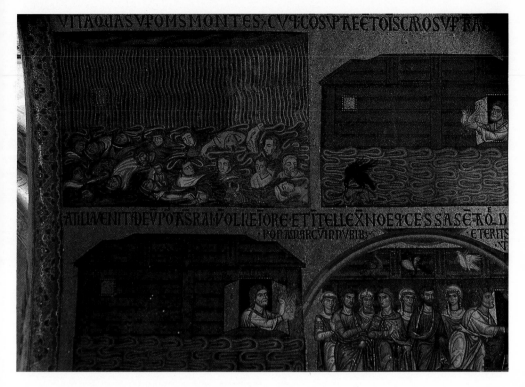

1   Mosaic of the Flood in the atrium of St. Mark's, 1982

27th Nov. 1845.

II (left) John Ruskin *South side of St. Mark's after rain* 1846

III John Ruskin *Detail of the south side of St. Mark's* 1846

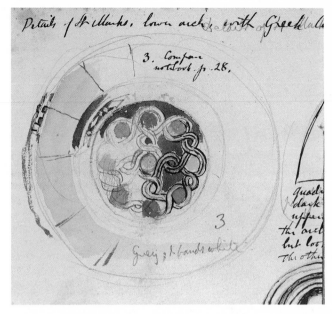

IV Gentile Bellini *Procession of the Cross in St. Mark's Square* (detail) 1496

V (left)   John Ruskin *Northwest angle of the façade of St. Mark's,* 1852

VI   First porch of St. Mark's from the west, 1982

VII   Window and spandrel of the second porch of St. Mark's, 1982

VIII (left)   John Ruskin
*Southwest portico of St. Mark's
from the loggia of the Doge's
Palace* probably 1849

IX   John Ruskin *Study of a
zigzag capital of the southwest
portico (St. M. Book)* 1850

X   South façade of St. Mark's,
1982

XI   J.W. Bunney *The west front of St. Mark's* 1877–82

XII West and south walls of the Treasury of St. Mark's, 1982

XIII Old marbles framed by nineteenth-century replacements on the north side of St. Mark's, 1982

XIV (right) Looking east from the south nave aisle, beside the Baptistery door, 3 p.m., 9 February 1982

xv   North arcade of the nave from the south nave aisle near the Baptistery door, noon,
5 February 1982

XVI Mosaic of King David in the south nave aisle, 4.30 p.m., 12 February 1982

XVII   Looking over the screen into the eastern dome, 10.30 a.m., 9 February 1982

XVIII   The central dome and part of the eastern dome, 9.30 a.m., 11 February 1982

XIX   The interior from south of the west central door, 1.30 p.m., 9 February 1982

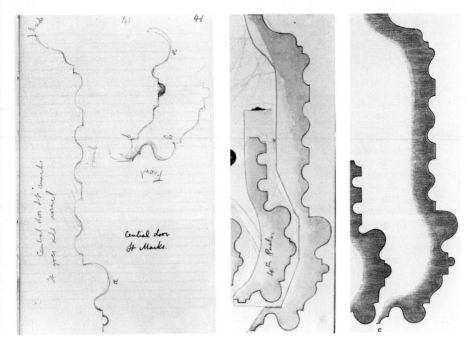

22 John Ruskin *Study of the moulding of the central door of St. Mark's (Bit Book)* 1850–52

23, 24 John Ruskin *Plan of the moulding of the central door of St. Mark's* 1852–53 (left 1852–53; right *Stones III*, 1853)

demands, he concludes that though he cannot use it, 'I see that great pains have been taken with the present plate and shall most willingly pay what it has cost – knowing that these failures are unavoidable'.[37] This must have stung Le Keux into redoubled effort, for a magnificent plate of the lily capital – surely the most sensitive architectural engraving of the nineteenth century – graces the second volume of the *Stones*.[38]

Despite this and a few lesser successes, Ruskin was deeply disappointed with the illustrations of the *Stones* – especially the crowded plates of capitals, bases, mouldings and other details abstracted from his drawings. The fate of one moulding, on the left jamb of the central door of St. Mark's, is representative. Ruskin begins his pencil sketch, top left, at the 'Inside', runs out of paper two-thirds of the way through, and completes the sketch, with two versions of the moulding as seen below *a*, out to the 'Front' of the jamb, mid-right. Though this jamb is now in a sorry state, it is still possible to read Ruskin's sketch closely against the bottom of the moulding as one stands beside it. In his ink drawing for the engraver Ruskin lines up the outside edges with a ruler, and, while most of the curves are reproduced with tolerable accuracy, several are distorted. Note the deeper bite of the top two concave curves and also the way in which the first convex curve above *a* in the pencil sketch is, in the ink drawing, pinched in upon itself. The published version compounds these distortions. The small convex curve below *a* in the sketch has been transformed into a jigsaw-puzzle extrusion, the second convex curve from the top has been much tightened, and almost every entry of a straight into a curved line has been modified. While the printed *Stones* version is still recognizable against the moulding, an attentive eye will quickly detect its vulgarization of the original. Though few of his readers would have noticed such inaccuracies, Ruskin was not – where optical fact was at issue – one to be satisfied with slovenliness. The text of the *Stones* frequently criticizes its plates,[39] and he later hoped to reissue the book with new illustrations.[40]

When he came to accept that *Examples* would have to be suspended after only three of its projected twelve volumes (LV.66) had been published, and that the *Stones* could only be made a popular success by replacing much of his visual analysis with a dramatic historical plot and those passages of 'improving' prose which have lengthened so many school speech days, Ruskin made a desperate effort to cram some of his analytical work into a 'Final Appendix' (11.265–88), the bleak pages of which were so seldom even cut by purchasers of the book (11.xxii). Looking back morosely on the whole undertaking, he remarks in *Praeterita* that research for the *Stones* had left 'Six hundred quarto pages of notes for it, fairly and closely written, now useless. Drawings as many – of a sort; useless too' (35.483). That the remnants relating to St. Mark's are far from useless, constituting a significant and – in a real sense – new contribution to our understanding of one of the world's great buildings, it is one of the aims of the following five chapters to demonstrate.

2 THE GREAT CADENCE
West front: large-scale considerations

RUSKIN asserts in *The Seven Lamps* that the west front of St. Mark's is, 'in its proportions, and as a piece of rich and fantastic colour, as lovely a dream as ever filled human imagination' (8.206). An architect, George Wightwick, responded: 'To *us* it is a very *un*-lovely nightmare. . . . we think it extremely ugly'.[1] The chief ground for this difference in taste is summed up in one phrase from Ruskin's description: 'a confusion of delight'. To tidy minds, the concepts of confusion and delight are mutually exclusive. Ruskin, on the other hand, always revelled in the sins committed by the artist against optical precision. His belief that 'All beautiful lines are drawn under mathematical laws organically *transgressed*' (29.81) typifies his response not only to organic forms, but also painting and large- and small-scale architectural design. It explains his loathing of the precise 'restoration' of mediaeval structure and ornament by engineers such as Eugène Viollet-le-Duc and G.B. Meduna, chief architect of St. Mark's during the disastrous rebuilding of the 1860s and 1870s (see Chapter 8), and is based on an understanding of facts about visual perception which the Gestalt psychologists were only to begin studying a generation later.[2]

p. 9

The west façade of St. Mark's first captured Ruskin's analytical attention in 1846, when he noted in his diary its 'amazing variety of composition' (D1.339). None of the arches of the four lateral porches sweeps a full semicircle. The northern two, however, 'approach so nearly to it as to make one suspect that the others . . . must have yielded'. The difficulty of estimating magnitude in viewing these arches intrigues Ruskin:

56
79

> It seems to me that of the two lateral arches of the lower storey the outermost is the widest, but the look of this again is most marked in the southern pair; and it is rendered doubtful by the innermost rising highest towards the cornice, which makes it look narrower. I paced them, but on twelve paces the extra space tells little and could not be proved, especially as the columns are differently set under the arch. (D1.339)

Strangest of all, the porticoes at the north and south ends 'are entirely different in proportion, the southern one being both lower beneath the cornice and considerably wider than' its counterpart, and 'having no under arch, but being open through, and its columns I think lighter'. The four lateral arches of the upper storey are also unequal,

25

9

25 St. Mark's from the west, 1860–65

the inner pair in this case being wider. Ruskin suggests that this
inequality, together with a subtle shift of the upper arches toward the
centre relative to their lower counterparts, gives a 'pyramidal, yet
varied, arrangement to the whole' (D1.340).

25

From this perceptive beginning, he moves on in the *Seven Lamps*
to a detailed analysis which is the more remarkable for having been
written without further viewing of the building itself:

The entire front is composed of an upper and lower series of arches,
enclosing spaces of wall decorated with mosaic, and supported on ranges of
shafts of which, in the lower series of arches, there is an upper range
superimposed on a lower. Thus we have five vertical divisions of the
façade; *i.e.* two tiers of shafts, and the arched wall they bear, below; one tier
of shafts, and the arched wall they bear, above. In order, however, to bind
the two main divisions together, the central lower arch (the main entrance)
rises above the level of the gallery and balustrade which crown the lateral
arches.

The proportioning of the columns and walls of the lower storey is so
lovely and so varied, that it would need pages of description before it could
be fully understood; but it may be generally stated thus: The height of the
lower shafts, upper shafts, and wall, being severally expressed by *a*, *b*, and *c*,
then *a*:*c*::*c*:*b* (*a* being the highest); and diameter of shaft *b* is generally to the
diameter of shaft *a* as height *b* is to height *a*, or something less, allowing for

52

the large plinth which diminishes the apparent height of the upper shaft: and when this is their proportion of width, one shaft above is put above one below, with sometimes another upper shaft interposed: but in the extreme arches a single under shaft bears two upper, proportioned as truly as the boughs of a tree; that is to say, the diameter of each upper = 2/3 of lower. *12, 30* There being thus the three terms of proportion gained in the lower storey, the upper, while it is only divided into two main members, in order that the whole height may not be divided into an even number, has the third term added in its pinnacles. So far of the vertical division. The lateral is still more subtle. There are seven arches in the lower storey; and, calling the central arch *a*, and counting to the extremity, they diminish in the alternate order, *a, c, b, d*. The upper storey has five arches, and two added pinnacles; and these diminish in *regular* order, the central being the largest, and the outermost the least. Hence, while one proportion ascends, another descends, like parts in music; and yet the pyramidal form is secured for the whole, and, which was another great point of attention, none of the shafts of the upper arches stand over those of the lower.

It might have been thought that, by this plan, enough variety had been secured, but the builder was not satisfied even thus: for . . . always calling the central arch *a*, and the lateral ones *b* and *c* in succession, the northern *b* and *c* are considerably wider than southern *b* and *c* [here Ruskin errs slightly; see below], but the southern *d* is as much wider than the northern *d*, *p. 54* and lower beneath its cornice besides; and, more than this, I hardly believe that one of the effectively symmetrical members of the façade is actually symmetrical with any other. (8.208–9)

Unpublished notes written between 1849 and 1852 carry the analysis further. Up to the level of the gallery the façade is

composed of the five great vaults or porches which protect the doors, with the broad piers that sustain them. The Vaults (the second & fourth being waggon vaults, the rest, half domes) are covered with mosaic. the spandrils sheeted with white alabaster. and each adorned by a single oblong panel of *xi* sculpture: The massy piers being first sheeted with alabaster. and then entirely veiled by two ranges one on the top of the other of marble & porphyry pillars (Add.46).

The porticoes at the ends of the façade contain

vaults of the same height – but of less than half the width of the great porches, [and] are added, partly to give greater space to the upper gallery – partly to give more complicated proportion to the arch series of the façade, which by their addition, is arranged in a proportion of seven terms instead of five. . . . The reader cannot but feel the value of the finishing notes, as it were of the great cadence, given by the two small flanking arches (Add.50).

The rectangular panels of sculpture set in the spandrels also help secure 'a harmonious relation among the parts'. They are 'set in two surges or waves – instead of on a horizontal line – in order to connect the three flanking arches more closely: and emphasize them: the intermediate panel being set highest' (Add.52). Next,

103 the upper part of the church – which rests on the nave walls (xyyz in the plan) is not of the Byzantine period: It was originally round arched like all the rest – as may still be seen in the not inaccurate representation of it in the xxxi old mosaic of the first porch; but was raised into ogee curves & decorated with niches in the Gothic times (Add.46).

Ruskin also notes the effect of the domes. Domes are native to 'the East', where their aim is 'to concentrate light upon their orbed surfaces', and where 'the bulging form may be also delightful, from the idea of its enclosing a volume of cool air'. But their 'chief charm is, to the European eye, that of strangeness', and at St. Mark's they are delightful largely because of their context:

I enjoy them in St. Mark's chiefly because they increase the fantastic and unreal character of St. Mark's Place; and because they appear to sympathize with an expression, common, I think, to all the buildings of that group, of a natural buoyancy, as if they floated in the air or on the surface of the sea. (9.183–4)

But it is the irregularity of 'the whole arrangement . . . in which the builder has varied every magnitude in this *generally* symmetrical composition' (Add.50) that strikes Ruskin most forcibly. Thus the arch of the north portico is 'both narrower & higher than [that of] the south', and this 'difference in width is balanced by a greater interval between it & the first porch'. (The restorers were soon to 'correct' this mediaeval refinement by widening the southern pier; compare *2, 25,* xi pre-restoration photographs with a later view.)[3] The arch of the first *56* porch is 'half a foot broader' than the second (Ruskin's figures are 20 ft and 19 ft 6½ in.), but 'is a flatter arch – & does not touch the gallery above', while its neighbour does, 'and therefore looks much *79* narrower than it really is'. The arch of the fifth porch 'is not flattened so as to fall short of the gallery – but – which answers the same purpose – widened by eight inches: measuring 20 ft 8 in', while the fourth 'measures only 19 ft 10 in'. Thus, while one's first impression is

of a central mass, with a pair of equal minor masses and one terminal; still smaller on each flank: – that is to say such arrangement as is expressed in a closer form in the leaf group – a

26, 27

– the more subtle effect upon the eye is that of the leaf group *b.* in which each intermediate lobe of the lateral series expands. & becomes a centre to the flanking group. (Add.51)

54

It must be pointed out that in a shortened discussion of these arches in Chapter 5 of *Stones II* Ruskin fiddles his numbers to bolster his claim that the builders display 'an intense perception of harmony in the relation of quantities' (10.153): the 'space' of the two archivolts flanking the central porch being given as 19 ft 8 in. and that of the succeeding pair as 20 ft 4 in., with Ruskin praising this 'subtle difference of eight inches on twenty feet' (10.153). A conscience-stricken footnote admits these are averages: 'of the two arches stated as 19 ft. 8 in. in span, one is in reality 19 ft. $6\frac{1}{2}$ in., the other 19 ft. 10 in., and of the two stated as 20 ft. 4 in., one is 20 ft. and the other 20 ft. 8 in.' (10.153n). In the manuscript for the *Stones* Ruskin had at first contemplated 19 ft 6 in. for the two arches flanking the central porch and 20 ft 6 in. for the succeeding pair: figures even more arbitrary – if less 'subtle' – than the averages finally published. Temptation arose because, unlike Ruskin's other measurements of the west front, these depended partly on visual estimates. Photographs indicate why. 56, 62 Only with the help of a heady assistant, using ladders resting against the delicate Ice Plinth, and keeping a tape taut across a span of 20 to 30 p. 66 feet, could direct measurements be taken. Ruskin's alternative for the first porch was used for all five: 'from wall pier to wall pier is 22 ft 6 56 in. The arch falls more than a foot on each side – especially on Clock [north] side within it. I should estimate it at 20 ft. for pure span' (SMB.52l). While Ruskin's figure of 22 ft 6 in. for the opening between the wall piers is probably as accurate as his other direct measurements (my figure, taken at the base in 1982, was 22 ft $7\frac{1}{4}$ in., but the porch was restored in the late nineteenth century and again in the early twentieth), the process by which he guesses some $2\frac{1}{2}$ ft off it seems crude at best.[4]

Happily, both the method whereby he arrived at, and the use to which he put, these elastic numbers are most untypical of Ruskin's study of St. Mark's. Some two hundred of his measurements of the lower storey of the west front were checked in 1980. The overwhelming majority still tallied within narrow limits,[5] and cases of disagreement – especially in parts of the first and fifth porches, and the southwest portico – can be confidently attributed to restoration. Ruskin's hundreds of careful measurements of the dimensions of piers, columns, plinths, doors, bases, and of the carved archivolts within the four lateral porches, all tell of asymmetry within a superficially symmetrical arrangement. He believes that the subliminal tension caused by such irregularity draws 'the whole building . . . into one mass' (8.205) in the observer's eyes,[6] and, realizing that such a claim would seem far-fetched to the 'pontifical rigidities of the engineering mind' (15.174n), points out that

28 Atrium of St. Mark's, 1860–65

29 View from northwest, 1860–65

The eye is continually influenced by what it cannot detect; nay, it is not going too far to say, that it is most influenced by what it detects least. Let the painter define, if he can, the variations of lines on which depend the changes of expression in the human countenance. The greater he is, the more he will feel their subtlety, and the intense difficulty of perceiving all their relations, or answering for the consequences of a variation of a hair's breadth in a single curve. Indeed, there is nothing truly noble either in colour or in form, but its power depends on circumstances infinitely too intricate to be explained, and almost too subtle to be traced. And as for these Byzantine buildings, we only do not feel them because we do not *watch* them (10.154).

Ruskin is convinced, too, of the falsity of one of the nineteenth century's most famous dogmas, that '*there should be no features about a building which are not necessary for convenience, construction, or propriety*', and that '*all ornament should consist of enrichment of the essential construction of the building*'.[7] St. Mark's flouts such restrictions as blatantly as it disdains precise axial symmetry. Its north and south porticoes, for instance, are 'of *no use whatever* except to consummate the proportions of the façade' (10.153). The number and beauty of the façade columns lead him to suggest that

Exactly in proportion to the importance which the shaft assumes as a large jewel, is the diminution of its importance as a sustaining member; for the delight which we receive in its abstract bulk, and beauty of colour, is altogether independent of any perception of its adaptation to mechanical

56

necessities. Like other beautiful things in this world, its end is to *be* beautiful; and, in proportion to its beauty, it receives permission to be otherwise useless. . . . [At St. Mark's, therefore,] we must be constantly prepared to see . . . with admiration, shafts of great size and importance set in places where their real service is little more than nominal, and where the chief end of their existence is to catch the sunshine upon their polished sides, and lead the eye into delighted wandering among the mazes of their azure veins. (10.102–3)

The 'unstructural' nature of the façade columns is proven by the fact that many, 'left visibly with half their capitals projecting beyond the archivolts they sustain', are 'little more than mere bonds or connecting rods between the foundation and cornices' (in the atrium, *28* some are entirely free-standing). Indeed, 'the whole system of architecture' of St. Mark's 'is in great part to set forth the beauty and value of the shaft itself' (10.448).[8]

In 1850, Ruskin measured the dimensions and relative positions to each other, to the piers or backing walls, and to the outer edge of the plinth on which they stand, of the shafts and bases of the first storey of the west front. This work, together with measurements of the shafts and many of the bases of the second storey, prompted some general observations:

the upper range is about two thirds of the height of the lower. The fact is that the proportions are continually varying – for though the architrave & plinths are always at the same height, the shafts . . . by no means match each other, and their differences are accommodated by the help of the goodnatured capitals & bases – which stretch or shorten themselves as need may be. But this very difference of size only delights the architect the more by enabling him to confuse the eye among changing proportions. (Add.x–9)

63, 70
XXXIII

The difficulty of obtaining perfectly matching columns from a collection of spoils was converted by the architect from apparent disadvantage into aesthetic triumph:[9]

His only means of obtaining [precise] symmetry will . . . be, in cutting down the finer masses to equality with the inferior ones; and this we ought not to desire him often to do. And therefore . . . we must expect to see shafts introduced of size and proportion continually varying, and such symmetry as may be obtained among them never altogether perfect, and dependent for its charm frequently on strange complexities and unexpected rising and falling of weight and accent in its marble syllables: bearing the same relation to a rigidly chiselled and proportioned architecture that the wild lyric rhythm of Aeschylus or Pindar bears to the finished measures of Pope. (10.104)

Ruskin records his response to this 'lyric rhythm' within a horizontal range of capitals and shafts in a number of drawings.

126
4, 42
51, 81

Relationships established through superimposition are even more intriguing. The *St. M. Book* contains many diagrams showing the idiosyncratic placement of one range of columns over another. Since the shafts of the first storey average about 9 ft, the second about 7 ft, in height, with their girth varying from 4 ft 6 in. for the largest of the lower range, to 2 ft for the smallest of the upper, the upper shafts are necessarily 'more numerous than the lower' (10.449). Ruskin, anticipating modern speculation, relates the superimposition at St. Mark's to that of 'the Pisan Romanesque' (9.245).[10] Critics are wrong to think this arrangement 'barbarous':

Nothing is more singular than the way in which this kind of superimposition . . . will shock a professed architect. He has been accustomed to see, in the Renaissance designs, shaft put on the top of shaft, three or four times over, and he thinks this quite right; but the moment he is shown a properly subdivided superimposition, in which the upper shafts diminish in size and multiply in number, so that the lower pillars would balance them safely even without cement, he exclaims that it is 'against law,' as if he had never seen a tree in his life.

Not that the idea of the Byzantine superimposition was taken from trees, any more than that of Gothic arches. Both are simple compliances with laws of nature, and, therefore, approximations to the forms of nature. (10.449)

As studies in the *St. M. Book* demonstrate, the scheme of superimposition at St. Mark's puts the two storeys into relationships that prevent the eye from imposing precise patterns on what it sees. None of the upper shafts is 'either exactly in, or positively out of, its place' (8.205) in relation to the lower tier, and such teasing irregularity aids further in the perceptual binding of the building.[11]

42, 51

While horizontal and vertical relationships between the columns are of great optical importance, Ruskin is equally insistent upon the role of the columns in articulating the dimension of depth. He had criticized Bellini's painting for its relative lack of 'light and shade . . . in rendering the character of the relieved parts' (3.209). The fault is severe in Ruskin's eyes, because the three-dimensional interplay between column and wall has a decisive influence on the chiaroscuro and colour of the façade:

IV

4, 25, 29
XI, XXXI

the position here given to it [the shaft], within three or four inches of a wall from which it nevertheless stands perfectly clear all the way up, is exactly that which must best display its colour and quality. When there is much vacant space left behind a pillar, the shade against which it is relieved is comparatively indefinite, the eye passes by the shaft, and penetrates into the vacancy. But when a broad surface of wall is brought near the shaft, its own shadow is, in almost every effect of sunshine, so sharp and dark as to throw out its colours with the highest possible brilliancy; if there be no sunshine, the wall veil is subdued and varied by the most subtle gradations of delicate half shadow, hardly less advantageous to the shaft which it relieves. And, as far as regards pure effect in open air . . . I do not know anything whatsoever in the whole compass of the European architecture I have seen, which can for a moment be compared with the quaint shadow and delicate colour, like that of Rembrandt and Paul Veronese united, which the sun brings out as his rays move from porch to porch along the St. Mark's façade. (10.448–49)

Otto Demus discusses the chiaroscuro created by the columns in terms which, though less detailed, are in essential agreement. He seems hardly to have been aware that in this and other instances he was anticipated by Ruskin.[12]

Nowadays, sadly, the 'most subtle gradations of delicate half shadow' behind the shafts have, in large part, been swallowed up into a sooty grey of varying intensity. Since the backs of the shafts, which are not washed by rain as are at least some of their faces, are in many cases coated with calcium sulphate and soot, the multiple reflection of light between wall and columns is also restricted. Two colours that especially attracted Ruskin – the 'blue veins, that rise and sink beneath the polished surface'[13] of the 'grove of golden marble' (10.448) – have been stifled in a pitted texture that in the summer of 1980 was often reminiscent of discoloured concrete. The veins of

61

many of the vertically striated shafts, especially the *cipollino* (no. 44 in Ruskin's plan of the fourth porch is a prime instance), have become deepening channels for acidic runoff. With mere surface play of colour seriously impaired under most conditions of light, the 'translucency and glow of marble' (33.139), of 'transparent alabasters' (8.81), can be imagined only after one has examined the six lovely alabaster columns of the nave.[14]

p. 168

While study of exterior colour and chiaroscuro in the light of Ruskin's commentary is a gloomy business in the 1980s, his analysis of form can still be read against the church with surprising ease. To trace, in the *St. M. Book*, his progress across the façade is to become aware of the astonishing energy, precision of attention, and disdain of personal comfort[15] with which Ruskin indulged a visual appetite that was

a sort of instinct like that for eating or drinking. I should like to draw all St. Mark's . . . stone by stone, to eat it all up into my mind, touch by touch. (10.xxvi)

He approaches the building in the spirit of self-limitation that also governs his study of the Alps:

Mont Blanc and all its aiguilles, one silver flame, in front of me; marvellous blocks of mossy granite and dark glades of pine around me; but I could enjoy nothing . . . until at last I discovered that if I confined myself to one thing, – and that a little thing, – a tuft of moss or a single crag . . . I began to enjoy it directly, because then I had mind enough to put into the thing (5.183–4).

His fondness for detail has often been regarded as a weakness. But Ruskin, accumulating his understanding of the great façade in the same way that Tolstoy builds his conception of a human personality or Proust the ambience of a remembered childhood, knows that

Greatness can only be rightly estimated when minuteness is justly reverenced. Greatness is the aggregation of minuteness; nor can its sublimity be felt truthfully by any mind unaccustomed to the affectionate watching of what is least. (7.230)

It is because he devoted so much attention to the details surveyed in the following two chapters that he was able to write the evocation of the west front with which this book opened.

3 BOUND WITH ALABASTER
The west front: horizontally continuous or repeated features

THOUGH Ruskin planned separate studies of each portico and porch, he comments in passing on elements that are common to all. It will be helpful to consider these horizontally continuous or repeated features first.

Plinths and Associated Mouldings

Ruskin distinguishes four 'plinths' in the lower half of the façade and names them, in ascending order, the 'Basic', 'Second', 'Great', and 'Ice' plinths.[1] They assume varying positions of recession or projection with respect to each other. Ruskin is especially intrigued by the curious relations between the upper two, and the often bewildering complexity of their mediation between other elements in the composition.

25, 29, 30

XXXIII

The two lower plinths constitute the 'base', which is

one of the most embarrassing parts of the structure. – It appears to have been restored, along the façade & northern side – at a period comparatively recent – and on the southern side, partly torn away, partly replaced by renaissance plinths . . . & the restorations have been so frequent – so confused – and in many places so dextrous, that it has become altogether impossible to form any conjecture as to the original condition of this part of the building: The base however along the west front is at present consistent with itself, & harmonizes with the effect of the whole, so that, whatever its date, it is worth while to examine its arrangement for its own sake, even were it not necessary to do so, in order to comprehend that of the superstructure.

XII

The first elevation then, above the pavement of St Marks Place is a step – or plinth about a foot high, more or less according to the height of the pavement itself. It retires with the line of the wall piers, in the main entrances or porches, that is to say the first & third – but it forms a raised floor in the other three porches, chequered with red and white marble: It is faced all along with panels of red marble, enclosing slabs of white; or nearly white; some of the pieces being more or less veined. The outer edge of this lowest plinth is represented by the line marked with small letters, a b, c, &c. in the series of plans.[2]

42

43, 57
60, 78

Above the Basic Plinth

rises another, about a foot and a half high, and falling about 1 ft 2 in. back from the lower plinth along the fronts of the piers: on this member of the

42

30 The northwest portico and part of first porch, 1860–75

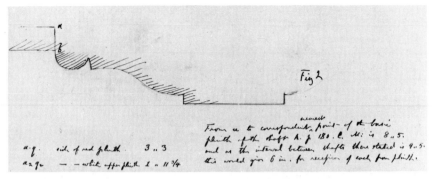

31 John Ruskin *Profile of the frame moulding of the Second Plinth* (Worksheet 129), 1849–50

base the lower pillars of the porches stand, and it forms a convenient seat, about two feet wide, between the bases of these pillars, the lower plinth forming the step to it. The common people sleep or lounge upon it nearly all day.[3] *56*

This plinth 'is panelled like the other'. Its frame is of 'white marble' and has the section drawn full size in Worksheet 129, fig. 2 (read *31* sideways). The panels are mostly 'white marble. very pure and transparent; and . . . pale veined grey and white or yellow & white *XI* alabaster let in', but in 'the great entrance door and door on the north' this Second Plinth is 'panelled with splendid dark green marble, and some pieces spotty red' (M.190l,r). This panelling, like that of the Basic Plinth, is 'simply but exquisitely finished' (9.334); its marble 'slices [are] rather thin. about ab – or not much more' (M.190). The outer edge of the Second Plinth is marked by capital letters on Ruskin's plans of the porches.

The horizontal moulding linking the Second Plinth to the wall, seen unobstructed on the south wall of the Treasury, is continuous *XII* behind the bases of the façade columns. This moulding prevents the *30* eye from dwelling upon the joining of plinth and wall, 'which would give an effect of instability'. It accomplishes this 'by attracting the eye to two rolls, separated by a deep hollow'. These 'bold projections'

entirely prevent the attention from being drawn to the joints of the masonry, and besides form a simple but beautifully connected group of bars of shadow, which express, in their perfect parallelism, the absolute levelness of the foundation. (9.334–5)

The moulding, a 'nearly perfect' type of what Ruskin calls the 'steep' basic profile, is 'peculiarly beautiful in the opposition between the bold projection of its upper roll, and the delicate leafy curvature of its lower' (9.338). *32*

33 The Great Plinth in the fifth porch, 1982

The Great Plinth imposes a strong horizontal thrust between the
25 upper and lower columns. As one nears the porches, the shadow it
33 casts in the intervals between the lower capitals becomes more
34 striking until, at close range, it becomes dominant. The Great
30 Plinth's most prominent feature is the 'upper bold dentil' (SMB.41),
    hand-cut and rugged, but replaced in parts of the building during the
p. 118 1860s and 1870s by diminutive specimens that Ruskin loathed. Its
35 lower edge bears a flower moulding, carved between two rows of
    dentils, which 'is perfectly flat and beautifully smoothed and the
    interstices cut down from it more or less steeply' (SMB.21). It
    accompanies the Great Plinth around most of the church, but breaks
p. 95 free to lead a visually delinquent and structurally precarious existence
    in the central porch.

64

34 The Great Plinth and the Ice Plinth in the fifth porch from below, 1980

35 John Ruskin *Floral Moulding at the base of the Great Plinth* (St. M. Book) 1850

36 John Ruskin *Profile and elevation of two mouldings at St. Mark's* (Stones I, 1851)

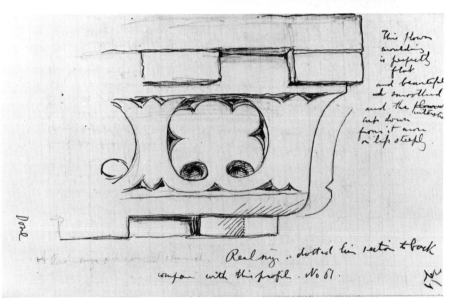

Surmounting the upper columns is the Ice Plinth, so named because this 'thin slab looks like a crust of ice' (SMB.19). Its delicacy (the flower pattern similar to that at the base of the Great Plinth) delights Ruskin, and its eccentric dartings and windings within and around the porches – which led one English observer to describe it as a 'Barbarism'[4] – are noted with satisfaction. The only portions of its soot-encrusted length that look remotely ice-like today are those most regularly favoured by the overfed pigeons which are, unaccountably, considered sacred to St. Mark's.

A fifth horizontal course provides the wall with a finishing accent of great piquancy. Its leaves project so strongly that a deep bar of shadow is caught under almost any angle of sunlight, its upper edge undulating against the brighter marble above. Ruskin considers this 'one of the earliest examples in Venice of the transition from the Byzantine to the Gothic cornice', admiring the 'well-directed thought of the sculptor' in the curling of the leaves and naturalistic enlivening of Byzantine forms:

the old incisions are retained below, and their excessive rigidity is one of the proofs of the earliness of the cornice; but those incisions now stand for the *under* surface of the leaf; and behold, when it turns over, on the top of it you see true *ribs*. (9.370)

Ruskin's engraver has lined the base of the cornice with diminutive dentils. In the original, they are huge and irregular. For all this magnificence of overhanging shadow and incident, Canaletto substitutes a flimsy cornice of the suburban sitting-room variety.

Capitals

Ruskin believes that in all fine architectural ornament, 'whatever order or class of it we may be contemplating, we shall find it subordinated to a greater, simpler, and more powerful' (9.301). The skilled designer fixes his attention first 'upon the arrangement of the features which will remain visible far away' (9.297), ensuring that these are 'divided first into large masses, and these masses covered with minute chasing and surface work which fill them with interest, and yet do not disturb nor divide their greatness' (9.303). Such planning for distant effect is evident in many capitals at St. Mark's:

Whether we examine the contour of the simpler convex bells, or those of the leaves which bend outwards from the richer and more Corinthian types, we find they are all outlined by grand and simple curves, and that the whole of their minute fretwork and thistle-work is cast into a gigantic mould which subdues all their multitudinous points and foldings to its own inevitable dominion. (10.161)

66

37 John Ruskin *Study of a lobed capital at St. Mark's* 1849–52

38 The northwest portico from the northeast, 1982

While exquisite at close range, such capitals retain bold articulation at a distance from which their finer subdivisions become invisible. In this respect, they are superior to even the finest Venetian Gothic capitals which 'Seen near . . . are the most incomparable study I have yet had . . . but their effect, seen from below, is not so good as Byzantine work. they are too fine to be traceable in distance' (M2.70).[5]

Ruskin's remarks tally more closely with his drawings and old photographs than with present grimy reality. Note how the *37, v* governing curves of the lobed capitals of the northwest angle maintained visual command at intermediate range in 1852. In 1982 *38* the same capitals presented a confused mass of dark greys against the black of their deeper recesses. Some capitals are distorted in apparent *61, x* articulation by white channels cut through the soot by streamlets of *xi* rainwater. J.W. Bunney's painting suggests what the distant effect of the capitals must have been when Ruskin first saw them: two horizontal bands of richly articulated bosses standing out from the shadows cast by the plinths they sustain. The effect in the summer of 1980 was of two bands of smudge, occasionally relieved by bursts of radiance where bits of marble had been broken, or washed by adventitious runoff.

Despite such falsification of their intended visual effect, the capitals still justify, when examined closely, Ruskin's praise of their variety and inventiveness ('the designs of the capitals of St. Mark's alone would form a volume' – 10.165).[6] That the concave capitals should do so is a special triumph, since the form imposes a restrictive method of working:

the sculptor of the concave profile must leave masses of rough stone prepared for its outer ornament, and cannot finish them at once, but must complete the cutting of the smooth bell beneath first, and then return to the projecting masses (for if he were to finish these latter first, they would assuredly, if delicate or sharp, be broken as he worked on) (9.381).

A 'foreseeing and predetermined method' is thus demanded, with the sculptor 'sure to reduce the system of his ornaments to some definite symmetrical order before he begins' and to carve more cautiously 'than if he could finish all as he worked on' (9.381–82). The concave is the 'disciplinarian capital', and there is danger of its repressing 'the power of the imagination', so that 'the indolence which cannot escape from its stern demand of accurate workmanship, seeks refuge in copyism of established forms' (9.382). At St. Mark's this danger is overcome. Even its Corinthian capitals, though founded on classical Corinthian, are in Ruskin's opinion more

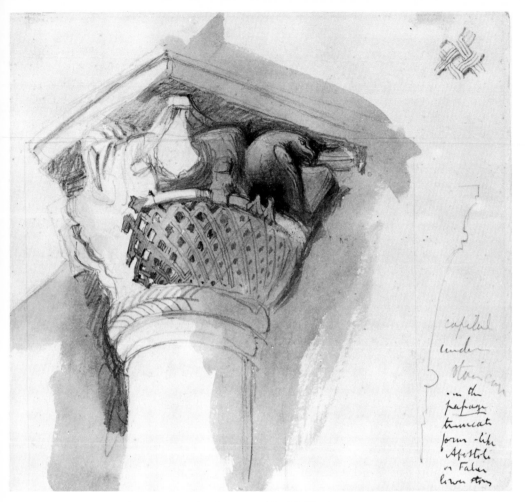

39 John Ruskin *Sixth-century capital in the atrium of St. Mark's* 1849–52

'picturesque' (11.322), more naturalistic in treatment of the acanthus, than their prototypes (10.24; 160). Indeed, some exhibit a mixture of leaf types (10.23), or unorthodox disposition of leaves, as in the drifted acanthus of the central porch (11.322). Though sometimes carelessly cut and always indifferent to precise symmetry, these capitals 'are indisputably more *natural* than any Greek ones, and therefore healthier, and tending to greatness' (10.161). Ruskin finds those utilizing bird and animal motifs especially delightful.

64

39, XXIII

The concave capital, however, was not as 'naturally pleasing to the Byzantine mind' as the 'bold convex or cushion shape' (10.158). Even in Corinthian capitals, the Byzantines tended 'to modify the concave profile by making it bulge out at the bottom', often adding a convex curve at the top also (10.158–9).[7] The convex profile, offering the sculptor a 'smooth surface' which is 'laid before him, as a piece of paper on which he can sketch at his pleasure', allowed a more imaginative, extemporaneous treatment:

> the mind of the sculptor, unshackled by the niceties of chiselling, wanders over its orbed field in endless fantasy; and, when generous as well as powerful, repays the liberty which has been granted to it with interest, by developing through the utmost wildness and fulness of its thoughts, an order as much more noble than the mechanical symmetry of the opponent school, as the domain which it regulates is vaster. (9.382)

37   Ruskin's favourites are those in which the bell is divided by 'recesses into separate lobes or leaves, like those of a rose or tulip, which are each in their turn covered with flowerwork or hollowed into reticulation' (10.165), or by even more sophisticated preliminary
53, 54   subdivision.

Though Ruskin refers to the capitals of St. Mark's as 'Byzantine', he is aware of their variable provenance, and the derivative nature of many. Citing evidence that the apse capitals of San Donato, Murano, 'were cut for their place' and are thus 'tests of Venetian workmanship' (11.270), he argues that many capitals commonly assumed to be imports from Constantinople are 'true Venetian work' (11.271). Ruskin's account of the transition from Byzantine to Gothic forms in Venetian capitals (11.272–3; D2.458–9), presupposes an active local school, influenced not only by Constantinople but also by the Lombardic Romanesque.[8] His belief that a rich current of Venetian sculpture supplemented Byzantine spoils in providing St. Mark's with its unparalleled collection of capitals is shared by many later writers.

40, 41 John Ruskin *Studies in archivolt decoration: the dentil* (*Stones I*, 1851)

Dentilled arches

The optical importance of the dentil is evident in almost any view of St. Mark's. As dominant as those defining the upper and lower edges of the Great and Ice Plinths are the dentils which accentuate the large arches. In the first volume of the *Stones* Ruskin outlines the thinking which might have led to their employment. The outside of the building is sheeted with an

30, 62

88, VIII

alabaster covering, literally marble defensive armour, riveted together in pieces, which follow the contours of the building. Now, on the wall, these pieces are mere flat slabs cut to the arch outline; but under the soffit of the arch the marble mail is curved, often cut singularly thin, like bent tiles, and fitted together so that the pieces would sustain each other even without rivets. It is of course desirable that this thin sub-arch of marble should project enough to sustain the facing of the wall; and the reader will see . . . that its edge forms a kind of narrow band round the arch (*b*), a band which the least enrichment would render a valuable decorative feature. Now this band is, of course, if the soffit pieces project a little beyond the face of the wall-pieces, a mere fillet . . .; and the question is, how to enrich it most wisely. It might easily have been dogtoothed, but the Byzantine architects had not invented the dogtooth, and would not have used it here, if they had; for the dogtooth cannot be employed alone, especially on so principal an angle as this of the main arches, without giving to the whole building a peculiar look, which I can no otherwise describe than as being to the eye, exactly what untempered acid is to the tongue. . . . What, then, will be the next easiest method of giving interest to the fillet?

V

40

Simply to make the incisions square instead of sharp, and to leave equal intervals of the square edge between them. [Also shown] is one of the curved pieces of arch armour, with its edge thus treated; one side only being done at the bottom, to show the simplicity and ease of the work. This ornament gives force and interest to the edge of the arch, without in the least

41

diminishing its quietness. Nothing was ever, nor could be ever invented, fitter for its purpose, or more easily cut. . . . Its complete intention is now, however, only to be seen in the pictures of Gentile Bellini and Vittor Carpaccio; for, like most of the rest of the mouldings of Venetian buildings, it was always either gilded or painted – often both, gold being laid on the faces of the dentils, and their recesses coloured alternately red and blue. (9.324–5)

In a passage intended for the second volume of the *Stones*, Ruskin adds:

the eye is never wearied of the dark & dotted piquant chains of these simple mouldings, following the curve of the arches upon the marble surface, like the line of the fishers net, floating on the lagoons in the moonlight. (Add.57)

Carvings in low relief

Ruskin takes pains in the *Stones* to justify the 'first broad characteristic' of St. Mark's, and 'root nearly of every other important peculiarity in it', its 'confessed *incrustation*' (10.93). Suppressing a sentence in the manuscript which had suggested that a person thinking the building made of solid marble 'has been deceived only by his own ignorance', he deals with the ethical problem more wittily by explaining that the visitor may

see that every slab of facial marble is fastened to the next by a confessed *rivet*, and that the joints of the armour are so visibly and openly accommodated to the contours of the substance within that he has no more right to complain of treachery than a savage would have, who, for the first time in his life seeing a man in armour, had supposed him to be made of solid steel. (10.95)[9]

The sculptural consequence of this incrustation is that

over the greater part of the edifice there can be *no deep cutting*. The thin sheets of covering stones do not admit of it; we must not cut them through to the bricks; and whatever ornaments we engrave upon them cannot, therefore, be more than an inch deep at the utmost. Consider for an instant the enormous differences which this single condition compels between the sculptural decoration of the incrusted style, and that of the solid stones of the North, which may be hacked and hewn into whatever cavernous hollows and black recesses we choose . . . in which any form or thought may be wrought out on any scale, – mighty statues with robes of rock and crowned foreheads burning in the sun, or venomous goblins and stealthy dragons shrunk into lurking-places of untraceable shade: think of this, and of the play and freedom given to the sculptor's hand and temper, to smite out and in, hither and thither, as he will; and then consider what must be the different spirit of the design which is to be wrought on the smooth surface of a film of marble, where every line and shadow must be drawn with the most tender pencilling and cautious reserve of resource, – where even the chisel must not strike hard, lest it break through the delicate stone, nor the mind be permitted in any impetuosity of conception inconsistent with the fine discipline of the hand. Consider that whatever animal or human form is to be suggested, must be projected on a flat surface; that all the features of the countenance, the folds of the drapery, the involutions of the limbs, must be so reduced and subdued that the whole work becomes rather a piece of fine drawing than of sculpture (10.105–6).

In keeping with his insistence that ornament be conceived as part of the total composition,[10] Ruskin concentrates upon bas-reliefs which were designed for specific locations. These are, on the west front, pre-eminently the spandrels of the door of the first, and correspond- 56, 79, XI ing windows of the second, fourth and fifth porches. While less naturalistic than the figures lining many a Gothic portal, such works exhibit exquisite sensitivity to their visual context, subordinating 'every form to architectural service': there is not 'a line in them which could be taken away without injury, nor one wanting which could be added with advantage' (10.108).

The six rectangular reliefs set into the spandrels between the western arches are positioned in a pattern which, Ruskin believes, aids in the optical unification of the façade, and in which he later pp. 53, 185 discerns also a symbolic significance. But many panels at St. Mark's illustrate a tendency 'to admit the insertion of fragmentary sculptures . . . rather with a view of displaying their intrinsic beauty, than of setting them to any regular service' in an architectural sense (10.96). Ruskin admires the 'respect for the works of others' which led the architect to save 'every relic with which he was entrusted' (10.96). Though suspicious of carving which is not designed as part of the building, and is not therefore *architectural* sculpture' (9.284; 23.168), he is charmed by a number of such panels, analysing one in some detail, and in 1876–77 attempting a brief stylistic survey of some pp. 82, 183 important specimens on the north and west façades. He favours those featuring peacefully opposed animals, while the 'groups of contend- 50, 124 ing and devouring animals are always much ruder in cutting, and take somewhat the place in Byzantine sculpture which the lower grotesques do in the Gothic' (10.168). Though these animal reliefs lack 'variety of invention, except only in the effective disposition of the light and shade, and in the vigour and thoughtfulness of the touches which indicate the plumes of the birds', the sculptors always 'secure variety enough to keep the eye entertained, no two sides of 95 these Byzantine ornaments being in all respects the same' (10.169). Bellini's painting and remnants of gilding on the inner spandrels of IV the porches indicate that the bas-reliefs were meant to be seen

in shadow against light; an effect much calculated upon by their designer, and obtained by the use of a golden ground, formed of glass mosaic inserted in the hollow of the marble. Each square of glass has the leaf gold upon its surface protected by another thin film of glass above it, so that no time or weather can affect its lustre, until the pieces of glass are bodily torn from their setting. The smooth glazed surface of the golden ground is washed by every shower of rain [though not on the inner spandrels], but the marble usually darkens into an amber colour in process of time; and when the whole ornament is cast into shadow, the golden surface, being perfectly reflective, refuses the darkness, and shows itself in bright and burnished VI light behind the dark traceries of the ornament. Where the marble has retained its perfect whiteness, on the other hand, and is seen in sunshine, it is shown as a snowy tracery on a golden ground (10.169).

13, XII The panels of the south Treasury wall are regularly washed by rain. They have by now lost at least a millimetre of their surfaces.[11] But from a range of three or four yards one can still appreciate the 'exquisite grace' (10.108), the 'most tender pencilling' (10.106), of their 'snowy tracery'.

4 A CONFUSION OF DELIGHT
Porticoes and porches of the west front

Ruskin worked from south to north in studying the façade in 1849–50, but since the ground plans and tables of measurements he prepared for publication take the reversed order (numbering the porches 1 to 5 from north to south), it is followed here.

The northwest portico

An early plan indicates that special emphasis was to be placed on the porticoes.[1] They are 'the most exquisite pieces of architectural proportion with which I am acquainted in Europe' (Add.50), admirable equally for form and colour. A drawing of the northwest portico in 1852, prepared on the spot with the aid of daguerreotypes, is Ruskin's largest drawing of St. Mark's.[2] A manuscript fragment describes it as the 'frontispiece' to an intended number of *Examples*, showing

the upper portion of the portico, as seen from the north west: It was impossible to include the whole elevation of the portico in one view – unless much more of the flanking architecture had been introduced – and the scale of the whole reduced nearly one half. (Add.x–12)

An 'accurate elevation' giving 'the proportion of all the parts' (Add.x–12,52) has disappeared, but a photograph from Ruskin's collection elucidates his analysis. The portico

presents us with examples of nearly all that is interesting in the structure of the building. The two large lower [nos 2 and 3] & two small upper pillars on the right side . . . are parts of the great ranks of pillars which form the entire facade: and are like all the rest backed by the firm wall. But the single pillar on the left is quite isolated – and sustains the whole weight of the angle of the church. To this pillar let us first direct our attention.

It is given with the two above it . . . [but] in reality, although only two pillars are seen in the elevation, it bears three, & a square mass of masonry (on which the arch of the portico is sustained) arranged on the top of its capital . . . but it is only when observed from the angle of the church that the three pillars are seen. At all points, however – the shaft looks able for its work. but the effect of strength is given by its perfect proportion: not by sturdiness . . . . the reader will be able at once to determine for himself whether the proportions are pleasing or not (Add.52).

The disposition of the three upper shafts exhibits both structural and aesthetic calculation:

42 The northwest angle, 1982

notice especially that the thickest . . . measuring 3 ft 2 in. round, while the other two measure 2 ft 10 in., & 2 ft 11 in. – is used for the outer angle. so as to balance the mass of masonry . . . at the opposite or inner angle. and to get the whole weight thrown as much as possible diagonally on the [lower] capital (Add.53).

In order to make the increased bulk and importance of this upper angle shaft

more manifest to the eye, the old builders made the shaft *shorter* as well as thicker, increasing the depth both of its capital and the base, with what is to the thoughtless spectator ridiculous incongruity, and to the observant one a most beautiful expression of constructive science. Nor is this all. Observe: the whole strength of this angle depends on accuracy of *poise*, not on breadth or strength of foundation. It is a *balanced*, not a propped structure; if the balance fails, it must fall instantly; if the balance is maintained, no matter how the lower shaft is fastened into the ground, all will be safe. And to mark this more definitely, the great lower shaft *has a different base from all the others of the façade*, remarkably high in proportion to the shaft, on a circular instead of a square plinth, and *without spurs* while all the other bases have spurs, without exception . . . . all expression of *grasp* in the foot of the pillar is here useless, and to be replaced by one of balance merely (10.450).

Though one must question the notion that the column's foundation is irrelevant,[3] it is hard to resist Ruskin's plea that we

feel what the old builder wanted to say to us, and how much he desired us to follow him with our understanding as he laid stone above stone.

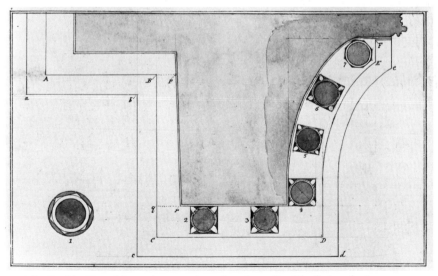

43 John Ruskin *Plan of the northwest portico and northern side of the first porch* 1850

And this purpose of his is hinted to us once more, even by the position of
43 this base in the ground plan of the foundation of the portico; for, though
itself circular, it sustains a hexagonal plinth *set obliquely to the walls of the
church*, as if expressly to mark to us that it did not matter how the base was
set, so only that the weights were justly disposed above it. (10.450)

The retention of this oblique setting in restorations of the 1880s and
1909–13[4] indicates – when compared with the brutal treatment of
the southwest angle a few years earlier – the success of the campaign
for preservation begun by Ruskin and Count Zorzi in 1877.[5]
v   Comparing the massive, yet compact, capital of the lower corner
shaft with the two to its right, Ruskin asks his reader to

observe the difference in the treatment of that of the great shaft – which has
hard and serious work to do – all-alone – from that of the others, and . . .
whether he supposes that architects who believe in the 'five orders' ever
dream of such adaptations of form to service (Add.55).

47 This capital

44 has the loveliest section I ever saw. carefully given on No 170, more
especially its lovely inner line: which I only saw by the accident of its lower
basket work being all broken away: and it is indeed only formed by the
chisel within side of the basket, by a kind of instinct – and it is of no use,
except like a kind of fine under anatomy, ruling the outside lines: but when
these are gone, *it* is left. – not so smooth as I have drawn it. for the chisel
works roughly in the dark – but quite as beautiful in main contour . . . .
Then i marks the piercing . . . where the basketwork ceases to be cut clear.
. . . From h to g is the *surface* of the lily which . . . falls entirely within the
basketwork. the lily itself is cut down to a third level, which is somewhat
roughly chiselled; the lily is no where cut *clear*. but well undercut. so as to
define it all sharply: and nearly $\frac{3}{4}$ of an inch deep
Then h_2f. is the profile of the basketwork on the angle. – it would be a little
more sloping: but follows close on the the [*sic*] lily line – which being here
given through the side (the centre of lily makes the fh_2 hardly slope
enough[)] But h_2i. always comes vertical – returning even a little perhaps,
towards i. (M.204–5)

The capital is 'the most finished example I ever met with of the
convex family, to which, in spite of the central inward bend of its
profile, it is marked as distinctly belonging, by the bold convex curve
45 at its root' (9.386). A huge plate in *Examples* gives details of this
capital and its counterparts of the southwest portico 'on their actual
scale' (11.332). They are 'without exception the most subtle pieces of
composition in broad contour which I have ever met with in
architecture' (10.164). Studied statically they are remarkable
enough. But they stand at the corners most frequently passed by

78

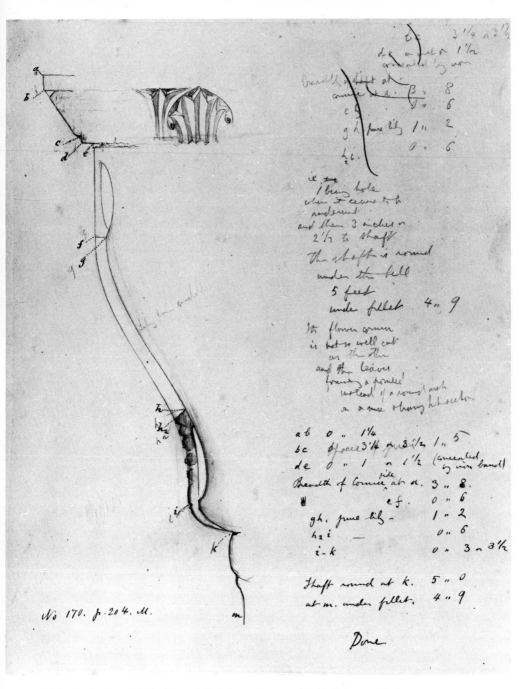

44 John Ruskin *Study of the lily capital of the northwest angle* (Worksheet 170) 1850

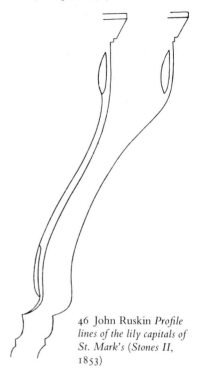

45 John Ruskin (engraved by R.P. Cuff) *Details of the lily capitals of St. Mark's* (*Examples*, 1851)

46 John Ruskin *Profile lines of the lily capitals of St. Mark's* (*Stones II*, 1853)

46 pedestrians, and Ruskin examines their effect on the moving eye. Three profile lines are identified: the innermost line of the bell behind the lily (left, inner line); the line of the profile of the basket work, taken through the side of the capital (left, outer line); and the outer profile of the capital at its angle (right):

the reader will easily understand that the passing of the one of these lines into the other is productive of the most exquisite and wonderful series of curvatures possible within such compass, no two views of the capital giving the same contour. (10.164)

One wishes cinematography – in addition to the daguerreotype and photograph he exploited so gratefully – had been available to Ruskin.

The lily capitals moved him deeply:

no amount of illustration or eulogium would be enough to make the reader understand the perfect beauty of the thing itself, as the sun steals from interstice to interstice of its marble veil, and touches with the white lustre of its rays at midday the pointed leaves of its thirsty lilies. (10.165)

80

47 John Ruskin (engraved by J.H. Le Keux) *Lily capital of the northwest angle of St. Mark's (Stones II, 1853) 1852*

In 1982 these capitals looked as if they were made of pitted concrete. Plundered from the sixth-century church of St. Polyeuktos in Constantinople[6] and placed in the most accessible positions at St. Mark's to draw attention to their grace and craftsmanship, they now testify to the disaster that has gradually overtaken the exterior.

42, 91

The lily capital supports a massive abacus (corresponding to the Great Plinth of the main structure) which forms the base for the three porphyry shafts of the second storey. Its sides are 3 ft 8–9 in. long, 1 ft 4 in. high (to bottom of dentils), and 'white' in colour (SMB.561,57). Though anything but white now, this abacus still boasts the huge dentils admired by Ruskin (views taken in 1852 and 1982 give identical counts).

v

1, 42

The bases of the second-storey columns stand upon square plinths brought to within $\frac{1}{2}$ in. of each other and 'cemented. so as to bind all into one solid plinth. about 4 in. within the edge of abacus' (SMB.57). The two western bases have profiles, carefully drawn by Ruskin, containing cavettos of 'remarkably fine conic sections – not circles', and are made of 'deep red Verona' marble (SMB.58), which is now crumbling badly. The three porphyry shafts are the best-preserved elements in the angle. They have not been rotated or interchanged as were their counterparts of the southwest portico: present joints and scars still match closely with the 1852 drawing. Of their three splendid capitals, he singles out the second from the north on the west face, drawing it in tiny format for the *Stones* and describing it as 'highly characteristic' (10.160). Deichmann agrees, placing it with a group of similar thirteenth-century capitals inspired by two sixth-century spoils at St. Mark's (also drawn by Ruskin).[7] Glancing up further we come finally to 'the bold and grotesque gargoyle' at the upper angle. Its position, at 45 degrees to the main axes of the church, proves it was 'plainly made under Lombardic influence' (10.357).[8]

42, v

49

39

48

The 'richly decorated sub arch' of the portico is measured and described. Its 'span . . . under soffit is 5 ft 10 in.', its 'height above upper surface of great plinth' is 7 ft 6$\frac{1}{2}$ in., and 'it has 4 ft 10 in. of pure stilt: more perfectly defined at the masonry joint than I have ever seen it'. The arch is, 'as seen by the measures – flat above the stilt . . . and this makes the stilt so defined' (SMB.551). Ruskin praises the 'most exquisite leafage' of the face carving (Add.56).

30, XXXVI

At this point Ruskin reached the top of his ladder, recording that he 'could not reach' for measurement the 'uppermost' arch of the portico (SMB.551). He could, however, admire the relief of peacocks set into its backing wall.[9] The outer chain pattern receives close attention. He draws the section of its 'little horny triangles' and 'balls in concave side of square' (SMB.55), returning later to note the exact

50

82

48 Grotesque figure on the northwest angle, *c.* 1880

49 John Ruskin *Bird capital of St. Mark's* 1851–52

50 Relief of peacocks in the northwest portico

sequence of circles and squares and the fact that the left side has one more such element than the right (SMB.80). The hasty engraving for *Stones II* (plate 11), however, reverses the sides of the chain and falsifies other details,[10] with Ruskin trimming his description (10.169) to match the reversal. In a regularized parody which Ruskin cannot have designed, this panel became the cover-motif for the *Stones* (reproduced at 9.liv). His admiration for its 'effective disposition of the light and shade' (10.169) is still evident a quarter century later in two fine watercolours, though he had by then given up trying to get the chain right.

    Glancing back from these drawings to his 1852 study, one is struck by Ruskin's earlier reticence about colour. A wash gives some sense of the generally light tones of the alabaster incrustation, but the porphyry shafts are scarcely differentiated from the others. This caution is only slightly less pronounced in a companion drawing of

XXXI
XXXVIII
V

83

the southwest portico. An intention to use these drawings for engraving may supply a partial explanation. Equally important is Ruskin's crushed awareness of his inability to reproduce 'the most subtle, variable, inexpressible colour in the world' (10.115). Attempts to do so are 'hopeless from the beginning', and it is 'dangerous for me to endeavour to illustrate my meaning, except by reference to the work itself' (10.113–15). The porticoes epitomize all Ruskin finds most attractive, yet most elusive, in the building:

It would be easier to illustrate a crest of Scottish mountain, with its purple heather and pale harebells at their fullest and fairest, or a glade of Jura forest, with its floor of anemone and moss, than a single portico of St. Mark's. (10.115)

The first porch

The two sixteen-sided shafts linking the northwest portico and the first porch are numbered 2 and 3 in Ruskin's plan of the lower storey. The superimposed columns 'are for a wonder above the lower' here (SMB.54), though even this correspondence (see pre-restoration photographs) was not precise. Moving south, we reach the first porch.

Ruskin's study of the setting of shafts and associated members helps explain some of the present oddities of the porch. His measurements of the bases, girths of shafts, and distances of bases from the edge of the Second Plinth tally closely with the present structure. However, his figures for the gaps between the bases on the north side indicate a westward displacement of bases 4, 5 and 6 since 1850. The gap between the 'proximate outer angles' of bases 4 and 5 has grown from 1 ft $5\frac{1}{4}$ in. to 1 ft 6 in.; between 5 and 6 from 1 ft $3\frac{1}{4}$ in. to 1 ft 5 in.; and the 'minimum distance between side and proximate angle' of 6 and 7 from 1 ft $4\frac{1}{2}$ in. to 1 ft 6 in.[11] This change helps explain the lack of parallel between the upper and lower columns of the north side. The strong present tilt to the left of the upper columns seen from the west (compare the photograph taken before restoration with a modern one) also receives partial explanation when comparisons are made with Ruskin's diagram (SMB.51): the capitals of all five have been shifted closer to the wall.

In a study of the south side of this porch, drawn in 1850, the top diagram gives the positions of the first-storey bases on the Second Plinth, while the lower shows the 'Abaci of lower shafts in situ under great plinth'. Ruskin notes that the outer line of the Great Plinth 'should be a regular curve', and gives its relationship to the edge of each abacus at lower right. The 'five upper shafts are shaded in

84

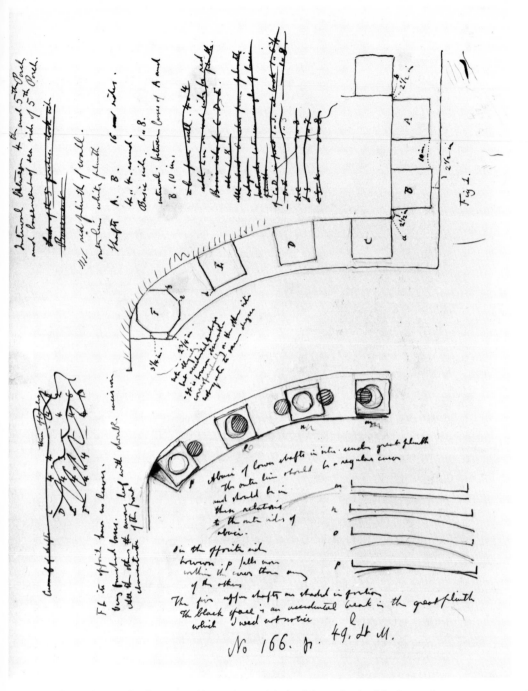

51 John Ruskin *Study of relations of bases, abaci and shafts of the south side of the first porch* (Worksheet 166) 1850

85

52 John Ruskin *Prophet in the left spandrel of the inner arch of the first porch* 1850–52

position' (small circles) to show their relations to the abaci (squares) and shafts (larger circles) of the lower storey. The present structure *42* conforms to Ruskin's diagram, and since his measurements for the gaps between the lower bases on the south side agree almost exactly with comparisons taken in 1980,[12] it appears this side of the porch has not been seriously disturbed. Ruskin finds the porch

excessively remarkable for the way in which the great plinth stops against the tympanum – giving place to the belt of basreliefs which cross it *30, 82* [compare the fifth porch]. and which seem fragments built in as they chanced to come: A very singular adoration of Magi & Shepherds: – and various single figures under the shell canopy. (SMB.49l).

The curious juxtaposition of these carvings has also intrigued later scholars.[13]

56 The arch over the doorway is daguerreotyped and partially measured (Ruskin bypasses the 'line of this internal arch' for 'fear of injuring carving' – SMB.52l). He finds that 'a gap behind it shows the real arch is brick & that the stone is only a facing. It is most masterly in effect – stone with interstices filled with gold mosaic. but rudely cut on close examination' (SMB.52). In a passage intended for the *Stones*, Ruskin writes:

86

the principal skill of the Byzantine sculptor is always shown in the decoration of the face stones . . . [where] he expatiates with the most exquisite freedom – and it would need a volume of plates to give the reader an adequate idea of the grace & power of the sculpture in the archivolts of St Marks alone . . . in general – the sculpture is kept flat – & the effect obtained, or relieved. by gold & colour. . . . The interstices of the marble carving are filled with mosaic – the gold being used for the principal ground: and the colour in delicate points: in process of time the marble darkens slightly . . . and the whole design is seen relieved in darkness upon a luminous field. (Add.57–58)   VI

A pencil drawing shows the prophet carved in the left spandrel. 52
Ruskin must have been sketching from an elevated lateral position, for the prophet's gaze – intent upon the viewer – arrests attention in a way that surpasses the usual effect of the original.[14]

The four 'beautiful capitals' (SMB.49l) with double spurs at the 54
western ends of the second storey exhibit

the union of breadth of mass with subtlety of curvature, which character-
ises nearly all the spurred capitals of the convex school. Its plan is given in 53
[the figure]: the inner shaded circle is the head of the shaft; the white cross, the bottom of the capital, which expands itself into the external shaded portions at the top. Each spur, thus formed, is cut into a ship's bow, with the Doric profile; the surfaces so obtained are then charged with arborescent ornament. (9.385)

Deichmann believes these 'completely unique' works may, like the lily capitals, have come from the sixth-century church of St. Polyeuktos in Constantinople.[15] Their compliance with Ruskin's ideal of delicate ornament which maintains effective articulation at a distance is still apparent from ground level, and in Ruskin's drawing, XXXIII
made at longer range in cleaner times.   XXXI

53 John Ruskin *Plan of double-spurred capital* (*Stones I*, 1851)

54 Double-spurred capital on the south side of the first porch, *c.* 1880

55 The northern
columns of the first
porch, 1980

56 The first and second
porches of St. Mark's,
1860–75

The second porch

56 Ruskin's study of the shafts between the first and second porches reveals several idiosyncrasies. The columns surmounting the sixteen-
57 sided shafts of the first storey (nos 12 and 13) are not directly above them, nor is their displacement in this respect equal – that over no. 12 being further off centre. The measurements also show the 'clock-ward shaft' of the second storey (the great clock is on the north side of the Piazza) 'an inch farther in from the clockward side of great plinth than the other from the sea ward' (SMB.53). Slight alterations have occurred in the placement of columns 12 and 13 since 1850. The
51 interval between their bases, given by Ruskin as 10 in., was in 1980 almost an inch wider, suggesting an attempt to lessen the difference between the two storeys.

57 Ruskin's figures for the distances between bases 14–19, between their southern reciprocals 20–25 (not shown), and between these bases and both their backing walls and the front of the plinth HIK on which they stand, agree closely with measurements taken in 1980.[16] Several peculiarities noted by Ruskin may thus be studied with assurance that this second porch has been left relatively undisturbed. He finds the sides of bases 15, 16, 18 and 19 all between 1 in. and 1½ in. shorter than those of bases 14 and 17. Thus, though all are 'distant about 4 inches from line H.I.[K.]', nos '15 & 16 being smaller, are not in contact with wall. so also 18 & 19'.[17] The irregularity is recorded

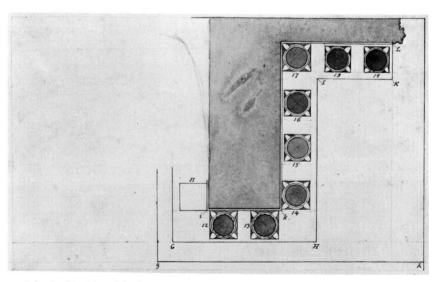

57 John Ruskin *Plan of the first storey of the northern half of the second porch* 1850

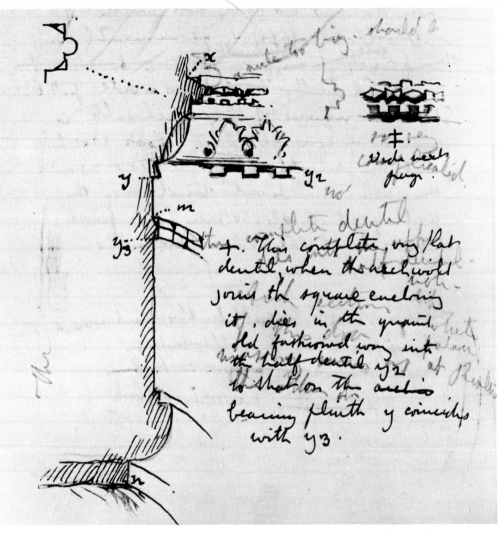

58 John Ruskin *Section and details of left side of archivolt/spandrel of the window of the second porch* (St. M. Book) 1850

in Ruskin's plan. More significant visually are the variations in girth of the second-storey shafts, from 2 ft $6\frac{1}{2}$ in. and 2 ft $7\frac{1}{2}$ in. (north and south respectively measured 'halfway up') in the pair flanking the inner arch of the porch, to 3 ft 5 in. and 3 ft 6 in. (north and south) in the most westerly pair. Immediately behind this outside couple stands a pair more than half a foot less in girth (2 ft $9\frac{1}{2}$ in. north; 2 ft 11 in. south). These smaller shafts 'are curious in their marked effect on the eye' (SMB.66).

The archivolt of the upper window is daguerreotyped[18] and studied with care. Ruskin sketches (in what must have been a most

56

VII

59 John Ruskin (engraved by J.C. Armytage) *Archivolt/spandrel of the window of the second porch* (reversed image) (*Stones II*, 1853)

58 awkward position) its section and mouldings, noting that the 'complete, very flat dentil' y3, 'when the archivolt joins the square
VII enclosing it [to the left of the third raised ball from the bottom], dies in the quaint old fashioned way into the half dentil y2' (SMB.66l). The
59 archivolt and spandrel[19] appear in the *Stones* in a reversed plate of whose inadequacy Ruskin was aware:

It is left a fragment, in order to get it on a larger scale; and yet . . . it is too small to show the sharp folds and points of the marble vine-leaves with sufficient clearness. The ground of it is gold, the sculpture in the spandrils is not more than an inch and a half deep, rarely so much. It is in fact nothing more than an exquisite sketching of outlines in marble, to about the same depth as in the Elgin frieze; the draperies, however, being filled with close folds, in the manner of the Byzantine pictures, folds especially necessary here, as large masses could not be expressed in the shallow sculpture without becoming insipid; but the disposition of these folds is always most beautiful, and often opposed by broad and simple spaces, like that obtained by the scroll in the hand of the prophet seen in the Plate.

The balls in the archivolt project considerably, and the interstices between their interwoven bands of marble are filled with colours like the illuminations of a manuscript; violet, crimson, blue, gold, and green, alternately: but no green is ever used without an intermixture of blue pieces in the mosaic, nor any blue without a little centre of pale green; sometimes only a single piece of glass a quarter of an inch square, so subtle was the feeling for colour which was thus to be satisfied. [A footnote adds: 'The fact is, that no two tesserae of the glass are exactly of the same tint, the greens being all varied with blues, the blues of different depths, the reds of different clearness, so that the effect of each mass of colour is full of variety, like the stippled colour of a fruit piece.'] The intermediate circles have golden stars set on an azure ground, varied in the same manner: and the small crosses seen in the intervals are alternately blue and subdued scarlet, with two small circles of white set in the golden ground above and beneath them, each only about half an inch across (this work, remember, being on the outside of the building, and twenty feet above the eye), while the blue crosses have each a pale green centre. [The MS (p. 60) mentions the small crosses of red, green and blue 'introduced also in the interstices of the spandrel above – forming the only interruption to its breadth of marble & gold'.] Of all this exquisitely mingled hue, no plate, however large or expensive, could give any adequate conception (10.115–16).

Ruskin apparently attempted a coloured plate before reaching this despairing conclusion.[20] In the present polluted state of the relief it is impossible even to identify the marble in which it is carved.[21] Many tesserae have fallen out, but some sense of the colour described by Ruskin may still be felt. Indeed, despite the bad state of the columns and incrustation flanking the lower window, some lovely hues still emerge in this porch. The eight blue/green and cream breccia shafts of the second storey are marvellous, and the alabaster shafts below – their veins set in wavelike patterns to each other – still yield in some lights the gold/azure combination so admired by Ruskin.

VII

VIII

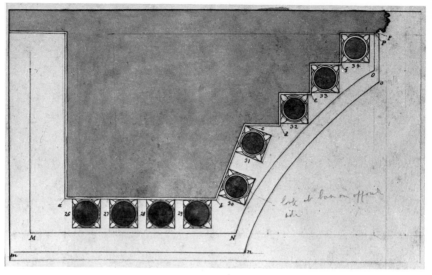

60 John Ruskin *Plan of the first storey of the northern half of the third porch* 1850

The wall piers at both sides of the third (central) porch

4, 62, 79   Ruskin notes some interesting facts about these piers. Their eight lower shafts, nos 26–29 and 40–43, all approximate to 4 ft 8 in. in girth.[22] However, the bases of 26–29, though the same size as those of 40–43, are more widely separated – by an average of about an inch. To achieve even this much uniformity, the columns of the southern pier have been so strongly displaced from the centre that, while on the north there is a gap of some 5 inches between the base of

60   no. 26 and the north edge of its backing wall (*a* in Ruskin's plan), its southern reciprocal, no. 43, meets the south edge of its backing wall

78   without leaving any gap at all (*s* in plan of fourth porch).

    The twelve upper shafts of these piers vary strikingly in girth, from 2 ft 7 in. to 3 ft, measured 'halfway up'.[23] With their capitals

126   and Ice Plinth, they inspired several remarkable drawings in 1876.

61   They were in a shocking state in 1980, with patches of soot and calcium sulphate dominating cavities (often following vein lines) where the surface had eroded.

The third porch

62   The central porch remains – in the placement of its lower columns at least – largely unaltered since 1850. Ruskin is struck by the 'curious and delicate curve' *o n*, the 'most remarkable feature' of the entire

94

61 Second-storey columns
between the third and fourth
porches, 1980

Basic Plinth of the church, and draws a careful diagram, with *60*
measurements and instructions to aid in its geometrical reconstruction (M. 189–90).[24]

The unexpected endings and angles of the Ice Plinth and the *63, 70*
cornice over the second-storey capitals – the 'lie of the line by the
curve' (SMB.43l) – fascinate Ruskin. Perhaps the strangest feature is
the manner in which the upper columns are supported. The Great
Plinth, surmounting the lower capitals throughout the rest of the
façade, vanishes abruptly between nos 30–39, and its 'lower flower
cornice . . . continues alone carrying first the upper shafts then the
archivolts' of the three inner recessed arches. Odd as such lessening of *62, 66*
support (for second-storey columns which are taller here than in the
rest of the façade) may be, Ruskin discovers even greater defiance of
normal procedure in the placement of the upper over the lower
columns. In his study of the three columns surmounting the
porphyry shafts 30 and 31 and their southern counterparts 38 and 39 *60*
(not shown), he had first thought both upper central shafts
overlapped at least one shaft below. Looking more carefully, *63*

I see I am wrong in putting even the edge of the central one over that of the
great one below. Nothing is more strange in the church than the carrying
of this central shaft on the cross bit of the thin flower cornice. not $4\frac{1}{2}$ inches
thick. It is actually set on a plank of stone (SMB.40).

Meanwhile, the Great Plinth has left a ghostly reminder of itself, as if

62 Third porch of St. Mark's, 1860–65

63, 67 calculated to delight Ruskin: 'its upper bold dentil . . . runs along . . . behind the three shafts', deep in shadow, until it meets the outermost of the inner three arches (SMB.41).

The six upper shafts provide another surprise. While the two outer pairs measure 3 ft 3 in., the inner measures 3 ft 4 in. (north) and 3 ft 2 in. (south) in girth: 'These are the innermost shafts. It is odd that one should be larger & the other smaller. They evidently put in the odd ones'.[25]

63 Upper columns and soffit of the second sculptured arch of the north side of the third porch, 1860–75

64 John Ruskin *Capital of the third porch* (*Examples*, 1851)

The capitals of lower columns 30–39 are described in 1879 as the 'first leaves I ever drew from St. Mark's' (24.288). One of these 64 capitals (almost certainly the second from the door, south side)[26] is 'evidently founded on the antique Corinthian, but infinitely more picturesque, and worked with leaves which, instead of being pointed, are forked at the extremities'. These 'are represented as drifted round the capital by the wind, and the idea is several times repeated, both in the porch and in other parts of the church' (11.322).[27] The capital drawn by Ruskin is 'worked in white marble' and stands on a shaft of 'dark porphyry', which gives 'brilliancy to the crystalline whiteness which is to serve for ground to the sharp dark touches of the Byzantine chisel' (11.322). This reads sadly today, 61 though the architect may not have intended the capital to be seen white. Bellini shows the inner eight of these ten capitals gilded.[28] IV

The arches of the porch are studied carefully. The outermost of the 62 three inner arches spans 21 ft between its outer edges, 'and the space 66 between this and the soffit of innermost is divided I think equally in 3', the innermost measuring 11 ft 10 in. between the bottom edges of its soffit. While this inner arch rises 7 ft 9½ in. 'above the flower plinth

97

65 Carvings on the face of the innermost arch of the third porch

66 Inner three arches of the third porch, 1860–75

of capitals', it 'has 2 feet more of pure stilt and then the outer arches follow it keeping parallel of course becoming more and more semicircular' (SMB.46–7). The great outer arch is set unevenly over the opening defined by the angles of the wall below. The angle 'falls about 5 or 6 inches on Clock [north] side and 3 on sea side – inside of sculptured soffit of greatest archivolt' (SMB.47).

Close attention is given to the decorated arches. The '*inner* archivolt has on its outside a series of figures much crowded. in a twined wreath of cylindrical stems with vineleaves'. Ruskin finds the 'twining of it & small fillings most lovely: and ingenious. but inelegant on the whole' (SMB.45). Its inner edge carries 'a long bead instead of dentil' (SMB.46), unlike the other two sculptured arches. On its soffit are 'two monstrous figures upholding the leaves out of which the rolling frieze [?] rises'. The northern figure 'has two serpents out of his mouth who bite his limbs'. Glancing at the southern figure, however, Ruskin's visual acuity falters, and he writes (with averted gaze?): 'the other has two biting her breasts'.[29] Overcoming his double vision, he looks up to note:

animals generally *dead* or *devouring each other* are mixed among the leafage: several birds however eating the fruit as usual. Part of this archivolt I have daged [daguerreotyped]. Two dark birds: it is remarkable for the development of its *poppy* heads: in great numbers (SMB.45–6).

67 Capitals and carvings of the inner arches of the third porch

68 Carvings on the soffit of the innermost arch of the third porch
69 Carvings on the face of the second decorated arch of the third porch

70 Face of the outer carved archivolt of the third porch, 1860–75

The daguerreotype is missing, but a photograph belonging to the *73*
Guild of St. George shows the animals and foliage.[30] Comparing
such carvings with those of the Duomo of Verona, he writes that
though the latter have 'greater motion and spirit' they display
'infinitely less grace and science'. At St. Mark's,

> however rude the cutting, every line is lovely, and the animals or men are
> placed in any attitudes which secure ornamental effect, sometimes
> impossible ones, always severe, restrained, or languid. . . . the Eastern
> torpor is in every line, the mark of a school formed on severe traditions . . .
> but with an exquisite sense of beauty (9.428).

Comparing this sculpture with that of the other two carved arches of
the central porch in the late 1870s, however, Ruskin finds it 'mere
twelfth century grotesque, unworthy of its place' (24.291).

    The face of the second carved arch – 'a series of female figures now *66*
unintelligible as the painted inscriptions on their scrolls are gone' –
arouses mixed feelings. The figures are 'very graceful, but forced in *67, 69*
attitude', and their 'features are ugly & mindless when seen close.
even disagreeable' (SMB.42). He attempts a catalogue of the seventeen
figures, noting that their scrolls 'are broad – almost square only
rolled at end: have had inscription in good plain latin letters'
(SMB.41l). Bellini shows 'the chain of figures . . . gilded. and their *IV*
scrolls are grey; on dark (blue?) ground. effect very beautiful'
(SMB.72l). In *St. Mark's Rest* Ruskin relates this archivolt to the
mosaic and cornice above it, noting *62*

> those steps of stone ascending on each side over the inner archivolt; a
> strange method of enclosing its curve; but done with special purpose. If you
> look in the Bellini picture, you will see that these steps formed the rocky
> midst of a mountain which rose over them for the ground, in the old
> mosaic; the Mount of the Beatitudes (24.290).

The sculpture now wins unqualified approval, but its interpretation
still puzzles him:

> I am not sure yet of anything in this archivolt except that it is entirely
> splendid twelfth-century sculpture. I had the separate figures cast for my
> English museum, and put off the examination of them when I was
> overworked. The Fortitude, Justice, Faith, and Temperance are clear
> enough on the right – and the keystone figure is Constancy, but I am sure of
> nothing else yet: the less that interpretation partly depended on the scrolls
> (24.291).[31]

    The soffit of this arch contains 'the superb sculpture of the *63*
months', daguerreotyped, partially drawn,[32] and interpreted briefly
in the *St. M. Book* (pp. 42, 44, 45). A comparison between these

Months and those of Spenser's *Faerie Queene* is placed in the Gothic section of the *Stones*, for Ruskin finds them 'treated with the peculiar spirit of the Gothic sculptors . . . this archivolt is the first expression of that spirit which is to be found in Venice' (10.321). Though his unfamiliarity with standard Byzantine cycles of the Months results in a few questionable assertions, the suggestion of Gothic influence is plausible.[33] His interpretations (remarks about Spenser excluded) follow:

The sculptures of the months are on the under-surface, beginning at the bottom on the left hand of the spectator as he enters, and following in succession round the archivolt; separated, however, into two groups, at its centre, by a beautiful figure of the youthful Christ, sitting in the midst of a slightly hollowed sphere covered with stars to represent the firmament, and with the attendant sun and moon, set one on each side, to rule over the day and over the night.

73l

The months are personified as follows: –

63 1. JANUARY. *Carrying home a noble tree on his shoulders, the leafage of which nods forward, and falls nearly to his feet.* Superbly cut. . . . His sign, Aquarius, is obscurely indicated in the archivolt by some wavy lines representing water . . . .

2. FEBRUARY. *Sitting in a carved chair, warming his bare feet at a blazing fire.* . . . His sign, Pisces, is prominently carved above him ['two fat fish' (SMB.44)].

71 3. MARCH. Here, as almost always in Italy, *a warrior* . . . . His sign, the Ram, is very superbly carved above him ['the winged lion painted on his shield and a capital ram above him' (SMB.44)] . . . .

4. APRIL. Here, *carrying a sheep upon his shoulder.* A rare representation of him. In Northern work he is almost universally gathering flowers, or holding them triumphantly in each hand. . . .

73 5. MAY *is seated, while two young maidens crown him with flowers.* A very unusual representation, even in Italy; where, as in the North, he is almost always riding out hunting or hawking . . . .

6. JUNE. *Reaping.* The corn and sickle sculptured with singular care and precision, in bold relief, and the zodiacal sign, the Crab, above, also worked with great spirit. . . .

72 7. JULY. *Mowing.* A very interesting piece of sculpture, owing to the care with which the flowers are wrought out among the long grass. . . .

8. AUGUST. Peculiarly represented in this archivolt, *sitting in a chair, with his head upon his hand, as if asleep; the Virgin* (the zodiacal sign) *above him, lifting up her hand.* This appears to be a peculiarly Italian version of the proper employment of August. [It is common in Byzantine cycles; see Demus 1960, p. 154.]

9. SEPTEMBER. *Bearing home grapes in a basket.* . . .

10. OCTOBER [not shown]. *Wearing a conical hat, and digging busily with a long spade.* . . .

67 11. NOVEMBER. *Seems to be catching small birds in a net.* I do not remember

71 March and April. Soffit of the second decorated arch of the third porch

72 July, August and the grapes of September. Soffit of the second decorated arch of the third porch

73 Carvings on the soffits of the innermost (right) and second of the decorated arches of the third porch, 1860–75

him so employed elsewhere. [Again, typically Byzantine, though usually given to October]. . . .

12. DECEMBER. *Killing swine*. . . . (10.316–21)

Ruskin's praise is echoed by Demus, who considers these carvings the work of 'an artist of great talent',[34] while G.H. Crichton places them 'among the finest reliefs of their kind'.[35]

The carvings of the outer arch are not mentioned in the *St. M. Book*, but two passages in the *Stones* indicate Ruskin's admiration. Contrasting the 'graceful, fixed, or languid' figures of Byzantine sculpture with the 'Northern Energy' of the Lombardic and Gothic schools, he states in *Stones I*:

If the great outer archivolt of St. Mark's is Byzantine, the law is somewhat broken by its busy domesticity; figures engaged in every trade, and in the

62

103

preparation of viands of all kinds; a crowded kind of London Christmas scene, interleaved (literally) by the superb balls of leafage, unique in sculpture (9.428).

70 Ruskin is confusing the face carving with that of the soffit, containing
74–76 the Trades. A more careful study for *Stones II* confirms his feeling that this sculpture exhibits the transforming influence of a powerful new style. While much of the earlier sculpture of Venice features
73r 'grotesque animals scattered among leafage, without any definite meaning',

> the great outer entrance of St. Mark's, which appears to have been completed some time after the rest of the fabric, differs from all others in presenting a series of subjects altogether Gothic in feeling, selection, and vitality of execution, and which show the occult entrance of the Gothic spirit before it had yet succeeded in effecting any modification of the Byzantine [architectural] forms. (10.315)

When he returns to St. Mark's in the late 1870s, this arch receives prominent notice. Its carving consists,

62, 70 to the front . . . of leafage closing out of spirals into balls interposed between the figures of eight Prophets (or Patriarchs?) – Christ in their midst on the keystone. No one would believe at first it was thirteenth-century work, so delicate and rich as it looks; nor is there anything else like it that I know, in Europe, of the date: – but pure thirteenth-century work it is, of rarest chiselling. (24.286–7)

Ruskin's dating and praise are echoed by later writers.[36]

The Trades of the soffit are 'equally rich, and much more animated' than the face carvings (24.288). In 1877 he lists the fourteen subjects, from left to right, in a letter to Rawdon Brown.[37] However, in *St. Mark's Rest* he suggests that 'read from right to left, Oriental-wise, the order would be more intelligible' (24.289).[38] Ruskin's interpretations are:

1. Fishing.	8.	Masonry.
2. Forging.	9.	Pottery.
74 3. Sawing. Rough Carpentry?	10.	The Butcher.
4. Cleaving wood with axe. Wheelwright?	11.	The Baker.
75 5. Cask and tub making.	12.	The Vintner.
6. Barber-surgery.	13.	The Shipwright.
7. Weaving.	14.	?

Keystone – Christ *the Lamb*; *i.e.*, in humiliation.

Demus agrees with all but two of these readings, giving no. 7 as Shoemaking (Ruskin had written 'Weaving? very difficult to make out' to Brown), and no. 9 as 'Selling of milk and cheese' (again,

74–76 Details of the Trades Cycle on the soffit of the outer arch of the third porch

Ruskin had queried: 'Potters? or Water carriers?'). Like all subsequent commentators Ruskin finds the fourteenth figure enigmatic: 'a sitting figure, though sitting, yet supported by crutches.' He 'cannot read this symbol: one may fancy many meanings in it', but guesses: 'The rest of old age?' (24.288–89).[39] Especially impressive are the 'two beautiful angels' of the keystone, the 'beautifully clear and forcible' carving of nos 2, 3 and 5, and the realism of nos 4 and 8 ('the workers lay mortar with trowel just like ours').[40] Ruskin concludes: 'there is little work like them elsewhere, pure realistic sculpture of the twelfth and thirteenth centuries' (24.290). Demus considers the reliefs, which he dates about 1260, 'by far the most complete and most lifelike representations of the Trades in mediaeval sculpture'.[41]

But the balls of leafage on the outer face evoke Ruskin's strongest response. He had etched one for *The Seven Lamps*, writing: 'It looks as if its leaves had been sensitive, and had risen and shut themselves into a bud at some sudden touch, and would presently fall back again into their wild flow' (8.121). An 1850 notebook entry headed 'Spiral feeling of Venetians' compares the leaves and balls to 'sea waves'

76

70
18

whirling about 'a ball of foam' (M2.36). In 1877 he draws the ball
xxxiv next above, with the bird underneath. The verve and dash of the
drawing are worthy of the original, strengthening Ruskin's claim
that one cannot 'at all know how good' such sculpture is, 'unless you
will learn to draw' (24.287):

> You see, in the first place, that the outer foliage is all of one kind – pure
> Greek Acanthus, – not in the least transforming itself into ivy, or kale, or
> rose: trusting wholly for its beauty to the varied play of its own narrow and
> 77 pointed lobes. . . . it is as nearly as possible the acanthus of early Corinth,
> only more flexible, and with more incipient blending of the character of the
> vine which is used for the central bosses. You see that each leaf of these last
> touches with its point a stellar knot of inwoven braid . . . the outer acanthus
> folding all in spiral whorls.
>
> Now all the thirteenth-century ornament of every nation runs much
> into spirals, and Irish and Scandinavian earlier decoration into little else.
> But these spirals are different from theirs. The Northern spiral is always
> elastic – like that of a watch-spring. The Greek spiral, drifted like that of a
> whirlpool, or whirlwind. It is always an eddy or vortex – not a living rod,
> like the point of a young fern. (24.287)

By 1877 Ruskin had discerned an influence even stronger than the
Gothic on this swirling foliage, as on much else at St. Mark's – the
spirit of ancient Greece:

> 64 The first leaves I ever drew from St. Mark's were those drifted under the
> breathing of it; these on its uppermost cornice, far lovelier, are the final

perfection of the Ionic spiral, and of the thought in the temple of the Winds. (24.288)[42]

The carvings of this arch, described by Demus as 'the crowning achievement of Venetian Ducento sculpture',[43] are now in ruinous condition. The lacy pattern of the lower ball has been eaten away; the bird that Ruskin drew has few feathers left to lose.[44] Ruskin wrote in 1879 that he had cast two of these balls for St. George's Museum as 'the most instructive pieces of sculpture of all I can ever show there' (24.287). Did he foresee the day when his casts might also become the best three-dimensional record of those superb carvings?[45]

18

77, xxxiv

The fourth porch

79

The shafts of the fourth porch appear to have been left in peace between 1850 and 1980. Ruskin's figures[46] show that those of the lower storey vary in base circumference between 3 ft 8 in. and 4 ft 5 in., and that the builders attempted to match them as closely as possible between the north and south sides. The pair showing the largest discrepancy, no. 47 and its reciprocal 52, measuring 4 ft 2 in. and 4 ft 5 in. respectively, are placed in positions that make them difficult to match in normal viewing. Nos 44 and 55, at the front, are identical in girth (4 ft 1 in.) and both of *cipollino*. Sulphurous acid, reaching St. Mark's in rain and pungent mists, had by 1980 reduced column 44 to the likeness of a rotting tree stump, while the 'beautiful verd antique bases' of nos 49 and 50 framing the lower window, whose profile Ruskin drew full-size (WS.165), were shapeless lumps of crumbling stone.

78

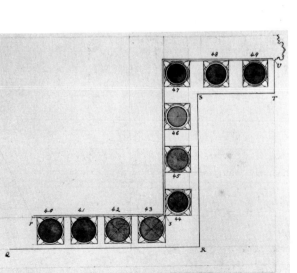

78 John Ruskin *Plan of the north half of the fourth porch* 1850

79 The fourth and fifth porches, *c.* 1875

Ruskin measures the second-storey shafts at their bases, and discovers a variation in girth between 3 ft 4 in. and 2 ft 6½ in. The four smallest, framing the archivolt of the upper window and measuring from north to south 2 ft 9 in., 2 ft 8 in., 2 ft 6½ in. and 2 ft 10 in., are 'noticeably small'.[47] The Ice Plinth here 'carries about as much of the *back* of the arch with mosaic as it does of its sides' (SMB.34). Ruskin, like more recent writers, connects the carving of the inner archivolt stylistically with that of the fifth porch.[48]

The fifth porch

The fifth porch and southwest portico were greatly altered in restorations that took place during the twelve years before the Ruskin/Zorzi protest of 1877 (see Chapter 8). Ruskin's notes provide much detail against which the present structure can be evaluated.

The shafts, bases and capitals of the southern half of the fifth porch 79 were reset. The photograph shows their unstable condition, caused by rebuilding to the edge of the porch, sometime between about 1870 and 1877. Ruskin's 1850 diagram of the positions of the upper shafts (unshaded circles) over the abacus heads of the lower shafts is 81 reproduced with added white circles showing the setting of the upper shafts in 1980. It is difficult to determine how much of the change in relative positions is due to alterations in the upper, how much to changes in the lower, columns. Certainly the latter were moved. Stains on the bottom of the Great Plinth marking former positions of the lower abaci, a dangling metal dowel used for the old fastening of one of these abaci, and cement patches covering holes left by others, were visible in 1980.

While the dimensions of the individual bases and shafts of the entire first storey still tally with Ruskin's figures, the positions of the bases and shafts of the southern half of the porch have all changed with respect to each other, the plinth on which they stand, and the 80 backing wall.[49] To give one of many changes: the distances between the bottoms of shafts 62–65 have all increased: between 62/63 by 1¼ in., between 63/64 by over 3 in., and between 64/65 by 2 in. This expansion of more than 6 in. in accumulated distances between the southern shafts is consistent with G.E. Street's observation in 1880 that the rebuilt portion of the façade had been moved about half a

80 Rough plan of the first storey of the fifth porch and southwest portico

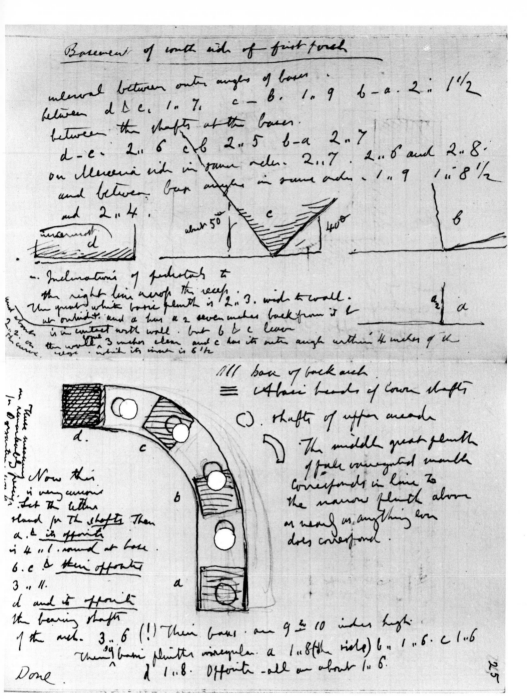

81 John Ruskin *Superimposition of shafts of the south side of the fifth porch* 1850 (present positions of shafts added in white)

82 John Ruskin *Inner arch and columns of the fifth porch* probably engraved *c.* 1852

p. 201 foot westward. That the molestation stopped at the southern half of the fifth porch is indicated by the fact that the intervals between the bases and shafts of its north side tallied closely in 1980 with Ruskin's figures.[50]

As always, the disposition of shafts of variable girth intrigues him. The outer pair (58 and 65) measure 4 ft 1 in., the next two pairs 3 ft 11 in., and the shafts flanking the lower window only 3 ft 6 in. The latter appear to sustain more weight (the arch above) than the others, and Ruskin notes: 'Highly curious – the main bearing shafts smallest'.[51] The circumference at the bottom of the upper shafts varies from 3 ft 3 in. for the western couple to only 2 ft 8 in. for those framing the carved archivolt (SMB.28l–r). This inner pair has dissimilar bases. That to the south has 'a most unusual thing the rude base . . . of which the lower member . . . is octagonal – all worked in one piece with shaft', and while its height is 11 in., all the others of the second storey are some 2 inches shorter (SMB.28). Such irregularity in height and profile is compounded by striking differences in decoration:

those on the Sea [south] side having very rich & elaborate angle leaves [a note adds: 'later work. evidently. very refined in cutting'] but on the Merceria side plain leaves flat at point. with one rounded rib (SMB.28l–r).

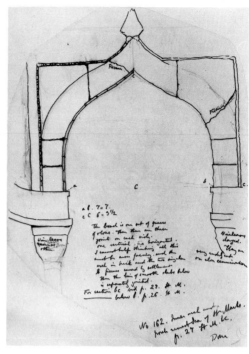

83 Inner arch of the fifth porch, daguerreotype, 1849–52

84 John Ruskin *Study of the inner arch of the fifth porch* (Worksheet 162) 1850

Above the Ice Plinth 'there is nothing whatever but the plain waggon vault of the flat arch which is 9 ft 6 in. high above it exactly under the soffit' (SMB.29) and decorated with 'the vile modern mosaic' (SMB.23).

An engraving of the inner arch, intended for *Examples*,[52] was made 'partly from Daguerreotype – & partly from materials – but not from nature'.[53] One of the daguerreotypes survives, and the 'materials' – a worksheet and five pages in the *St. M. Book* – explain how he produced such a detailed drawing without having the building before him. The worksheet records the main lines and dimensions of the archivolt, its stonework, and 'two singular fissures caused by settlement'. It is cross-referenced to two notebook pages (one is reproduced here) illustrating, with measures, the 'Section at side of arch through the daged Vine Capital', and referring in turn to the full-sized drawing of the 'flower cornice' occupying *a b* on the page shown. Another page analyses the reversed curves of the outer and inner edges of the archivolt (SMB.30). These details enable Ruskin to correct for converging verticals and distorted curves in his daguerreotype. Two more pages study the section and carving of the leaf moulding:

113

This is one of the rudest leaf mouldings though rich which I have met with   It is all worked in rude ridges . . . but exquisite effect given to it by the gold mosaic rudely cemented into its interstices. . . . rolled leaf border [its section is the curve drawn beside Ruskin's writing], in rude ridges . . . The leaves bearing the ridges in centre. – instead of *depressions*. a form quite new to me . . . and perhaps the simplest possible   It is not easy to draw however but it is in this way [sketch at left] and interstices touched with gold [many tesserae missing in 1982].

Such studies made possible the authenticity of Ruskin's more finished drawings.

The southwest portico

Ruskin claimed in 1879 that the restored southwest portico was merely a 'vile model' of the original (10.115n). Bunney's careful
_{XI} painting of 1877–82 records the shocking contrast between the old and new incrustation (since partly remedied). No less dramatically, Ruskin's studies and daguerreotypes prove that the structure itself has been greatly modified since the 1850s.

The most obvious change involved a widening of the pier between the fifth porch and the portico, observable by comparing a
_{12, 25} daguerreotype and Ponti's pre-restoration photograph (c.1860–65) with Bunney's painting (1877–82). A desire to secure symmetry with the corresponding northern pier is betrayed by the wider spacing of
₈₀ the two lower columns (nos 66 and 67) and those surmounting them,
₈₉ as well as the placing of a new statue between the latter to mirror that to the north.[54] The widened spandrel between the arches of the fifth porch and southwest portico and the broader frame surrounding its rectangular bas-relief can be seen in the same comparison, while the
₇₉ 1870s photograph shows a break where the old brickwork met the new. Finally, the plinth sustaining the lower columns possessed only three panels before the restoration and now, like its northern counterpart, boasts four. This plinth was 7 ft $4\frac{1}{4}$ in. long in 1850 (ws.133 and M.196l). It is now almost a foot and a half longer at 8 ft $8\frac{1}{2}$ in.

The western aspect of the portico has been altered. In Ponti's
_{2, 25} photographs the outer edge of its upper wall slopes inward as it rises (still true of the northwest corner), in keeping with Ruskin's notion
_{p. 52} that the façade was designed to draw the eye both upward and inward. This refinement was removed by the restorer's plumb-line. Ruskin's measurements demonstrate, moreover, a substantial move to the south by the corner lily column (no. 69). Whereas its distance
₈₀ from no. 68 was, 'at root of shafts, 8 ft 7 in.' in 1850 (M.180), that

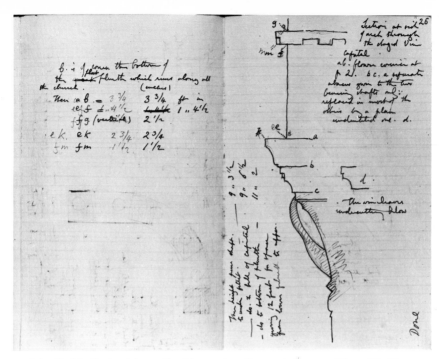

85 John Ruskin *Study of the profile of the members (from capital to top of Great Plinth) sustaining the right side of the inner arch of the fifth porch (St. M. Book)* 1850

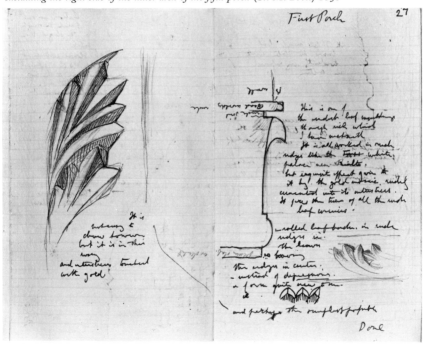

86 John Ruskin *Study of the leaf moulding of the inner arch of the 'First' [i.e. fifth] porch (St. M. Book)* 1850

interval is now 9 ft 4½ in. Another change is observable by comparing Ruskin's careful diagram of the basic plinths and pavement slabs of nos. 68 and 69 with the present structure. Whereas the western edge of the Basic Plinth of column 69 ('B' in Ruskin's diagram) stood a good deal west of that of 68 ('C'), the two are now virtually even (see Ruskin's large watercolour of the portico, done *c.* 1849, for confirmation, from another angle, of the old dispositions). That the placement of no. 69 westward of the Basic Plinth of the main body of the west front ('q_2' in Ruskin's diagram) might have been part of a deliberate scheme of the old builders was either overlooked or deliberately ignored by the restorer, G.B. Meduna.

Moving to the east and south of the portico, we may regard the present structure as a rough model against which Ruskin's record can be read. In the 1849 watercolour,[55] the view, almost identical with that given in two daguerreotypes, was taken from the second storey of the loggia of the Doge's Palace.[56] To the change in relative positions of columns 68 and 69 already noted must be added a shift in the diagonally opposed columns 68 and 70. The gap between them in 1850 'at root of shafts' was 13 ft (M.180), and is now 14 ft ¾ in. Such large differences indicate drastic rebuilding. Only the third interval, between southern columns 69 and 70 measured at 'the root of the shafts', still agrees, at 9 ft 5 in., with Ruskin's figure.[57] Shaft 69 has been turned: its veining, which in Ruskin's drawing descends from left to right in harmony with that of no. 70 (the reversed image of the daguerreotype confirms this), now descends from right to left. Such optical details, probably unnoticed by the restorer, were important to the men who first positioned these shafts.

The capitals of the second storey have been drastically rearranged. While all four of the south face were of the zigzag type before reconstruction, the second from the west is now a small leafy

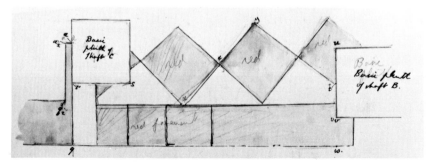

87 John Ruskin *Study of the disposition of bases and pavement of the southwest portico before its rebuilding* (Worksheet 129) 1849–50

88 John Ruskin *The southwest portico of St. Mark's* (*Examples*, 1851)

89 Part of the southwest portico, 1982

specimen. Deeply withdrawn into the shade beside its scintillating   *89*
partner, it is painfully out of place in the composition. While the two
southern capitals over the other lily column are still zigzags, much of
their visual effect was squandered by Meduna's inattention to detail.
Before restoration, these capitals were slightly recessed under their   *90*
cornice. Now they recede so far that they are drowned in shadow   *91, 92*
during the brightest hours of the day. Ruskin's studies had assumed
that the zigzag capital, 'in its place very effective and beautiful'
(9.383), is designed for bright illumination: 'The fillets . . . are cut an
inch deep down from its simple bell: whose contour is given more
truly at fig. 2' (M.203). These incisions produce the powerful shade
that gives the capital its piquant effect even at long distance. But each
band is itself subdivided (two variant sections are given at lower right
in Ruskin's study) by 'two sharp lines of shade', visible in nearer   IX
viewing, but not if the capital is itself in deep shadow.

Such disregard for finer points of design is not surprising when we
discover that the second-storey shafts were not even replaced in their
original order. Ruskin's daguerreotypes and drawings, as well as old

117

90 John Ruskin *Study of the southwest portico from the east*, 1849–52

91 The southwest portico from the southeast, 1982

92 The southwest portico from the east, 1982

photographs, show that before restoration both southern shafts over the southwest lily column were of the bulging porphyry type. One has been retained at the southwest corner; the other replaced by a slender shaft of green breccia. Changes to the upper walls were
88, VIII equally arbitrary. In an effort to match the northwest portico, angle
91, XI pilasters in red Verona, lacking in 1850, have been added. The geometrical relations between the panel, decorative circle, and arch
92 on the eastern side have all been altered. The top of the panel, which once touched the semicircular rings under the gutters, now falls
88 below them by at least half a foot.[58]

The prominence of the dentil bands over the capitals in Ruskin's 1851 engraving of the portico is striking when comparison is made with the present structure, even from closer range. Ruskin explains the difference in 1879:

118

The ancient dentils are bold, broad, and cut with the free hand, as all good Greek work is; the new ones, little more than half their size, are cut with the servile and horrible rigidity of the modern mechanic. (24.421)

Comparing new with old, we find a ratio of about 3:2 (in the lower plinth at the right it is almost 2:1) in numbers of dentils occupying the same space. Lamenting many similar 'wanton and inconsiderate changes made in the mouldings which it was pretended to reproduce' (24.409), Ruskin writes:

Imagine a Kensington student set to copy a picture by Velasquez, and substituting a Nottingham lace pattern, traced with absolute exactness, for the painter's sparkle and flow and flame, and boasting of his improvements as '*plus exacte*'! That is precisely what the Italian restorer does for *his* original; but, alas! he has the inestimable privilege also of destroying the original as he works, and putting his student's caricature in its place! (24.421)

94 John Ruskin *Study of a capital on the north façade of St. Mark's* 1849–52

93 St. Christopher; north façade

95 Alexander the Great; north façade

5 PEACOCK'S FEATHERS IN THE SUN
The north and south sides

Apart from the westerly portion drawn in 1852, only a few details of   v
the north side receive Ruskin's attention. The lobed capitals are   p. 68
drawn separately and admired for their chiaroscuro in distant effect.
Backing the arch to their left are some bas-reliefs which, apart from   124
the artful asymmetry of their composition, intrigue him by their
placement. 'The way the tondi are set', he writes, 'reminds me of
planets swimming in space' (SMB.8ol). A second-storey capital under
the next arch to the east is studied in a small sketch that combines   94
frontal aspect with information about curves of profile: 'The
deepening of relief of cross, which is vertical, while bell curves in,
highly curious'.[1]

    Notes made in 1876–77 on some of the larger sculptures (24.253n)
virtually exhaust his study of the lower half of this façade. Beginning
from the east, the 'large St. Christopher'   93

unites Byzantine with what seems to me later characters in a lovely way; at
any rate it is exquisitest work of this Byzantine school; all the proportions
of the lateral shafts, leaves of capitals, etc., as fine as can be. You cannot
examine it too long or too carefully.

Demus considers this a thirteenth-century work, carved for its place.
Its large size permitted the saint to 'be seen by passers-by and thus
protect them from sudden death'.[2] A series of carvings, all dated by
Ruskin 'thirteenth-century transitional work', comes next: three
panels at the top of the north transept wall, identified as 'St. John, St.
Matthew, and St. Luke' (the middle figure is actually Christ; St.
Matthew is at his right, while St. Luke sits above and to the left of the
Porta dei Fiori), 'St. Mark sitting' to the right of, and 'St. John the
Evangelist standing' over, the doorway, as also the 'door itself and   127
the bas-relief above it'.[3] As so often, most later investigators agree
with Ruskin's dating.[4] Next comes the

small horizontal panel with sacrifice of Isaac, a quaint little piece of late
work [in this context, 'late' means thirteenth- or fourteenth-century]
imitating the Greek symbolical manner; that is to say, the thicket is one
small tree, the ram caught in it stands quietly beside its stem, the altar is a
slender pillar with fire on the top, and the interference of the Deity
represented only by a hand emerging from the foliage.[5]

The next panel mystified Ruskin:

95   A goddess of light – what goddess I can do no more than guess, and mean to find out. The orb beneath her is radiated; she shakes flames from the long torches in her hands, and is ascending in a chariot driven by griffins, the wheels put far away on the right and left, merely as signs they are there. Entirely Eastern-Greek in treatment, no doubt an imported sculpture.

The 'goddess' is now generally accepted to be Alexander the Great, and the 'flames' at the ends of the 'torches' appear to be small animals. Ruskin's suggested provenance, however, seems as plausible as a number of later theories, one of which relates the panel to similar works produced in Constantinople about 1080.[6] Finally, the most

v   westerly panel is 'St. George standing. The worst'.

    The carvings of the upper storey[7] are examined closely in a notebook of 1849–50. Ruskin discerns

three distinct periods of transition – if not four: in the Gothic work of the upper story. The niches and statues on the north side are pure and early, and full of interest. On the south side: still fine but less perfect: To the front: very far inferior: These are three; only the difference between the north &

3   south sides not well defined: Then the crocketing and statues on the finials are of the latest and most extravagant time. – of most delicate marble, while the archivolts are of Istrian stone. They are wonderfully cut in and out – but utterly vulgar and distorted in thought and execution – if I saw them on Milan cathedral – of which they strongly remind me; or in a stone masons yard in the New road, I should speak of them with nothing but detestation. They have heads of the commonest classical types (M.205–6).

Ruskin's suggested sequence is close to that of a recent scholar, who also relates some of the northern finial statues to contemporary sculpture at Milan Cathedral.[8]

97   Ruskin finds one tabernacle 'superior to all the rest . . . the last of all – farthest back from the square on North side, and on the projecting angle':

It is the simplest possible plan of a niche: it has four sides, eight massy simple slabs of stone: cut into the cusps and mouldings: and a flat top with a hole in the centre – no vaulting whatever: then the pyramidal canopy is set on this level slab: This plan of niche is adopted in more elaborate works and an imitation vaulting filled in with plaster: but I like the simple and massy masonry of these square ones better. I am not certain of the jointing – but there is one joint certainly through the apex of each arch. and the other fitted at each angle among the dentils. how curiously manly and simple as opposed to the filigree niches with rib vaulting of even earlier times – Bayeux for instance in the north. (M.211–12)

96   The *St. M. Book* elucidates finer details. One page gives

the dentil at the top showing joints and the curious *intaglio* diamond, new to

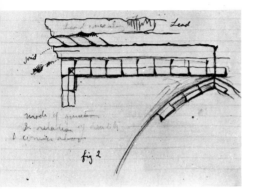

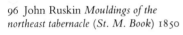

96 John Ruskin *Mouldings of the northeast tabernacle* (*St. M. Book*) 1850

97 Northeast tabernacle of the upper storey, 1982

98 John Ruskin *Details of the northeast tabernacle* (*St. M. Book*) 1850

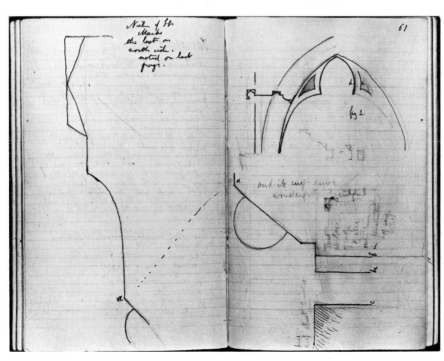

me at angle of dentil. and the neat touching of the apex of arch under centre of dentil block. All should be much neater than I have drawn it. (M.212)

98 Another gives, in fig. 1,

the profile of cusp – wonderfully pure and beautiful for this style. cut clear. and at p 61.l. continued on p 61. [bottom] is the section of arch moulding real size. note that the dentil is small and flat as compared with angle dentil – (which from its mode of turning is necessarily bold:) the cavetto singularly shallow: the roll as singularly bold. The line b. at p 61. is section at base and apex of of [sic] arch. b_2 at penetration of cusp. c. the cusp itself, ought to be about 2 inches wide – ie. d.e. in fig 1.

97 This niche would be perfectly beautiful but for its leaden flowers [in the spandrels] a great fault. common to all the rest. (M.212)

Ruskin notes: 'Its shafts have no bases', and the capitals are 'somewhat roughly cut when seen close but very perfect in effect' (M.212). Under the canopy stands

a very noble, slightly colossal armed figure – Michael? [so identified also by Goldner] which has chain mail under a jointed cuirass – or rather jointed body armour. This figure appears to me about the time and workmanship of the two best angels of the Doges palace – those of south east & south west angles. it has finely chiselled features in repose, and a hairy demon under its feet; which however is very weak & poor. another instance of failure in grotesque. This beautiful niche may be given as a central type of Venetian Gothic – equally removed from Byzantine on the one side – from late florid work on the other. (M.212–13)

His 'central type' established, Ruskin considers the other tabernacles:

This niche is different from all the rest: but the others separate from it by different degrees: the likest to it are those next it on the north side of the church, as far as the north west angle: but they show these following differences. The arch dentil is run up at its apex into one of the retreats of the cornice dentil, instead of merely touching the side of a block; the turning of 96 the angle is only [a simple diagonal rather than the 'intaglio diamond'] . . . the arch is less pointed – and the cavetto of its section much deeper. All these northern niches have beautiful figures – quiet – severe & grand – the perfect type of what figures should be in external decoration – no Byzantine formalism in them – yet no modern luxuriousness. . . .

100, 101 Next to these niches may be classed those of the opposite or southern side: but their figures are far inferior and more modern. – their arches also in the management of the cusp. The final one, however next the Ducal palace, is here – most strangely – as on the other side – the best of the series: it is nearly the same in outer contour of arch as its beautiful opposite – it has the same shallow cavetto of section: the arch point is however run a little against or into the cornice dentil: – in the second niche – the intermediate one of south side the arch point is squeezed up into the dentil block. and in

124

99 The Ship Captain's Companion; north façade, 1982

the third – the angle niche south west. it is fairly run in to the half of cornice dentil – as in all the niches to the front

The third stage of difference is in the front [western] niches; whose figures are comparatively quite modern – forced, theatrical and poor – more especially the two kneeling ones at the angles. Their capitals are for the most part far inferior. – more rudely cut & more florid in design – except those of the north west angle already noted . . . and their cusps far inferior in line, as also those of the three towards piazzetta . . . . We have thus three marked periods in the working of the *pure* Gothic of St Marks; (without counting the red and vulgar traceries of the lower porches and windows) (M.213–14). XI VII

The tabernacles and associated figures Ruskin likes least are those by Niccolò Lamberti and assistants.[9] The prophets, angels, virtues and saints surmounting the upper arches please him even less, despite their distant effect. While these 'great arches and their first or under finials are, judging by their leaf sculpture without doubt of same period as the niches above and below', and 'have been originally without crockets, and have had plain leaf finials', the p. 10

extravagant crocketing – wildly cut a jour [right through] in white marble; is awkwardly pinned on afterwards – late 15th century of the worst kind. and the original simple finial is surmounted by a pedestal with bracket moulding – carrying a late and utterly vile statue. (M.215) 3, 97

Ruskin's response to another feature of these upper arches is equally severe. He places in the 'period of pure Gothic' of the northern tabernacles

the very singular wall niches between the arches on the north side which have cabled shafts leaning outwards against the archivolts; bending round them; the niches themselves curved outwards like a mitre. with a leaf ornament on each side very pure & good (M.215). 99

100 Upper part of the south façade before restoration, 1860–65

Filling these niches, however, are

99 some of the vilest modern statues conceivable – used as gutters for the roof – having urns or waterpots on their shoulders into which the leaden pipes are carried. These distorted monstrosities seem to have been put up in the 18th century (M.215).[10]

They are 'literally fit for nothing but a ship captain's garden at Bermondsey' (M.206).

p. 21   Ruskin's 1846 studies would lead one to expect much activity in 1849–52 on the south façade. In fact, it receives even less analytical

VIII attention than the north side. His large watercolour defines the limits of his eastward progress. A brief note gives the 'section of archivolt of great wide arch towards palace on side of St Marks'. It 'has a rose & leaf moulding of the earliest pattern', but 'is coarsely worked and looks added'. To its left, above 'the little shaft in the niche', is the 'loveliest' capital he has 'yet seen'. It has 'Birds with cross tails – and pine cones on angles' (SMB.101l).[11]

His chief interest on the south side can only be inferred from later comments. In 1877, lamenting Meduna's rebuilding, he writes nostalgically of 'the bright recess of your Piazzetta, by the pillars of Acre' where he once spent so many 'happy and ardent days' (24.405–6). The mosaics

126

especially were of such exquisite intricacy of deep golden glow between the courses of small pillars, that those two upper arches had an effect as of peacock's feathers in the sun, when their green and purple glitters through and through with light. (24.407)

So splendid was the colour 'that in old time I looked every day at this side of St. Mark's, wondering whether I ever should be able to paint anything so lovely' (24.408). No drawing by Ruskin of these upper arches has been found.[12] Comparison between an old photograph and the present structure permits identification of particular slabs of the purple-veined marbles which were removed.[13]

100

x

Drawings of 1846 and 1849 show another attraction of this side of the church: the so-called Pillars of Acre, drawn again memorably in 1879.[14] Ruskin seems to have regarded the space between these pillars, the south façade, and the west Treasury wall almost as an interior, describing it in 1879 as the 'sweetest of all sacred niches in that great marble withdrawing-room of the Piazzetta' (14.427). Under its colourful arches, moreover, stood the door (now fastened as a window) into the Baptistery – his favourite entrance to St. Mark's.

II, VIII

xxxv

101, XII

101 The south side of St. Mark's before restoration, before 1865

6 CHAPTERS TO BE WRITTEN
The interior

Ruskin's evocation of the interior of St. Mark's in *The Stones of Venice* is as effective as that of the west front. Just as a walk through constricted lanes had led, past various human impedimenta, to the shadowy pillars of the mouth of the Piazza and thence to the 'great light' of the square itself, so now a scandalized retreat from the inhabitants of the western porches ('knots of men of the lowest classes . . . basking in the sun like lizards') brings Ruskin and his readers to a door on the south side, and thence from the 'light and the turbulence of the Piazzetta' into the silent Baptistery:

xxx   We are in a low vaulted room; vaulted, not with arches but with small cupolas starred with gold, and chequered with gloomy figures: in the centre is a bronze font charged with rich bas-reliefs, a small figure of the Baptist standing above it in a single ray of light that glances across the
102   narrow room, dying as it falls from a window high in the wall (10.85).

Ruskin meditates briefly on a tomb effigy, several mosaics, the ancient wall marbles ('translucent masses darkened into fields of rich golden brown, like the colour of seaweed when the sun strikes on it through deep sea' – now an assortment of grey nineteenth-century improvements), and the modern Venetian wickedness disporting itself so noisily outside. And though the Serenissima is in imminent danger of annihilation at the hands of the Almighty (having, it seems, 'made her choice' to be 'hewn down, and cast into the fire'), Ruskin manages to shepherd his readers with some tranquillity into the main body of her great church:

It is lost in still deeper twilight, to which the eye must be accustomed for some moments before the form of the building can be traced; and then there opens before us a vast cave, hewn out into the form of a Cross, and divided into shadowy aisles by many pillars. Round the domes of its roof the light enters only through narrow apertures like large stars; and here and there a ray or two from some far-away casement wanders into the darkness, and casts a narrow phosphoric stream upon the waves of marble that heave and fall in a thousand colours along the floor. What else there is of light is from torches, or silver lamps, burning ceaselessly in the recesses of the chapels; the roof sheeted with gold, and the polished walls covered with alabaster, give back at every curve and angle some feeble gleaming to the flames; and the glories round the heads of the sculptured saints flash out upon us as we pass them, and sink again into the gloom. Under foot and over head, a continual succession of crowded imagery, one picture passing

128   *Continued on p. 145*

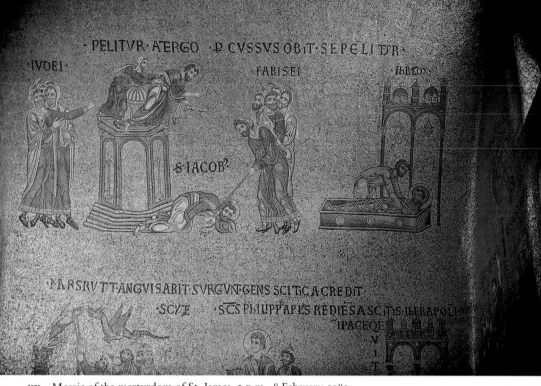

PELITVR·AERGO ·P·CVSSVS·OBiT·SEPELITR·

IVDEI· FARISEI IbELOD·

S·IACOB²

MARSKVT·TANGVISABIT·SVRGVNT·GENS·SCITICACREDIT·
·SCVI· SCS·PhILIPP·APLS·REDIESASCITIS·IbERAPOLI·
IPACEQI
VIT

xx Mosaic of the martyrdom of St. James, 3 p.m., 8 February 1982

xxi Parapet of north nave gallery and mosaic of Paradise from the south nave gallery,
11 February 1982

TRANS·HOSTIA·PETRVS·QVEM·RESERAT·DIGNIS·OMNIBVS·IPSE·VIRIS

No. 21. p. 44 ill.

XXII (left)   John Ruskin *Study of part of the north arcade of the nave (Worksheet 21)* 1849

XXIV (right)   John Ruskin *Details of the lunette over the Porta di San Giovanni (Gothic Book)* 1850

XXIII   John Ruskin *Study of a ram capital in the north arcade of the nave* 1849–52

1

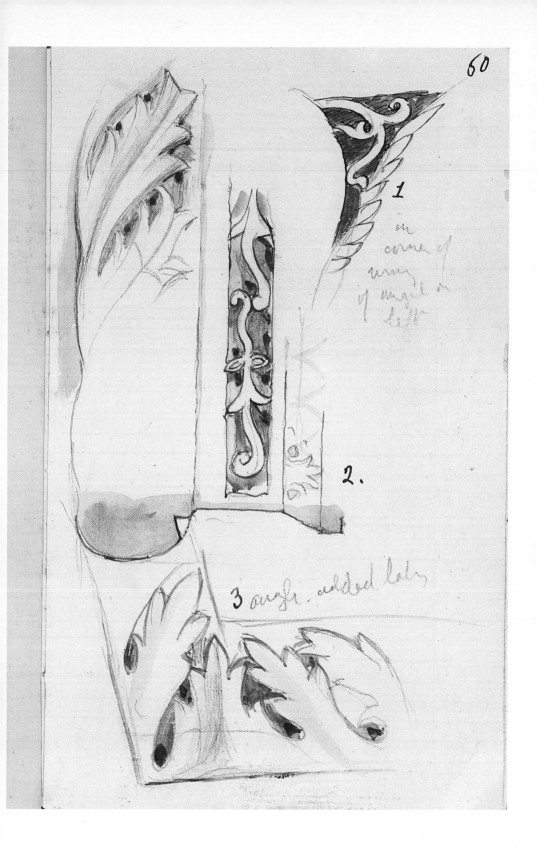

60

1

in
corner of
wing
of angel on
left

2.

3 angle. added later

PPHA

XXVI   Mosaic of the Doge and his People, 1 p.m., 12 February 1982

XXVII   John Ruskin *Study of mosaic of the Doge and his People* 1877

XXV (left)   Mosaic of Christ's Temptation and Entry into Jerusalem, 3.30 p.m., 11 February 1982

XXIX   T. M. Rooke *Mosaics of the eastern dome of St. Mark's* 1879

XXX   Detail of mosaic of the eastern cupola of the Baptistery, 3 p.m., 10 February 1982

XXVIII (left)   Mosaics of the eastern dome, noon, 12 February 1982

XXXI John Ruskin *Northwest portico and part of the first porch of St. Mark's* 1877

XXXIII   Mosaic, spandrel and columns of the first porch, 10.30 a.m., 18 February 1982

XXXII (left)   Mosaic of Salomé in the Baptistery, 10 February 1982

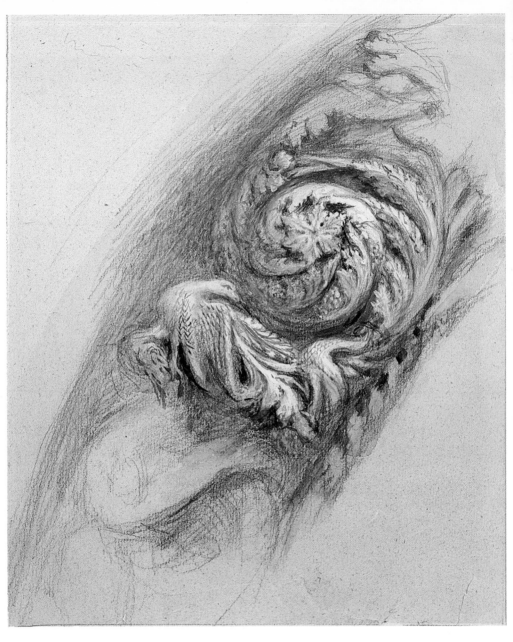

xxxiv   John Ruskin *Carved boss from the face of the outer central arch of St. Mark's* 1877

xxxv   John Ruskin *The Pillars of Acre and southwest portico of St. Mark's* (reversed image) 1879

xxxvii H.R. Newman *The horses of St. Mark's from the north* 1890

xxxvi (left) J.W. Bunney *The northwest portico of St. Mark's* 1870

XXXVIII   John Ruskin *Copy of part of the drawing of the northwest portico of St. Mark's made in 1877* (ill. XXXI) 1879

into another, as in a dream; forms beautiful and terrible mixed together; dragons and serpents, and ravening beasts of prey, and graceful birds that in the midst of them drink from running fountains and feed from vases of crystal; the passions and the pleasures of human life symbolized together, and the mystery of its redemption; for the mazes of interwoven lines and changeful pictures lead always at last to the Cross, lifted and carved in every place and upon every stone; sometimes with the serpent of eternity wrapt round it, sometimes with doves beneath its arms, and sweet herbage growing forth from its feet; but conspicuous most of all on the great rood that crosses the church before the altar, raised in bright blazonry against the shadow of the apse. And although in the recesses of the aisles and chapels, when the mist of the incense hangs heavily, we may see continually a figure traced in faint lines upon their marble, a woman standing with her eyes raised to heaven, and the inscription above her, 'Mother of God', she is not here the presiding deity. It is the Cross that is first seen, and always, burning in the centre of the temple; and every dome and hollow of its roof has the figure of Christ in the utmost height of it, raised in power, or returning in judgment. (10.88–89)

The passage creates a marvellous atmosphere of spatial mystery. Those glimmers of light, wandering through the shadows before striking the uneven floor, that gradual unfolding of hollows and ever deeper hollows, evoke a powerful three-dimensional impression. The sense of the spectator's movement through the building, the ever-changing vista from his entry at the Baptistery door, through the dark nave aisle with its glowing mosaics, and out into a position from which the screen and apse and higher domes become visible, is startling in its authenticity. Nothing could convey more effectively the confused wonder which movement and shifting angles of vision impart to the visitor upon his first entry into St. Mark's. XIV, XV XVI XVII, XVIII

This evocation of vagueness and mystery was fashioned from precisely focused observation. In a draft for the passage, Ruskin had written of the

huge square piers . . . either single or in double groups separated by a narrow arch – according to the weight they bear – imagine these massy piers connected by narrow galleries at half their height – sustained by shafts & arches which separate the body of the church into something correspondent to a nave & aisles – and form enclosures for chapels in the transepts – imagine smaller caverns cut out into a kind of labyrinthine darkness on each side of the choir . . . and the whole feebly lighted – partly by small apertures in the sides of the domes – partly by rose windows at the ends of the nave & transepts[.][1]

Though the final text may be more effective in evoking the impressions of a first visit, it is regrettable that Ruskin abandoned the analysis which was to have supplemented his superb introduction.

102 The Baptistery, looking northwest, 1860–65

The fragments that have been preserved contain perceptive study of large- and small-scale composition.[2]

Ruskin explains, in one of these omitted passages, that he has given ground plans for the churches of Torcello and Murano in *Stones II* (10. facing 22) because he 'could give them with some degree of completeness without confusing the eye or mind of the reader'; but at St. Mark's,

there are so many detached chapels, & nooks. & side porches, & chambers shrines & chapels, that if I give him a complete plan, he will probably, unless a professed architect give up all attempt to follow my description:

146

This woodcut then . . . is not a plan of St Marks, but an abstract of its plan: *103*
giving the essential parts of it and their relations, so that the eye can seize
them at once. I have omitted the sacristy – the chapels of St Isidore and St
[blank; Ruskin means Madonna dei Mascoli] – the Sala del Tesoro – and
several small chambers adjoining to it. . . . We have then. first – an
enclosure of solid walls in the shape of a blunt cross – roofed by five large &
six small cupolas, whose positions are represented by the shaded circles; &
supported upon waggon vaults . . . thrown across from pier to pier
between them – but not represented in the plan in order to avoid confusion.
These waggon vaults are of course connected with the cupolas by pieces of
triangular vaulting, of the form which the reader may see in a moment by
trying to cut an orange or apple into a cube. The eight pieces of skin left
when the cuts on all the six sides first meet each other, are of the form in
question. I shall call them angle vaults when I have occasion to refer to
them. but I have no intention of entangling the reader in a maze of roof
sections. . . .

The black spots in the body of the church represent the piers on which it
stands. The large square ones are those which carry the main waggon vaults
of the roof. they rise in huge and unbroken masses – sheeted with mosaic –
to the spring of these vaults, and would produce an effect of painful weight
were it not for the relief given to the eye by the intermediate shafts
represented by the small round spots, shafts each of one piece of alabaster.
exquisitely proportioned, and sustaining upon light stilted circular arches
rich galleries of carved marble running round the whole church at half the
height of the heavy piers. Each of the three great branches of the entire area   xv, xix
[i.e., nave and N. and S. transepts] is thus divided into nave and aisles – and
an exquisite lightness and complexity is given to the aspect of the whole
fabric, all the greater, because the aisles instead of being roofed at the top, as
in our gothic, are left entirely open, and the spectator looks up through the
narrow space between the light gallery and the outer walls, to the vaulting   xiv
and mosaic of the highest roof. The play of light & shade obtained by this   xviii
arrangement has always rendered St Marks a favourite subject with artists.
(Add. 42–3)

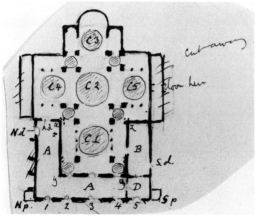

103 John Ruskin *Sketch
plan of St. Mark's* 1849–52

The combination of these graceful forms with the massive piers is one of the most striking features of the interior:

the very condition in St Marks, owing to the inferiority of inner substance [the brickwork], that the great piers are to be huge – square, & evidently rather above than beneath the bulk necessary for their office enables them to receive the gallery against their flanks, and even in some places to let it run through their mass, without the least appearance of want of harmony in the structure – but on the contrary with an infinite gain of general lightness & beauty – while the pure shaft and arch work is set to supporting the galleries themselves and the eye is gratified – in their minor portions by the most °perfect symmetry of proportion – and in the vast piers – by the splendour of surface? (Add. w5)[3]

Ruskin's readers must evaluate this arrangement in the light of their previous experience:

Now: if the reader has been diligent in the study or familiar with the forms, of Egyptian, early Greek – or early Norman architecture: he will be struck by the singular lightness and grace of this elevation – by the high stilting of the arches – the bold expansion of the capitals – and the delicate lines of the archivolts – But if he has on the contrary, been devoted to the study of the English or French middle Gothic – the impression made on his mind by this Byzantine design will be exactly contrary – he will be struck by the simplicity & solidity of its parts – by the massy singleness of its block shafts and the bold horizontality of its band of decoration. It appears thus to be an exact mean between the two schools of ponderous and slender architecture.

In like manner, a student of the Greek Doric, or of our Earliest English, or of the great Florentine Renaissance, schools, will be at once struck. & offended, by the excessive luxurious[ness] & minuteness of the ornament in the capitals and upper parapet. And a student of later Northern Gothic will be equally offended by the emptiness of the spandrils – & simple mouldings of the narrow archivolts. The design appears therefore also to be a mean between the two schools of highly decorated and perfectly plain architecture.

I do not on this ground allege it to be any nearer perfection than many examples of both the schools between which it strikes so equal a balance: but I wish the reader to remember continually . . . that this Venice is the Point of Pause – the dead water, between the currents of many opposing traditions & national feelings – and that we shall continually find in it either the root, or the reconciliation of many branches & divisions of human feeling of which elsewhere it is almost impossible to trace the fraternity. (Add.x–3)

An example is apparent as one stands under the Ascension dome:

The dome of St. Mark's, and the crossing of the nave and transepts of Beauvais, are both carried by square piers; but the piers of St. Mark's are set square to the walls of the church, and those of Beauvais obliquely to them

104 Angel at the southeast of the crossing under the
Ascension dome

. . . . their expression is altogether different, and in that difference lies one
of the most subtle distinctions between the Gothic and Greek spirit (9.122).

But each inner angle of the central piers at St. Mark's sustains, at the
level of the galleries, a carved angel set obliquely to the axes of the
building. This arrangement 'plainly' shows 'Lombardic influence'
(10.357).[4]

Ruskin's description of the 'vast cave', 'huge square piers', 'utmost
height', and 'faraway casement' of the interior contradicts his
subsequent pronouncement that the *impression of the architecture* of a
marble-incrusted building like St. Mark's *is not to be dependent on
size*', that 'none of the parts of the building' are 'removed far from
the eye', that 'we have here low walls spread before us like the pages
of a book, and shafts whose capitals we may touch with our hand'
(10.112–13). As so often when he is laying down the law rather than
using his eyes, Ruskin has pontificated his way into gross error. Only
eight of almost 600 capitals above ground level listed by Deichmann
– those sustaining the bronze horses – can be 'touched': the rest are far
above the tallest reach. While the columns and incrusted walls invite
close inspection, they stand many times the height of Goliath. It is
surely the combination of minutely attractive and sometimes
accessible detail with a sense of shadowy vastness, rather than the
exclusive dominance of either, that gives St. Mark's much of its
unique charm.

The incrustation which helped draw Ruskin into self-
contradiction is 'the first broad characteristic of the building' (10.93).
We may regard 'every piece of jasper and alabaster given to the
architect as a cake of very hard colour, of which a certain portion is to
be ground down or cut off, to paint the walls with' (10.98). The

149

marble rises 'Up to height of pillars . . . in broad upright bands of different kinds varying from a couple of feet to two yards broad. facing each other on opposite sides of the church';[5]

> the beauty of the veining in some varieties of alabaster is so great, that it becomes desirable to exhibit it by dividing the stone, not merely to economise its substance, but to display the changes in the disposition of its fantastic lines. By reversing one of two thin plates successively taken from the stone, and placing their corresponding edges in contact, a perfectly symmetrical figure may be obtained, which will enable the eye to comprehend more thoroughly the position of the veins. (10.104)

This practice, bitterly denounced by some,[6] is carried a step further on the piers. Here corresponding mirror-images occur, not merely across each face of the pier, but also between those faces as seen obliquely. Since the lighting of the two planes seen by the viewer is seldom uniform, their matching patterns are subtly differentiated in hue and tone. Extending the technique described by Ruskin into the third dimension thus increases an already remarkable richness of colour, and supports his claim that those who carried out the incrustation were more interested in displaying the 'intrinsic beauty' of their marbles than in enforcing a rigidly 'structural' style, that 'it is on its value as a piece of perfect and unchangeable colouring, that the claims of this edifice to our respect are finally rested' (10.96–7).

In many of the mediaeval mosaics, however, he discerns an attempt to help articulate the form of the building. They perform not merely colouristic and symbolic, but also 'architectural service'
(10.137n). In the central dome a remarkable feature is

> the interruption of the general aspect of the circle by the figure of the Madonna. A modern architect required to decorate a dome would assuredly have made it with the figures in all its compartments as nearly alike as might be; but in this case the twelve figures of the Apostles are arranged in unbroken series, with drapery in finely divided folds and of light colours; then come the two angels in white, with their wings bedropped with gold, and between these, that is to say, in the whitest part of the whole circle, is placed the Madonna, in a solid mass of dark blue drapery nearly black, and relieved only by three small golden crosses, one on each shoulder, and one on the part of the dress which falls over the
> forehead; this figure fronts the west door of the church, and its darkness gives light and brilliancy to all the rest of the dome. (10.137n)

This is an 'exquisite decorative arrangement', satisfying Ruskin's demand that ornament be subordinate to the total composition of the building it enriches.[7] Even more strikingly 'architectural' are the olive trees of the dome:

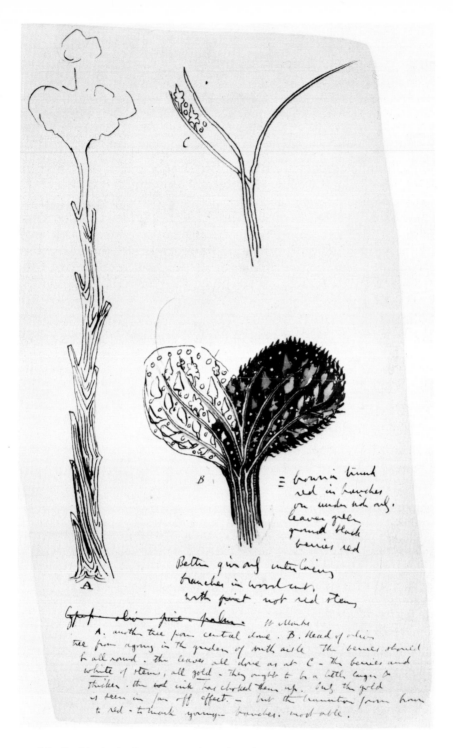

105 John Ruskin *Study of vegetation as depicted in several mosaics at St. Mark's* 1849–52

Trees, much smaller in size and much less conspicuous in position, would as well or better have indicated that the scene was on the Mount of Olives, but their tall stems and dark foliage are of admirable service in dividing, like so many slender pillars, the golden field of the vaults. In order to fit them for this architectural service, the branches are lopped off all up the trunks, and the foliage is only represented in the clustering heads. (10.136n–137n)

Other architecturally effective mosaics are the panels of 'saints – of which the Isaiah – David – Madonna – Solomon & Ezekiel' in the nave aisles are 'among the richest pieces of decorative work in the church', and the 'Death of St Philip . . . and of St James' in the 'Vault of south aisle', are 'admirable in ornamental power'.[8] Some mosaics on the vault of the north transept, 'more especially the Miraculous Draught of Fishes, the Calming of the Sea, and the Curing of the Cripple let down through the house-top', are also designed for ornamental effect:

In this latter subject . . . a piece of architecture is introduced necessarily. In that of the Miraculous Draught of Fishes a high tower, perhaps Capernaum, is introduced as a side scene, and in the Calming of the Sea, a great rock, but the main purpose of all these objects, like that of the trees in the central [dome] . . . is . . . decorative. (10.138n)

The Renaissance and later mosaics, in contrast, are usually conceived as separate pictures:

in the north Triforium . . . is Girolamo Piloto's Paradise – one of the best of the restored mosaics but of which the dead colours & . . . especially the great brick red mass in the centre – destroy the effect of that part of the church. It is most curious that the modern mosaics make it tawdry outside – & dull within[.][9]

The only exception is the 'great tree at the end of the [north] transept, representing the generations of Christ', which is 'good in its effect from below', while the 'other modern mosaics are better than whitewash and that is all' (10.138n). Ruskin especially despises one designer:

Exactly in proportion to a man's idiocy is always the size of the letters in which he writes his name on the picture that he spoils. . . . the spectator who wishes to know who destroyed the effect of the nave, may see his name inscribed twice over, in letters half a foot high, BARTOLOMEO BOZZA. (11.410)

Though sensitive to the architectural contribution made by the mosaics, Ruskin scrapped what would have been a much fuller discussion than emerges from these fragments. Indeed, his plans for 'anatomical analysis' were so severely curtailed that when preparing the chapter on St. Mark's he wrote – in a passage which, though numbered for the printer, was abandoned – that he could merely give an 'idea of the method of structure, and the character of the mouldings, by a detailed account of some of the more important parts'. Further revision reduced this to 'some *one* of the more important parts' (Add.42); then even this hope was frustrated. A scattering of manuscript fragments and drawings indicates that the arcades of nave and transepts were to have been among the subjects thus analysed.

The shafts and arches supporting the galleries are the most 'valuable pieces of stone & the most considered pieces of proportion, in the whole fabric' (Add.w–6). A sketch of the second and third columns of the north arcade of the nave, intended to aid in preparing   XV, XXII a careful plate, was made in 1849.[10] The shafts are 'solid blocks of alabaster. beautifully tapered . . . and containing each between 40 and 45 cubic feet of solid alabaster'.[11] They are

some two feet in diameter – (6 ft 2 in. round at the base –) and 15 feet high. I in vain endeavoured to ascertain their probable value – the sculptors to whom I applied saying that no such pieces of alabaster were now to be obtained – and that no definite price could therefore be set upon them. They have elaborate & singular capitals – of which some further account is given in the second chapter of the fourth part [never published; some MS fragments and drawings are printed in the following pages] – and sustain arches whose curves are singularly studied (Add.44).

The architect has designed these arches   XIV, XIX

to obtain as much lightness of effect as possible, without sacrificing the circular curve entirely; As the spectator regards them from below he imagines them to be stilted semicircles . . . but he will feel as if there were a peculiar charm and grace in the spring of the circle – more than of circles generally. If he ascends into the galleries opposite, he will discover the reason . . . . The curve is not circular . . . but brought at the apex into some approximation to that of a pointed arch. and there is the slightest possible suggestion of the horse shoe form at the base – the mouldings falling back a little as they first rise: This allowance for the perspective effect which in looking up at a round arch plainly stilted, flattens the upper part of the curve, and causes the perpendicular lines to appear slightly convergent, gives the peculiar charm to these arches as they are seen from below. and is a remarkable evidence of the subtle instinct of the Byzantine builders in the arrangement of ornamental lines. (Add.44)

Most of the nave arches clearly have the horseshoe shape when   XV viewed from the opposite aisles.[12]

The bases of the nave are studied in a careful worksheet. They are   *21* remarkable first for the appearance of a band or ring about the bottom of the shaft: so completely resembling an addition for protection that I at first supposed it so: it is a – b in section: projecting more or less: in one or two of the shafts hardly $\frac{1}{2}$ an inch. in others an inch   It is a separate slab put under the shaft – the section is confused both at a and b by the mortar: It is decidedly ungraceful.

21
XIX The most easterly base of the south arcade (B) differs in that its angles are 'occupied by heartshaped processes, the germs of those of the Doges palace . . . but entirely without decoration – heavy – blunt pointed – and reminding one a little of a shoe sole' (ws.20).

The capitals of the six nave columns

107
XXIII are of great importance. I have therefore drawn one of them large in [figure]. They are founded, as the reader will see at a glance, on the Corinthian and this seems to have been a general law for the principal bearing shafts of the early Venetian churches. Instead however of the usual insipid tendrils at the top of the Corinthian capital, four out of the six nave shafts have the fronts of rams seen in the drawing: the fore legs & horns being cut entirely clear from the bell of the capital; and the latter especially being remarkable for the boldness of their unsupported projection: for a full turn & a half of their spiral   The acanthus leaves themselves are also very daringly undercut . . . and the whole capital is one of the most fantastic of those which can be shown to have been cut for their present service in Venice, in the Byzantine period.[13]

Ruskin refers next to a lost illustration of a 'Renaissance capital of the best period. in order that every possible advantage may be given to the adverse cause' (his comments suggest the capitals of Sansovino's *106* nearby Loggetta):

the reader shall judge for himself which of the two is the more rational & beautiful form.

He will observe in an instant the main distinction: – namely that the Renaissance capital has no concentrating upper abacus: and throws out its sprawling & useless spurs far beyond the edge of the masonry it has to sustain. These projecting processes are not only seen at once to be utterly useless: but have nothing in themselves to excuse their prominence – they are dead scrolls – as devoid of interest as they are of strength: The Byzantine spurs on the contrary are animal forms, full of quaintness and picturesque value – and presenting in the coils of their horns alone, as much intricacy of design as there is in all the four Renaissance spurs put together. – but none of this intricacy is allowed to interfere with the main purposes of the capital – and its jutting heads & bending leaves are all gathered at the top into one effort of sustaining strength. . . . While however, on the one hand, this Byzantine capital is to be praised for its subduing the fancifulness of its decoration into visible service, it may on the other be an example to us of the manner in which lightness & elasticity under superincumbent weight,

154

106 Capital (a modern copy) of the Loggetta at the base of the Campanile of St. Mark, Venice

107 John Ruskin *Ram capital of the nave of St. Mark's* 1849–52

may be expressed wherever the architect wishes to do so – without any loss of richness in ornamental effect.[14]

The ram capital has one blemish: it is gilded. This fault, however, is grave, in modern eyes only . . . . The old Byzantines were not in the habit of using stucco ornaments in place of stone, – and however richly gilded they knew & felt that the carved work of their church was in marble – and enjoyed it accordingly. Our wretched modern hypocrisies have rendered us suspicious we can trust nothing but what proclaims itself – genuine – if even that; and cannot conceive the spirit which would overlay with gold what was already beautiful – *We* reserve our gilding for unworthiness: Nevertheless – I hold this indiscriminate gilding of sculpture to be an error . . . for no delicate form is so well seen when its surface is lustrous, as in the pure dead white of the marble. And the adoption of such a method, is the more to be regretted in this instance because the chiselling of the stone is deserving of such careful observation as is little likely to be given to its gilded contours.[15]

Relating the style of this carving closely to that of the apse capitals of San Donato in Murano (the position of which proves them 'to have been cut for their present service'), Ruskin concedes it is 'rough & coarse, & worked chiefly in deep alternate furrows & ridges', but 'in the management of these coarse lines there is a science & knowledge of effect which may well put the most refined modern execution to shame'. Referring again to the small drawing of the ram's head capital, he suggests that

xv

xxiii

155

In the effect of the entire capital . . . the reader will not I believe – see much absence of refinement, except that the rams stand somewhat clumsily on their legs. I therefore went up close to the work: and then drew one of the

108 heads separately . . . the archaic character of the chiselling may be seen at once – more especially in the rude suggestion of fleece. The crochecoeurs [kisscurls] used on the forehead bear a close resemblance to those of the Ninevite sculptures – but there is a little piece of artifice in the eye which belongs to a period of more advanced Naturalism. & which would delight even Edwin Landseer. Its peculiar stare is obtained by leaving the pupil flat – and incising a small furrow within a larger on its outer edge [Ruskin refers to another, missing, drawing of 'the eye alone – half the actual size'] . . . .

The same spirit of Naturalism interfering with the conventionality of the Corinthian capital is shown by the bending stalk and well copied form of the vineleaf which forms the bracket under the centre of the abacus: As this

XXIII
108 also can hardly be seen clearly enough in the first figure, it is given larger in [lower fig., which is mounted sideways] . . . . It will be seen that the leaf is completely expressed – but there is not a touch of the chisel to spare. The vine leaf occurs in one capital only – other natural leaves are used in the rest.[16]

The projection of the rams' heads is matched by that of the 'heads of

107 the leaves', which 'are equally daring in curl' (ws.22) in the central,
109, XV Corinthian, capitals of each arcade. A rapid memorandum shows Ruskin's determination that an intended engraving of the 'aisle of St Marks' should do justice to the shadows cast by these projections.

He notes next the 'white slender abacus' over the capitals. Though 'a mere continuation of the cornice of the piers', it is of 'consummate beauty'.[17] This abacus supports an architrave – 'on a level with the wall, though distinguished by a vigorous joint' – which he studies in several careful diagrams.[18] All in all,

the proportion of the whole arcade; the bold excess of the capital above the tapering shaft and the perfect purity and simplicity of the architrave, render these nave sides always delightful.[19]

The gallery is 'one of the most important decorative features of the whole edifice' (Add.w–6). Instead of the 'intrusive and unmanageable feature' it is in modern Protestant churches, it is 'indispensable to the effect of' St. Mark's, and 'actually enlarged to a size greater than is needful, and decorated in a most elaborate manner,

XIV that the eye may be attracted to it' (Add.44).[20] The side facing the aisle consists of 'a noble round arched parapet, with small pillars' (10.288) and simple capitals designed 'to express lightness' (9.140).

XV, XXI The nave side, in contrast, sustains a magnificent array of

solid slabs of richly sculptured marble – set between low square piers of red marble. We cannot examine them in detail – for all are different – and we

156

Central
Capital for
plate of
aisle of St Marks
Dot up. as usual
with blacks.

108 John Ruskin *Details of ram capital* 1849–52 (see colour ill. XXIII)

109 John Ruskin *Study of chiaroscuro of Corinthian capital in the nave: instructions for engraving* 1850–52

110 Panel on the north gallery of the nave

112 John Ruskin *Study
of a capital in the transept
of St. Mark's* 1851–52

111 John Ruskin
*Capital in the Baptistery
of St. Mark's* 1849–52

should need a separate plate for each . . . . that they were cut for distant effect is unquestionable – nothing can be more delightful than their appearance of sharpness and intricacy when seen from beneath – while they are rude and blunt when examined close by looking over the gallery. (Add.x–13)

Ruskin, like a recent commentator, is especially attracted by one *110, xv* 'rich' and 'beautiful' panel in the north arcade (10.285).[21]

These panels are 'surmounted by a final projecting cornice; which is necessary in order to crown the whole group of arches and parapet'. Since this member 'has of course – no supporting function', its design, instead of expressing the upward spring of a loaded cornice (9.366), is enriched with 'weak inlaid and current ornament':

The reader will I hope begin to appreciate the feeling with which the system of the lovely building is carried out, when he looks at the pattern of this cornice . . . . It is a chain of crosses enclosed in diamond shaped spaces: *xv, xxi* and singularly delicate in its distant effect – like a richly wrought piece of silver jewellery. (Add.x–13)

Ruskin finds another example of thoughtful adaptation of detail to *xiv* total effect in these arcades. The small leaf cornice of 'the great brick piers' is used 'not with true supporting function; but merely to mark the level of the spring of the archivolts – and to bind the alabaster coating together more securely'.[22] It is 'part of its duty to express this

158

inferior office – and to show by its slightness or method of decoration' that it is 'distinct from the true cornice of structural support'. The 'languor and delicate horizontal flow' of its floral pattern is 'exactly the character which marks this confession most plainly' (Add.x–11). But when a similar pattern is carried across onto the loaded abaci of the nave capitals, the difference in function

is instantly expressed by its taking the concave curve . . . which is besides *361*, XIV useful as being in greater harmony with that expression of lightness & elasticity which we have seen it is [in] their other features the aim of these capitals to express.[23]

The balance of Ruskin's surviving study of the interior in 1849–52 consists of notes and drawings of scattered details. Several other capitals are singled out. The one to the left of the doorway from the *111* Baptistery into the nave is admired for 'the life and character of the *102* curves', and

the irregular and fearless freedom of the Byzantine designers, no two parts of the foliage being correspondent; in the original it is of white marble, the ground being coloured blue. (11.271)

Ruskin's captivation by this beautiful, eccentric, but probably not 'Byzantine',[24] capital – easily overlooked because of the striking XXXII Salomé in the mosaic above – was inevitable. It is built into the wall on two sides, and the lively and asymmetrical design of the south face shown in the drawing is different from that of the eastern face.

A capital which Ruskin has drawn to minute scale is one of six of *112* this type supporting the eastern arcades of the transepts.[25] It is 'one of the most delicate' of the concave capitals,

remarkable for the cutting of the sharp thistle-like leaves into open relief, so that the light sometimes shines through them from behind, and for the beautiful curling of the extremities of the leaves outwards, joining each other at the top, as in an undivided flower. (10.157)

Such subordination of detail to strong articulating lines explains the effectiveness of these capitals in distant viewing.[26] At the same time, their carving, which Deichmann dates late eleventh century, exhibits 'as completely living leaves as any of the Gothic time' (10.161). Here is that combination of 'natural truth' with 'the melodies and organization of design' (16.289n) which characterizes Ruskin's favourite ornament.

It is illuminating, after viewing these capitals, to take a few steps laterally and inspect some Gothic specimens (1384) on the great screen. A pencil note scribbled on one of the worksheets remarks that these 'capitals if not gilded would be wonderful – crisp fanciful –

113 Capital of the screen of St. Mark's

114 Angle spur of a base in the Baptistery

finished & sharply undercut but all bad in feeling' (WS.141). The abrupt twist of this ending is elucidated in a journal entry which reiterates praise of the carving but complains that its disposition is 'ineffective'. While not 'over luxuriant' – a fault of later 'corrupt' Gothic such as that of the upper external arches (11.10–13) – these
113 capitals are 'bad in composition and effect'. The capital shown in the
112 photograph, when compared with that in Ruskin's drawing, explains his unease. The screen capitals lack that clear articulation which Ruskin praises in earlier, 'Byzantine' capitals, and are, he concludes, 'cramped and ungraceful' (M.200).

The base of the most westerly column on the south side of the Baptistery is described in the *Stones* as

> The most beautiful base I ever saw, on the whole . . . [Its northeast angle spur] is formed by a cherub, who sweeps downwards on the wing. His two wings, as they half close, form the upper part of the spur, and the rise of it in the front is formed by exactly the action of Alichino, swooping on the pitch lake; 'quei drizzo, volando, suso il petto.' But it requires noble management to confine such a fancy within such limits. (9.343)

Curiously, this praise is not reflected in an illustration among the twelve spurs engraved in Ruskin's accompanying plate. A closer
114 look may explain the omission. This is not the face of a 'cherub', but a bearded and battleworn follower of Lucifer.[27]

The lunettes of the Porta di San Giovanni and Treasury door are studied in detail. They – like their counterparts over the northern door and first and fifth western porches – are

160

115 Lunette over the Porta di San Giovanni

116 John Ruskin *Angel in the left spandrel of the Porta di San Giovanni* (*Gothic Book*) 1850

117 John Ruskin *Apex of the lunette over the Porta di San Giovanni* (fragment of Worksheet 118) 1850

fantastic forms derived from the Arabs, and of which the exquisite decoration is one of the most important features in St. Mark's. Their form is indeed permitted merely to obtain more fantasy in the curves of this decoration. The reader can see in a moment, that, as pieces of masonry, or bearing arches, they are infirm or useless . . . . They are of course, like the rest of the building, built of brick and faced with marble, and their inner masonry, which must be very ingenious, is therefore not discernible. They have settled a little . . . and the consequence is, that there is in every one of them, except the upright arch of the treasury, a small fissure across the marble of the flanks. (10.291–92)

103 The Porta di San Giovanni (Ruskin's 'Arabian Door', marked A.d in his plan) is the most unusual. Ruskin praises 'the amazing refinement of the Byzantine workmanship', especially the 'beautiful angels'.[28] Though the latter are 'not well cut – the folds of the dresses are mere incisions: and the features hard & bad', the 'grace of position and *116* conception' are 'perfect'. He notes 'the flow of the hair' which is 'graceful though formal' and sympathizes 'so entirely with the flowing roll of leafage' surrounding the arch (M.149–50). Another *117* drawing shows the 'Top of the arch . . . . The hair of the principal figure, as that of the angels flowed like the leaf roll, is in reticulated *xxiv* curls' (M.154). Other details are sketched in the *Gothic Book*:

115
1. Ornament filling the interstice of the left hand angels left wing above [to the right of the angel's halo]. . . . 2. leaf moulding – hollow ornament and section, springing from the lintel on the [bottom] right: In all these hollow ornaments there is no real undercutting. It is cut deep down. and then cleverly set drill holes give it its point; both in the leaf and the tendril . . . . Observe again. the forked leaf. peculiarly Byzantine. 3. Turn of the angle on the [bottom] right of arch. leaves added in the 14th century at the time of the architrave (M.150l).

At top left is the foliage of the original leaf roll, with drill holes, above the bottom right corner of the lunette. Ruskin is intrigued by 'the left hand angels left wing . . . . a recess cut deep down behind the roll, enough to put ones hand into, of which I cannot conceive the use' (M.153; one wishes he had speculated). Comparison between the *115, 116* head of this angel as drawn by Ruskin and the view given in the photograph provides further evidence of the considerable relief of the carving.

Three Gothic tombs are studied.[29] That of Doge Giovanni Soranzo (1329) in the Baptistery[30] is a 'plain sarcophagus' with 'no effigy, and only three small figures on its sides'. In the centre is 'John *118* the Baptist, holding the Lamb, within a circle' and 'on each angle a *119* bishop holding a book'. Ruskin finds these figures 'very stiff and cheaply cut', but 'the expression of the faces good and grave'. The

118 Tomb of Doge Soranzo in the Baptistery: John the Baptist

119 Tomb of Doge Soranzo in the Baptistery: a Bishop

leaf cornice is praised for its bold projection and the sharp cutting of its outer edges.

The dentils have been gilded, the ground between them painted blue. The leaf plinth has all its flowers and leaves gilded, and the ground red; a bar of blue seems to have been struck across beneath the roots of its leaves. (11.294–5)

Traces of blue were visible between the dentils in the winter of 1982.

The 'exquisite tomb of St. Isidore' (*c.* 1355) receives more detailed analysis:

The sarcophagus itself is laid under a round arched recess behind the altar,

163

and is of workmanship so superior both to that of the ornaments of the recess itself in which it lies, and to that of all the other sepulchral monuments in Venice, that it might at first be supposed to be by the hand of a foreign master. Close examination of its ornaments has however induced me to believe that it is an extraordinary effort by the best Venetian master of the period, and that it owes its superiority to the affection and zeal with which it has been worked, not to the skill of foreign hands. One of its most remarkable features is the superiority of the flower ornamentation to the recumbent statue, the latter, though highly finished, being hard and ungraceful, in some places unnatural, in its lines. The sculptor had just arrived at the point when he could thoroughly master the disposition of the lines of vegetation, but not the more difficult contours of the human form. This circumstance is alone sufficient to distinguish it from the works of the Pisan and Florentine schools; and as the flower mouldings themselves, refined though they be, are yet entirely modelled on Venetian types, I believe we may safely consider this monument as a kind of high-water mark for Venetian sculpture in the middle of the fourteenth century. (11.299)[31]

Ruskin's complaint that 'the darkness of the chapel is so great that it is almost impossible to see even the front' of the tomb has been rendered harshly inappropriate by a spotlight. His further comments may be tested in detail against the original:

The three projecting portions are each wrought into a square-headed niche, with a shell lightly traced on the back of it behind the horizontal lintel, this lintel being sustained by two spiral shafts, whose length is eked out by pedestals below, and short pilasters above – a most ungraceful arrangement, but redeemed by the loveliness of the carving with which it is charged, and evidently adopted with the intention of keeping the sarcophagus square and quiet in its main lines (note about absence of Gothic feeling in Sarcophagus).

These niches are filled by three saints, of whom the one on the left, with a scroll, is the Baptist; the other two, bearing books, have no marks whereby they may be distinguished. Their drapery is well and freely cast . . . but there is an unmeaning smile in the faces, the lips being a little open, marking some inability in the sculptor to express his intention. In the panels between these niches are two most interesting bas-reliefs. In that on the left, St. Isidore, bound, is being dragged behind a horseman who scourges his horse at the gallop, over rocks and briers, in a wild country, these facts being expressed in sculptural language by a row of five bushes below the horse, and three trees in the distance, the ground being broken up into the usual formal upright fragments like pieces of starch, by which the mediaeval sculptors represent rocks. The galloping horse is wonderfully spirited for the period. Two warriors appear in the distance with small round shields, not larger than their helmets, the latter being conical and without crests – and the rest of the armour evidently meant to represent Roman costume. This is still more markedly the case in the other bas-relief, where the

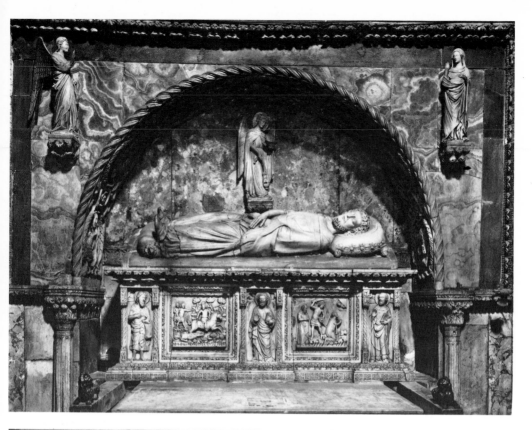

120 Tomb of St. Isidore

121 Tomb of St. Isidore: the Martyrdom of the Saint

executioner who beheads St. Isidore is in rich Roman mail. Christ appears to receive the martyr's soul, in the centre of an effulgence of rays which issues from a conical (cloud?) in the corner of the bas-relief (11.299–300).

This is close and delighted observation. But a tomb in the Baptistery, contemporary with that of St. Isidore and linked with it by Ruskin as 'the best existing examples of Venetian monumental sculpture' (11.95), elicits a response of a different order:

We hardly know if it be a tomb indeed; for it is like a narrow couch set beside the window, low-roofed and curtained, so that it might seem, but that it is some height above the pavement, to have been drawn towards the window, that the sleeper might be wakened early; – only there are two angels, who have drawn the curtain back, and are looking down upon him. Let us look also, and thank that gentle light that rests upon his forehead for ever, and dies away upon his breast.

The face is of a man in middle life, but there are two deep furrows right across the forehead, dividing it like the foundations of a tower: the height of it above is bound by the fillet of the ducal cap. The rest of the features are singularly small and delicate, the lips sharp, perhaps the sharpness of death being added to that of the natural lines; but there is a sweet smile upon them, and a deep serenity upon the whole countenance. The roof of the canopy above has been blue, filled with stars; beneath, in the centre of the tomb on which the figure rests, is a seated figure of the Virgin, and the border of it all around is of flowers and soft leaves, growing rich and deep, as if in a field in summer.

It is the Doge Andrea Dandolo, a man early great among the great of Venice; and early lost. She chose him for her king in his 36th year; he died ten years later . . . . (10.85–6)

The effigy is arresting enough when seen from the elevated angle,
123 and under the artificial glare, of the typical reference photograph.
122 Viewed from below as intended, and illuminated only by the slanting light of the window on the right, it is as moving as Ruskin's description.[32]
XIV, XV   Turning back to look into the main interior from one of Ruskin's favourite positions, one cannot help feeling that he left some of his strongest impressions unexpressed. A phrase emerging unexpectedly from the midst of an analysis of the red plinth which traverses the interior wall tells of 'the seats [formed by the top of the plinth] where I have often been so happy' (M.198). Anyone who has spent a few hours in the shadows engulfing those cool benches will understand one cause of that happiness for someone with Ruskin's sensitivity to colour. A diary entry made on 4 November 1851, while he was working on early drafts of his account of St. Mark's for the *Stones*, lists among

166

122, 123 Tomb of Doge Andrea Dandolo

Chapters to be written.
1. On colour . . . .
2. Light. Rays. . . .[33]

Probably largely because of the impossibility in 1851 of publishing acceptable reproductions of 'the most subtle, variable, inexpressible colour in the world' (10.115), the chapters were never written.

Though they are little more than useful memoranda, modern colour photographs taken under natural light help illustrate a few ways in which this interior satisfies Ruskin's notions about colour:[34]

the first necessity of beauty in colour is gradation, as the first necessity of beauty in line is curvature . . . the second necessity in colour is mystery or subtlety, as the second necessity in line is softness. Colour ungradated is wholly valueless; colour unmysterious is wholly barbarous. Unless it loses itself, and melts away towards other colours, as a true line loses itself and melts away towards other lines, colour has no proper existence, in the noble sense of the word. What a cube, or tetrahedron, is to organic form, ungradated and unconfused colour is to organic colour (16.423).

Even under the crude floodlighting so common in illustrations of St. Mark's (they are easily recognized by their black windows), the gradation – if not the mystery – of the colours is apparent. Under natural light, the gradation is astonishing. It has been claimed recently that as many as 'ten million colour variations between the neutral whites, greys and blacks, and all the different hues' are detectable by the human eye.[35] There could be few that are not visible during the changing light of a single day inside St. Mark's. A
xv view from the south aisle of the nave, taken at noon under silvery February light, shows part of the north arcade. The illumination is – as always in St. Mark's – uneven; consisting here partly of direct sunlight from the south windows, partly of light entering from every direction through the domes, partly of light reflected from the mosaics, floor, and marble incrustation. The response of the columns and spandrels of the arcade explains why alabaster was considered the most precious of marbles by the ancients,[36] – varying not merely the tones, but the actual hues, of the light they transmit. The variation in these three identical shafts is remarkable: the greyish pink of the most brightly-lit one on the right becoming a rusty orange in the darkest on the left, while its flax-blue veins have become a blackish blue. The
xiv, xv gradation across the spandrels is almost as striking. Considering
xix merely the impressions given by this group of photographs of the nave, one is at a loss to classify the alabasters present here. Are the nave shafts *Alabastro fiorito* ('Faint quince, finely striated with pink, rose and brownish grey'), *Alabastro ad onice* ('Grey, pink, violet, and

white') or *Alabastro rossastro venato* ('Pinkish, with veins of red, violet, and yellow')?[37] Are the spandrels sheeted with *Alabastro ametista dendritico* ('Delicate lilac hue, with foliated lines of darker shade'), *Alabastro a Pecorella carnino* ('Flesh colour'), *Alabastro a rosa venato* ('Veined rose colour'), or is it that alabaster whose colour reminds a modern authority of the hues seen under the human fingernail?[38] In fact, they may be all these and more, depending upon their illumination. Alabaster is translucent, and the depth and intensity of light's penetration may result in different hues emerging from the same kind of marble. Ruskin's perception in Italian skies of a

marble light. The towers at Arona stood against the bars of sky just as if the sky were solid alabaster[39]

evokes beautifully the sense of illumination from within that is so much a part of the mystery of St. Mark's. The glow of the nave columns when viewed from the shadow of Ruskin's seat against the wall – it appears most intense when the church is dimly lit and the eye accommodated to twilight – is an effect which the most patient photography cannot reproduce.

As one moves out to view the mosaics, the variability of colour increases. Gold which is piercing yellow near a window or where some rounded edge catches high light may be subdued to a rich brown a few feet away. The tonal ranges of blues and purples in the eastern dome (seen here from different angles and at different times of day) are astonishing. Everywhere one looks, from floor to ceiling, one sees infinite gradation of colour in materials which – if viewed under even lighting – would appear much more uniform. And each of those tones changes from minute to minute and season to season, in step with the changes in the sun's positions, and all the dependent angles of multiple reflection and refraction of its rays inside the building. The resultant colour combinations exemplify Ruskin's belief that

xx

xxv, xxviii

xvii, xxviii

No colour harmony is of high order unless it involves indescribable tints. It is the best possible sign of a colour when nobody who sees it knows what to call it, or how to give an idea of it to any one else. Even among simple hues the most valuable are those which cannot be defined; the most precious purples will look brown beside pure purple, and purple beside pure brown; and the most precious greens will be called blue if seen beside pure green, and green if seen beside pure blue. (16.424)

But hue and shading are only two factors. Of equal importance is the 'texture' of colour:

I mean the literal texture: namely the bloom, down, gritty surface – silky –

furry – vitreous – & c – as in flesh – feathers – rocks – dresses – water – mist –
& so on. Textures which give the final loveliness to the colour . . . .[40]

Compare, from one position in the nave aisle, the coarse grain of the
red Verona marble (arcade above nearby mosaic, or distant effect);
the hard shine of the floor under direct sunlight, yet as mellow as an
Impressionist fruit-piece in shade; the gemlike brilliance of individu-
ally articulated tesserae of a nearby mosaic, still scintillating, but
looking like richly woven tapestry at a distance. To such simple
variants in colour texture must be added those, caused by extremes of
illumination, in which photography is incapable of following the
eye. In St Mark's one often looks from deep shadow, through a space
filled with light, into another shaded space containing dimly-
glowing figures. When the intervening brightness is not too intense,
the camera may capture the distant colours and shapes with some
approximation of true effect. But when the cross-light is brilliant – as
in looking up into the central dome when its windows are blazing
with the late morning or early afternoon rays of a low winter sun –
those shapes seem to hover at greatly increased distances beyond a
veil of shimmering light. This effect of evanescence, of dematerializ-
ation of the holy figures in the dome – surely calculated by the
mosaicist in his conception of the Ascension[41] – is recorded by the
camera as an overexposure. Modern photography has not inval-
idated Ruskin's warning that in treating the colour of St. Mark's it is
'dangerous for me to endeavour to illustrate my meaning, except by
reference to the work itself' (10.115); for here are

colours for which there are no words in language, and no ideas in the mind,
– things which can only be conceived while they are visible (3.285–6).[42]

7 ONE GREEK SCHOOL
Studies of 1876–77: the mosaics

Five years after leaving Venice in 1852 Ruskin recalled

so much hard, dry, mechanical toil there, that I quite lost, before I left it, the charm of the place. . . . I have got all the right feeling back now, however; and hope to write a word or two about Venice yet, when I have got the mouldings well out of my head . . . .[1]

The mouldings must still have been casting baleful shadows when, at a lecture in 1859, he reportedly agreed with G.E. Street's remarkable claim that 'such a cathedral as Chartres is worth ten St. Mark's' (16.463).[2] Addressing the Royal Institute of British Architects in 1865, he curtly dismisses 'Byzantine, Indian, Renaissance-French, and other more or less attractive but barbarous work' (19.36). In 1867, 'Looking at St Mark's photograph in evening a dim gleam of the old feeling revisits' him,[3] and he returns to Venice after an absence of seventeen years in 1869, then again in 1870 and 1872. But though he writes from Venice in 1869 that 'the colours of architecture' are not 'visible to any one but me' (36.573) and proposes, in 1871, 'to get some pieces of colour there for the last time that it will be possible',[4] St. Mark's does not seem to have figured in his studies.[5]

Plans for a new edition of the *Stones*, to include 'new drawings, giving some notion of my old memories of the place',[6] bring him back to Venice in September 1876, but a day after arrival he finds the task 'like editing a volume of baby talk, without any fun in it' (24.xxxv). By January 1877 a new work on Venice has taken precedence. Entitled *St. Mark's Rest* (Chs 1–7, 10, published 1877; 8 and 11 in 1879; the rest in 1884), the book is only partially concerned with the old church. It is instead a selective presentation of a Venice of the imagination, invoking works of art as evidence of the old Venetians' highest ideals, 'symbols of another world' rather than 'the furniture of this'.[7] Ruskin approaches these symbols, not as an academic iconographer, but as one who deeply believes, or longs to believe, in the reality of the powers they signify. It is thus inevitable that the 'mystic and majestic thought' in which he had, in 1874, declared 'Cimabue . . . and the Byzantines generally' to be pre-eminent,[8] should draw him to the mosaics of St. Mark's, and an interest that had coexisted with the formalistic architectural analysis of 1849–52.

The medieval mosaics could be shown to be architecturally effective; but Ruskin had also argued in the *Stones* that they were part of a symbolic scheme which ultimately defined the whole building as one vast icon, 'the visible temple' becoming 'in every part a type of the invisible church of God' (10.135).[9] They are thus disposed in a doctrinally significant order (10.133–39). In the atrium, 'reserved for unbaptised persons and new converts', it was felt that, 'before their baptism, these persons should be led to contemplate the great facts of the Old Testament' – the 'Fall of Man', the 'lives of Patriarchs up to the period of the covenant by Moses', and finally 'the Fall of the Manna' which indicates 'to the catechumen the insufficiency of the Mosaic covenant for salvation . . . and to turn his thoughts to the true Bread of which that manna was the type'. Entering the central door ('the type of baptism') he saw, looking back, 'a mosaic of Christ enthroned' and holding an open book, on which is written: 'I AM THE DOOR; BY ME IF ANY MAN ENTER IN, HE SHALL BE SAVED.' The entrance was thus, for believers, 'a daily memorial of their first entrance into the spiritual Church'. Then,

the mosaic of the first dome, which is over the head of the spectator as soon as he has entered . . . represents the effusion of the Holy Spirit, as the first consequence and seal of the entrance into the Church of God. . . . From the central symbol of the Holy Spirit twelve streams of fire descend upon the heads of the twelve apostles . . . .

Next,

it was thought fittest that the worshipper should be led to contemplate . . . the past evidence and the future hopes of Christianity . . . namely, that Christ died, that He rose again, and that He ascended into heaven . . . . On the vault between the first and second cupolas are represented the crucifixion and resurrection of Christ, with the usual series of intermediate scenes, – the treason of Judas, the judgment of Pilate, the crowning with thorns, the descent into Hades, the visit of the women to the Sepulchre, and the apparition to Mary Magdalene. The second cupola itself, which is the central and principal one of the church, is entirely occupied by the subject of the Ascension. At the highest point of it Christ is represented as rising into the blue heaven, borne up by four angels, and throned upon a rainbow, the type of reconciliation. Beneath Him, the twelve apostles are seen upon the Mount of Olives, with the Madonna, and, in the midst of them, the two men in white apparel who appeared at the moment of the Ascension, above whom, as uttered by them, are inscribed the words, 'Ye men of Galilee, why stand ye gazing up into heaven? This Christ, the Son of God, as He is taken from you, shall so come, the arbiter of the earth, trusted to do judgment and justice.'

Beneath the circle of the apostles, between the windows of the cupola,

XVIII

172

are represented the Christian virtues, as sequent upon the crucifixion of the flesh, and the spiritual ascension together with Christ. Beneath them, on the vaults which support the angles of the cupola, are placed the four Evangelists, because on their evidence our assurance of the fact of the Ascension rests: and, finally, beneath their feet, as symbols of the sweetness and fulness of the Gospel which they declared, are represented the four rivers of Paradise, Pison, Gihon, Tigris, and Euphrates.

The third cupola, that over the altar, represents the witness of the Old Testament to Christ; showing Him enthroned in its centre, and surrounded by the patriarchs and prophets. But this dome was little seen by the people; their contemplation was intended to be chiefly drawn to that of the centre of the church, and thus the mind of the worshipper was at once fixed on the main groundwork and hope of Christianity, – 'Christ is risen,' and 'Christ shall come.'

This insistence that the entire scheme is subordinated to the Ascension dome is corroborated by the great twentieth-century student of the mosaics, Otto Demus.[10]

Ruskin had also, in the *Stones*, objected to the denigration of the mosaic figures by previous writers:[11]

I have to deprecate the idea of their execution being in any sense barbarous. . . . The character of the features is almost always fine, the expression stern and quiet, and very solemn, the attitudes and draperies always majestic in the single figures, and in those of the groups which are not in violent action; while the bright colouring and disregard of chiaroscuro cannot be regarded as imperfections, since they are the only means by which the figures could be rendered clearly intelligible in the distance and darkness of the vaulting. So far am I from considering them barbarous, that I believe of all works of religious art whatsoever, these, and such as these, have been the most effective. (10.130)

He had tried to 'penetrate into the feeling' (10.133) evoked in the mediaeval believer by these mosaics:

the great mosaics of the twelfth and thirteenth centuries covered the walls and roofs . . . with inevitable lustre; they could not be ignored or escaped from; their size rendered them majestic, their distance mysterious, their colour attractive. They did not pass into confused or inferior decorations . . . . They were before the eyes of the devotee at every interval of his worship; vast shadowings forth of scenes to whose realization he looked forward, or of spirits whose presence he invoked. And the man must be little capable of receiving a religious impression of any kind, who . . . remains altogether untouched by the majesty of the colossal images of apostles, and of Him who sent apostles, that look down from the darkening gold of the domes (10.132).

This passage shows how far Ruskin, already in the early 1850s, was capable of transcending the sectarian uneasiness that so often assailed him inside St. Mark's.[12]

But by 1877 mere empathy with mediaeval sensibility no longer suffices him. 'Every day', he writes of the 'enormous separation' in mental attitude between himself and his cautious and conventional friend Charles Eliot Norton, 'brings me more proof of the presence and power of real Gods, with good men' and – disregarding the objections such polytheism might have aroused in a Catholic churchman – declares that 'the religion of Venice is virtually now my own'.[13] This creed – one of a bewildering array adopted by Ruskin in the 1870s as his moods and longings, or the exigencies of argument, dictated – is accompanied by a strikingly different tone in his writing. The awed eloquence of the *Stones* is replaced in *St. Mark's Rest* by the cranky, proprietary impatience of a believer who suspects he may be casting his pearls before swine. As an initiated insider – almost, it seems at times, as one who thinks himself a reincarnate mediaeval Venetian – Ruskin bullies his 'Few Travellers Who Still Care' (24.195) from one mosaic to the next. Problems of dating are acknowledged, then waved aside with the impatience of a bear raiding an alerted apiary ('I believe, early twelfth-century – late eleventh it might be – later twelfth it may be, – it does not matter' [24.295]).

You must get hold of the man who keeps sweeping the dust about, in St. Mark's; very thankful he will be, for a lira, to take you up to the gallery on the right-hand side (south, of St. Mark's interior); from which gallery, where it turns into the south transept, you may see, as well as it is possible to see, the mosaic of the central dome.

Christ enthroned on a rainbow, in a sphere supported by four flying angels underneath, forming white pillars of caryatid mosaic. Between [actually, above] the windows, the twelve apostles, and the Madonna – alas, the head of this principal figure frightfully 'restored,' and I think the greater part of the central subject. Round the circle enclosing Christ is written, 'Ye men of Galilee, why stand ye at gaze? This Son of God, Jesus, so taken from you, departs that He may be the arbiter of the earth: in charge of judgment He comes. . . .'

Such, you see, the central thought of Venetian worship. Not that we shall leave the world, but that our Master will come to it . . . . Catholic theology of the purest, lasting at all events down to the thirteenth century; or as long as the Byzantines had influence. For these are typical Byzantine conceptions; how far taken up and repeated by Italian workers, one cannot say; but in their gravity of purpose, meagre thinness of form, and rigid drapery lines, to be remembered by you with distinctness as expressing the first school of design in Venice (24.291–2).[14]

Ruskin next orders the reader to look across at the shadowy

mosaic of Christ's Temptation and the more brightly lit Entry to
Jerusalem in the vault of the south transept: xxv

The upper one . . . is entirely characteristic of the Byzantine mythic
manner of teaching. On the left, Christ sits in the rocky cave which has
sheltered Him for the forty days of fasting: out of the rock above issues a
spring – meaning that He drank of the waters that spring up to everlasting
life, of which whoso drinks shall never thirst; and in His hand is a book – the
living Word of God, which is His bread. The Devil holds up the stones in
his lap.

Next the temptation on the pinnacle of the Temple, symbolic again,
wholly, as you see, – in very deed quite impossible: so also that on the
mountain, where the treasures of the world are, I think, represented by the
glittering fragments on the mountain top. Finally, the falling Devil, cast
down head-foremost in the air, and approaching angels in ministering
troops, complete the story. (24.293)

Assuming, no doubt partly for the sake of the ironic tone it allows
him to adopt, that his reader is – like Hippolyte Taine[15] – blind to
their aesthetic merits, he goes on:

Those were the kind of images and shadows they [the mediaeval Venetians]
lived on: you may think of them what you please, but the historic fact is,
beyond all possible debate, that these thin dry bones of art were nourishing
meat to the Venetian race: that they grew and throve on that diet, every day
spiritually fatter for it, and more comfortably round in human soul: – no
illustrated papers to be had, no Academy Exhibition to be seen. If their eyes
were to be entertained at all, such must be their lugubrious delectation;
pleasure difficult enough to imagine, but real and pure, I doubt not; even
passionate. In as quite singularly incomprehensible fidelity of sentiment,
my cousin's [Joan Severn's] least baby has fallen in love with a wooden
spoon (24.293–4).

The old Venetians 'did indeed find pleasantness in these figures; more
especially, – which is notable – in the extreme emaciation of them, –
a type of beauty kept in their hearts down to the Vivarini days [late
fifteenth century]' (24.294).

The next mosaic, appropriately, presents the Venetians' 'picture of
themselves, at their greatest time':

You must go round the transept gallery, and get the door opened into the
compartment of the eastern aisle, in which is the organ [the modern visitor
must make a more exciting journey: up the stairs beside the sacristy, out
onto the north exterior of the apse, around the apse, and into the southeastern gallery]. And going to the other side of the square stone gallery, and
looking back from behind the organ, you will see opposite, on the vault, a
mosaic of upright figures in dresses of blue, green, purple, and white,
variously embroidered with gold. xxvi

These represent, as you are told by the inscription above them – the Priests, the Clergy, the Doge, and the people of Venice; and are an abstract, at least, or epitome of those personages, as they were, and felt themselves to be, in those days. . . . the people of Venice in the central time of her unwearied life, her unsacrificed honour, her unabated power, and sacred faith. Her Doge wears, not the contracted shell-like cap, but the imperial crown. Her priests and clergy are alike mitred – not with the cloven, but simple, cap, like the conical helmet of a knight. Her people are also her soldiers, and their Captain bears his sword, sheathed in black.[16]

The faces of these figures

are *all* noble – (one horribly restored figure on the right shows what *ig*nobleness, on this large scale, modern brutality and ignorance can reach) (24.295).

Ruskin would have been even more indignant if he had seen the two execrable modern faces on the extreme left, as well as most of the drapery of the two left figures, which were missing in 1877.[17] Mercifully, they inhabit a corner that is shrouded in perpetual shadow.

Discovery of this mosaic brightened the last few days Ruskin was to spend working in St. Mark's. On 20 May 1877, studying the eastern mosaics, he had

found in St. Mark's the Duke and his people, and had a glorious hour, in the quiet gallery, with the service going on. I alone up there, and the message by the words of the old mosaicist given me (D3.953).

Ruskin felt he had received a special revelation. This Doge, 'serene of mind' among his people (24.296), provided a flattering vision of himself as Master, and his followers as Companions, of the St. George's Company which he had founded a few years earlier (30.xxxi) to foster communities – and eventually, an entire regenerate England – untainted by *laissez-faire* economics and modern factory industry. A little land and a few cottages had been obtained, and a small museum in Walkley, near Sheffield, was being furnished by Ruskin as an educational centre for the Companions (some of them labourers, many others Ruskin's friends), who pledged themselves to carry out the Master's principles.[18] On the very day he discovered the mosaic in St. Mark's Ruskin received – and interpreted as another 'sign' – a letter from some Sheffield workers who had earlier asked if they might 'rent some ground from the Company, whereupon to spend what spare hours they have . . . in useful labour' (29.98). Ruskin had been instructing these 'Yorkshire operatives' throughout the winter of 1876–77 in *Fors Clavigera* about the 'actual operations of St. George's Company' (29.13) and now the workers, to his intense delight, wrote that they 'had accepted my laws'. As supreme ruler over the Company its Master – with that magnanimity which only the highest office can confer – 'wrote to them in return that they should stand rentless' (D3.953).

Not totally hoodwinked by this sad little fantasy of himself as an autocrat, Ruskin writes more usefully the same day to one of his artist-assistants:

My dear Murray, – Can you join me on St. Mark's Place to-morrow at half-past nine, with your drawing materials? I am going up into the gallery, behind organ . . . to study a mosaic plainly visible, and of extreme beauty and importance. A sketch of it . . . will be the most important work you or I have yet done in Venice, and if it could be begun to-morrow I would wait [in Venice] till Wednesday to see it in some advancement. The figures are size of life, in dresses of exquisite dark richness, with white and black crosses for relief. Colours chiefly purple, green, and blue on the gold ground. (24.xl)

C.F. Murray's painting is reproduced in the Library Edition (24. facing 296). Much more exciting is the watercolour dashed off by Ruskin himself.[19] Seen from a distance, it gives a startling sense of xxvii actually viewing the mosaic within an architectural context that includes the projecting leaf moulding below and shadowy wall at the left. A separate sketch studies the Doge's head and – significantly – headgear. Two days after finding this 'best of all the St. Mark's p. 189 mosaics', Ruskin is still 'thrown into as complete a rear of confusion as ever yet in leaving a place' (D3.953) and, homeward bound four days after the great find, continues pondering the 'solemn message coming to me in St. Mark's, of other hope on earth, and work to be done first' (D3.954). Two years later, it remained for him the 'most precious "historical picture" . . . of any in worldly gallery, or unworldly cloister, east or west' (24.296).

After twitting readers of *St. Mark's Rest* ('Most Serene Highnesses of all the after Time and World') with their assumed inability to fathom the 'Duke's Serenity', he walks several steps north to examine the eastern dome. He had once considered its mosaics 'of xxviii inferior workmanship, and perhaps later than' those of the first and second domes (10.138n). Now he believes it 'must necessarily have been first completed, because it is over the altar and shrine' (24.296).[20] But he wishes to interpret, not date, this dome:

In it, the teaching of the Mosaic legend begins, and in a sort ends; – 'Christ, the King,' foretold of Prophets – declared of Evangelists – born of a Virgin in due time! (24.296)

While the prophets ranged round the Virgin foretell 'a good that is to be', the Evangelists, whose four emblems appear below, proclaim 'it is *here*':

the four mystic Evangelists, under the figures of living creatures, are not types merely of the men that are to bring the Gospel message, but of the power of that message in all Creation (24.297).

XXVIII The emblem of St. Mark then inspires an attack on guidebooks, scientific education, and the author of *The Stones of Venice* himself:

You will find in your Murray, and other illumined writings of the nineteenth century, various explanations given of the meaning of the Lion of St. Mark – derived, they occasionally mention (nearly as if it had been derived by accident!), from the description of Ezekiel. Which, perhaps, you may have read once on a time, though even that is doubtful in these blessed days of scientific education; – but, boy or girl, man or woman, of you, not one in a thousand, if one, has ever, I am well assured, asked what was the *use* of Ezekiel's Vision, either to Ezekiel, or to anybody else: any more than I used to think, myself, what St. Mark's was built for. (24.297)

Quoting the first chapter of Ezekiel, Ruskin interpolates comments insisting that while the old Venetians believed the prophet's testimony, and applied it to themselves, the degenerate tourist (who has not, he suspects, even 'a Bible with you') has lost such capacity:

'And this was the likeness of their faces: they four had the face of a Man' (to the front), 'and the face of a Lion on the right side, and the face of an Ox on the left side, and' (looking back) 'the face of an Eagle.'
    And not of an Ape, then, my beautifully-browed Cockney friend? – the unscientific Prophet! (24.298)

Evolutionary theory and attempts at rational explanation of the Bible have destroyed the faith which once gave potency to these images. The figure crowning the dome (or perhaps the seated Pantocrator in the apse below) inspires further wrathful commentary on Ezekiel's words:

'And above the Firmament that was over their heads was the likeness of a Throne; and upon the likeness of the Throne was the likeness of the Aspect of a Man above, upon it. . . . And when I saw it, I fell upon my face.'
    Can any of us do the like – or is it worth while? – with only apes' faces to fall upon, and the forehead [of a whore: Jeremiah 3.3] that refuses to be ashamed? Or is there, nowadays, no more anything for *us* to be afraid of, or to be thankful for, in all the wheels, and flame, and light, of earth and heaven? (24.299)

In the midst of this harangue – as much a lament for his own doubts as for his readers' supposed apostasy[21] – Ruskin turns briefly to aesthetic matters; but his 'notes have got confused, and many lost; and now I have no time to mend the thread of them' (24.300).[22] A passage on colour does disengage itself:

The decorative power of the colour in these figures, chiefly blue, purple, and white, on gold, is entirely admirable, – more especially the dark purple of the Virgin's robe, with lines of gold for its folds; and the figures of David and Solomon, both in Persian tiaras, almost Arab, with falling lappets to the shoulder, for shade; David holding a book with Hebrew letters on it and a cross (a pretty sign for the Psalms); and Solomon with rich orbs of lace like involved ornament on his dark robe, cusped in the short hem of it, over gold underneath. And note in all these mosaics that Byzantine 'purple,' – the colour at once meaning Kinghood and its Sorrow, – is the same as ours – not scarlet, but amethyst, and that deep. (24.301–2)[23]   xxviii

After another attack on his readers Ruskin returns to the mystic symbols under the dome:

The Ox that treadeth out the corn; and the Lion that shall eat straw like the Ox, and lie down with the lamb; and the Eagle that fluttereth over her young; and the human creature that loves its mate, and its children. In these four is all the power and all the charity of earthly life . . . . But the issue of all these lessons we cannot yet measure; it is only now that we are beginning to be able to read them, in the myths of the past, and natural history of the present world. The animal Gods of Egypt and Assyria, the animal cry that there is *no* God, of the passing hour, are, both of them, part of the rudiments of the religion yet to be revealed, in the rule of the Holy Spirit over the venomous dust (24.303).

The bullying preacher in Ruskin has succumbed briefly to the mythologist who had, in *The Queen of the Air* (1869), convincingly elucidated the symbolism of a number of important Greek myths. The mediaeval 'religion of Venice' is not, after all, the perfected ideal it is intermittently – for preaching purposes – assumed to be in *St. Mark's Rest*. Its very symbols derive largely from older religions, and even the rejection of it by modern atheists furthers the development of that religion of the future for which Ruskin yearns. Early in 1877, he had written:

all great myths are conditions of slow manifestation to human imperfect intelligence; and . . . whatever spiritual powers are in true personality appointed to go to and fro in the earth, to trouble the waters of healing, or bear the salutations of peace, can only be revealed, in their reality, by the gradual confirmation in the matured soul of what at first were only its instinctive desires, and figurative perceptions. (29.54)

This sounds remarkably modern, foreshadowing the thought of C.G. Jung and – in its Byzantine context – pointing irresistibly to

W.B. Yeats. It is symptomatic of Ruskin's uncertainty, however, that within two paragraphs of assigning a role to atheism in developing 'the religion yet to be revealed', he is ferociously attacking 'German and other' historians who questioned the evidence for the life of Christ (24.304).[24]

Readers of *St. Mark's Rest* – especially if previously acquainted with Ruskin only through the *Seven Lamps* and *Stones* – were in for greater surprises. His encounter with the mosaics after two decades of increasing absorption in classical Greek art and mythology[25] now led him to the revolutionary assertion that they are manifestations of an artistic and spiritual tradition that began long before Christianity. The 'intense first character' of all Byzantine art

is symbolism. The thing represented means more than itself, – is a sign, or letter, more than an image.

And this is true, not of Byzantine art only, but of all Greek art . . . . Let us leave, to-day, the narrow and degrading word 'Byzantine.' There is but one Greek school, from Homer's day down to the Doge Selvo's; and these St. Mark's mosaics are as truly wrought in the power of Daedalus, with the Greek constructive instinct, and in the power of Athena, with the Greek religious soul, as ever chest of Cypselus or shaft of Erechtheum. (24.280–81)[26]

Demus's claim that 'Greek statues and reliefs seem to have come to life in mosaic figures', that Byzantine art was able to transmit Hellenism to western Europe 'because of the ability of Western artists actually to *see* the *Greek* behind the *Byzantine*',[27] is anticipated in *St. Mark's Rest*.

The transmission of Greek spirituality through Byzantium into Western European art had already been touched upon by Ruskin in a lecture of 1874. Cimabue, a 'Greek of the Greeks, and Christian of the Christians', had treated 'Scripture history as a Greek Father of the Church'; at his touch the 'Byzantine traditions blossom suddenly'. But he and Giotto 'represent the new budding of an underground stem which has its root partly in Greece proper, partly in Egypt, and . . . the spirit-life which invented the forms of the throned gods and kings of Thebes is in the veins of Cimabue' (23.198–200).[28] In a sentence of startling beauty, Ruskin had claimed:

First of the Florentines, first of European men, Cimabue attained in thought, he saw with spiritual eyes exercised to discern good from evil, the face of her who was blessed among women; and with his following hand, made visible the Magnificat of his heart. (23.197)

XVIII   In the same spirit, Ruskin now points to the eastern and central
XXVIII domes of St. Mark's:

not a queen, nor a maid only, this Madonna in her purple shade, – but the love of God poured forth, in the wonderfulness that passes the love of woman. (24.281)

Such Christian symbols have antecedents in the figures on 'any good vase of the Marathonian time':

Black figures on a red ground, – a few white scratches through them, marking the joints of their armour or the folds of their robes, – white circles for eyes, – pointed pyramids for beards, – you don't suppose that in these the Greek workman thought he had given the likeness of gods? Yet here, to his imagination, were Athena, Poseidon, and Herakles, – and all the powers that guarded his land, and cleansed his soul, and led him in the way everlasting [Psalms 139.24]. (24.281)

This perception of spiritual continuity between ancient Greece and Byzantine Venice now gives St. Mark's a value in Ruskin's eyes that transcends even its aesthetic merits:

beyond all measure of value as a treasury of art, it is also, beyond all other volumes, venerable as a codex of religion. Just as the white foliage and birds on their golden ground are descendants, in direct line, from the ivory and gold of Phidias, so the Greek pictures and inscriptions, whether in mosaic or sculpture, throughout the building, record the unbroken unity of spiritual influence from the Father of light . . . down to the day when all their gods, not slain, but changed into new creatures, became the types to them of the mightier Christian spirits; and Perseus became St. George, and Mars St. Michael, and Athena the Madonna, and Zeus their revealed Father in Heaven.

In all the history of human mind, there is nothing so wonderful, nothing so eventful, as this spiritual change. (24.415)

Such application of Christian phraseology to Greek art and religion, the assertion that 'a Byzantine *was* nothing else than a Greek, – recognizing Christ for Zeus' (8.121n), is reinforced in remarks made about several mosaics in the Baptistery. Its eastern cupola is

xxx

very dark; – to my old eyes, scarcely decipherable; to yours, if young and bright, it should be beautiful, for it is indeed the origin of all those golden-domed backgrounds of Bellini, and Cima, and Carpaccio; itself a Greek vase, but with new Gods. (24.283)[29]

Here, as in the symbols under the eastern dome, lurks a strong undercurrent of pre-Christian symbolism:

That ten-winged cherub in the recess of it, behind the altar, has written on the circle on its breast, 'Fulness of Wisdom.' It is the type of the Breath of the Spirit. But it was once a Greek Harpy, and its wasted limbs remain, scarcely yet clothed with flesh from the claws of birds that they were. (24.284)

Though the figures flanking this image represent orthodox 'powers of the Seraphim and Thrones' and 'Above, Christ Himself ascends, borne in a whirlwind of angels', Ruskin's name for 'this narrow cupola' is 'the Harpy-Vault' (24.284–5).

The mosaics of the north wall of the Baptistery ('the most beautiful symbolic design of the Baptist's death that I know in Italy') could not be 'earlier than the thirteenth century' because they employ the Gothic trefoil (they are mid-fourteenth century), 'yet they are still absolutely Greek in all modes of thought, and forms of tradition' (24.285). Of the splendid Salomé, ridiculed by Taine for her 'dried-up joints of a consumptive patient',[30] Ruskin writes:

XXXII

> Herodias' daughter dances with St. John Baptist's head in the charger, on her head, – simply the translation of any Greek maid on a Greek vase, bearing a pitcher of water on her head. (24.283)

Though 'a princess of the thirteenth century in sleeves of ermine', she is 'yet the phantom of some sweet water-carrier from an Arcadian spring' (24.285).

While these mosaics reflect the continuity of ancient Greek with Byzantine artistic thought, those in the atrium seem alien to that tradition. They 'possess some qualities of thought and invention almost in a sublime degree', but are

17, 1

> different from the others of St. Mark's in being more Norman than Byzantine in manner; and in an ugly admittance and treatment of nude form, which I find only elsewhere in manuscripts of the tenth and eleventh centuries of the school of Monte Casino and South Italy. (24.291)[31]

These mosaics lack the spirituality of the best Byzantine art.

That spirituality, for Ruskin, is expressed primarily in the countenance. The one surviving mediaeval mosaic on the west front, depicting the thirteenth-century façade 'and the bearing of the body of St. Mark into its gates', contains figures of 'all the great kings and queens who have visited his shrine, standing to look on'. These personages, however, are 'not conceived . . . as present at any actual time, but as always looking on in their hearts' (24.286). Their faces are not mere portraits, but images of timeless spiritual presence. Ruskin is therefore outraged to find that

XXXI

XXXIII

> The three figures on the extreme right are restorations; and if the reader will carefully study the difference between these and the rest; and note how all the faults of the old work are caricatured, and every one of its beauties lost – so that the faces which in the older figures are grave or sweet, are in these three new ones as of staring dolls, – he will know, once for all, what kind of thanks he owes to the tribe of Restorers – here and elsewhere. (24.286)

124 Bas-reliefs on the north façade of St. Mark's

Similar considerations explain his curt dismissal of the prominent 'Christ in the Apse. horribly restored'.[32] In contrast, the figures in the central cupola of the Baptistery, though all 'very rude', are redeemed by a 'generally sweet & solemn' expression.[33]

The symbolic sculpture of Christ and the Apostles on the north façade manifests, for Ruskin, the same Greek spirit he discerns in the mosaics. It *124*

represents twelve sheep – six on one side, six on the other, of a throne: on which throne is set a cross; and on the top of the cross, a circle; and in the circle, a little caprioling creature.

And outside of all, are two palm trees, one on each side; and under each palm tree, two baskets of dates; and over the twelve sheep, is written in delicate Greek letters 'The holy Apostles'; and over the little caprioling creature, 'The Lamb.'

Take your glass and study the carving of this bas-relief intently. It is full of sweet care, subtlety, tenderness of touch, and mind; and fine cadence and change of line in the little bowing heads and bending leaves. Decorative in the extreme; a kind of stone-stitching or sampler-work, done with the innocence of a girl's heart, and in a like unlearned fulness. Here is a Christian man, bringing order and loveliness into the mere furrows of stone. Not by any means as learned as a butcher, in the joints of lambs; nor as a grocer, in baskets of dates; nor as a gardener, in endogenous plants: but an artist to the heart's core (24.241–43).

125 Bas-relief on the west front: St. George

This is 'very ancient symbolical Greek sculpture' (10.466); from 'such men Venice learned to touch the stone' (24.243). Later writers differ in their dating of the panel, but agree that, if not an early Byzantine original, it is a copy of one.[34]

XI   The six panels in the spandrels of the western arches show, in varying degrees, the influence of a new realism upon Venetian symbolic sculpture:

On the sides of the great central arch are St. George [left] and St. Demetrius [right], so inscribed in Latin. Between the next lateral porches, the Virgin and Archangel Gabriel, so inscribed, – the Archangel in Latin, the 'Mother of God' in Greek.

And between these and the outer porches, uninscribed, two of the labours of Hercules. I am much doubtful concerning these, myself, – do not know their manner of sculpture, nor understand their meaning. They are fine work . . . types, it may be, of physical human power prevailing over wild nature; the war of the world before Christ.

184

Then the Madonna and angel of Annunciation express the Advent.

Then the two Christian Warrior Saints express the heart of Venice in her armies.

There is no doubt, therefore, of the purposeful choosing and placing of these bas-reliefs. Where the outer ones were brought from, I know not; the four inner ones, I think, are all contemporary, and carved for their place by the Venetian scholars of the Greek schools, in the late twelfth or early thirteenth century. (24.252–53)

Ruskin's claim that matching pairs of images are placed meaningfully, and his suggested interpretation as one reads inward to the 'heart' of the church, are echoed in modern literature.[35] Most recent commentators date the central four within the period suggested,[36] and his puzzlement concerning the northern Hercules is matched by Demus's uncertainty as to whether it is fifth-century Italian, tenth-century Byzantine, or late Antique.[37] The stylistic relationships between the western panels have inspired wildly variable theories.[38]   xxxvi

Though not in Ruskin's opinion the best of these panels, the St.   125
George exhibits the growing realism of the period immediately preceding the Gothic phase in Venetian sculpture:

This, you see, is no more a symbolic sculpture, but quite distinctly pictorial, and laboriously ardent to express, though in very low relief, a curly-haired personage, handsome, and something like George the Fourth, dressed in richest Roman armour, and sitting in an absurd manner, more or less tailor-fashion, if not cross-legged himself, at least on a conspicuously cross-legged piece of splendid furniture . . . . (as at the side of the opera when extra people are let in who shouldn't be); only seven hundred years old. To this cross-legged apparatus the Egyptian throne had dwindled down; it looks even as if the saint who sits on it might begin to think about getting up, some day or other. . . . Unsheathing his sword, is not he?

No; sheathing it. That was the difficult thing he had first to do, as you will find on reading the true legend of him, which *this* sculptor thoroughly knew [see *Fors Clavigera*, letter 26: George refuses to fight for Diocletian against the Christians, and is martyred (27.479–81)]; in whose conception of the saint, one perceives the date of said sculptor, no less than in the stiff work, so dimly yet perceptive of the ordinary laws of the aspect of things. From the bas-reliefs of the Parthenon – through sixteen hundred years of effort, and speech-making, and fighting – human intelligence in the Arts has arrived, here in Venice, thus far. But having got so far, we shall come to something fresh soon! [Ruskin was in a later chapter to describe the   p. 104
carvings of the Trades of the central porch.] We have become distinctly representative again . . . desiring to show, not a mere symbol of a living man, but the man himself (24.243–45).

The finest of the six panels is the angel Gabriel between the fourth   79
and fifth porches, which 'appears to be by a better master than the

others – perhaps later; and is of extreme beauty'. His dating, early thirteenth century, is predicated on 'the manner of the foliage under the feet of the Gabriel, in which is the origin of all the early foliage in the Gothic of Venice' (24.253).[39]

While Ruskin's knowledge of mediaeval Venetian sculpture enables him to make thoughtful stylistic comments about these panels, he is not sufficiently absorbed in them visually to draw them. Instead, the drawings of 1876–77 reflect earlier interests: the colours of the west front; its columns and capitals; and sculpture which relates directly to architectural members such as arches and mouldings. One subject which proves most difficult is the upper range of shafts and capitals between the second and third porches. A growth, over one capital, of the plant Ruskin calls 'Erba della Madonna' (a common Venetian name is 'Occhi della Madonna') provided an irresistible picture, and on 16 September 1876 he complains in *Fors Clavigera*:

62

> I am weary, this morning, with vainly trying to draw the Madonna-herb clustered on the capitals of St. Mark's porch; and mingling its fresh life with the marble acanthus leaves (28.724).

p. 59 Ruskin is fascinated, as he had been a quarter century earlier, by the chiaroscuro created by the offsetting of the columns from the wall:

> Measure, weight, number. The glory of pillared architecture as opposed to a wall! (D3.913).

The diary records further hopes and disappointments, but by 8 November the 'Erba capitals' are still not done (D3.914). Ruskin's drawings have not been traced, but the Library Edition reproduces a photograph of one small ($5\frac{1}{4} \times 8\frac{3}{4}$ in.) watercolour. Despite the loss of colour, detail, and gradation of shadow involved in monochrome reproduction at fourth remove, the splendid interplay of projections and recesses, the delicate fall of the weed, the vigorous chiaroscuro of the capitals, the rendering of the dentils and leaf pattern of the Ice Plinth – all suggest a superb original.[40] Ruskin, however, felt he had failed:

126

> *November 29th. Wednesday.* A dismal day of all wrong, y[esterday]. More despondent in my walk on Lido sand than for many a day. Eyes bad, and photo better than my drawing of St. Mark's, very crushing. (D3.916)

70

In January 1877 Ruskin began writing his protest against the rebuilding of St. Mark's (see next chapter) and, fearing the whole façade might soon be destroyed as the southwest portico had been, undertook 'for spring work' a large drawing of the 'gold and purple' northwest portico (24.xxxvi). This subject caused even more

186

126 John Ruskin (engraved by Allen & Co.) *Shafts, capitals and Ice Plinth between the second and third porches* 1876

difficulty than the 'Erba capitals', with Ruskin complaining on 1 April, 'alas! am not what I was; eyes very different in painting St. Mark's' (D3.945), and on 7 May of being driven frantic

by one of my best friends standing by me in St Mark's place watching me paint – just at a difficult part – I *could'nt* tell her to go away, and made mistake after mistake, till I got into a perfect fever, and hav'nt recovered all day.[41]

He returned to England 'exhausted, by trying to paint, once more, a piece of St Mark's front', and lamenting: 'my eyes don't serve me now except for bold work'.[42]

The splendid drawing which caused such trouble is reproduced in colour here. Though not, as Ruskin's editors claim, the 'most elaborate and important of R.'s w.c. drawings of architectural subjects' (38.297) – even if discussion is restricted to St. Mark's, that of 1852 is larger, more detailed, more 'elaborate' – the painting provides a stunning record, 'left as the colour dried in the spring mornings of 1877' (24.413), of hues which observers of the present façade may not easily credit. Especially noteworthy are the delicately azure-veined golden alabasters, and the shadows between the columns and backing marbles.

In contrast to drawings which caused so much difficulty, the superb rendering of a fragment of the outer central archivolt was managed in one day. On 24 April 1877 he records: 'Got good

XXXI

V

XXXIV

drawing y[esterday] of St. Mark's archivolt ball' (D3.948). On 4 May another success is noted: 'Y[esterday] got bit of St. Mark's archivolt, unexpected, and much idea' (D3.950) – but if the reference is to a drawing, it has not been identified.[43] 'Exhaustion from multitudes of thoughts on recent explorations at St. Mark's' is recorded on 9 May, an entry for the previous day indicating that those thoughts concerned the 'upper mosaics' (D3.951).

Ruskin's study of St. Mark's in 1876–77 represents a considerable enrichment of the work of 1849–52. Shortly before leaving (and he had not yet discovered the mosaic of the Doge and his People) he writes: 'this Venice work a fine and necessary return on the old' (D3.951). He had found 'much more beauty than I used to' when doing the 'technical work of the *Stones*' (24.xxxvii), had made several fine drawings and, above all, had experienced before the mosaics the 'intimate relationship between the world of the beholder and the world of the image' which has been so well described by Demus:

> In Byzantium the beholder was not kept at a distance from the image; he entered within its aura of sanctity, and the image, in turn, partook of the space in which he moved. . . . Byzantine religious art abolishes all clear distinction between the world of reality and the world of appearance.[44]

Ruskin planned to return 'in November for another winter's work'.[45] But the watercolour of the Doge and his People was probably the last study he made at St. Mark's itself.

The building's place in his memory and imagination becomes vivid the following winter when, on the morning of 23 February 1878, Ruskin suffers a mental breakdown of such severity that a medical friend wonders 'whether he will ever again hold his pen or pencil for any end of use or enjoyment' (BD.66). During a milder disturbance in 1871, he had experienced a dream, sufficiently memorable to be mentioned in a lecture of 1872 and again in *St. Mark's Rest* (24.286), about

> a Venetian fisherman, who wanted me to follow him down into some water which I thought was too deep; but he called me on, saying he had something to show me; so I followed him; and presently, through an opening, as if in the arsenal wall, he showed me the bronze horses of St. Mark's, and said, 'See, the horses are putting on their harness.' (22.445–46)

The thoughts recorded in his diary during the two days preceding the seizure of 1878 (BD.99–102) include, on 21 February, a recurrence of the image of the fisherman ('leaving my nets'), much allusion to Rose La Touche, the Irish woman with whom he had been in love for years and who had died in 1875,[46] and – perhaps the surest sign that something is amiss – a dream 'of a beautiful restoration of a cathedral gate'. On the 22nd, thoughts of Rose are linked repeatedly with associations of the Venetian visit of 1876–77 and lines from *Othello*. Venetian references become entirely dominant toward the end of his last entry (Titian, Tintoretto, and the doges Andrea Gritti, Dandolo, and Selvo – the last of whom poses a visual problem which had arisen more than once in studies of the St. Mark's mosaics: 'Oh – dear doge Selvo, I want to know the shape of your cap, terribly').[47] After placing a letter from his gondolier as a bookmark in the Shakespeare he was reading, and on the verge of a mental collapse that has never been convincingly described or explained,[48] Ruskin makes a remarkable entry in his diary:

I am going to lock up with the Horses of St Marks. $\frac{1}{4}$ to one (20 minutes[)] by my Father's watch – 22nd February 1878 (BD.102).[49]

It would be foolish to attempt a precise interpretation of this suggestive imagery,[50] but it seems clear that at one of the more unsettled moments of his life a close and apparently comforting identification between Ruskin and his favourite building has asserted itself in his mind. The horses, standing guard over the 'cathedral gate' have become in some sense allies against a vaguely apprehended threat, and the image of a joint 'locking up' suggests that Ruskin, who had written his father in 1852 that 'whatever feelings of attachment I have are to material things' (LV.156),[51] senses a strong symbolic bond with the vulnerable building. We owe the survival of the old west front in part to the efficiency and sound tactical sense with which he had acted upon those feelings when the threat of its imminent rebuilding became apparent to him early in 1877.

127 The Porta dei Fiori (north façade) before restoration, before 1864

8 SERVILE AND HORRIBLE RIGIDITY
The campaign against rebuilding

'Ah,' he sed, 'it aint so with St. Marks.' I asked him who he wos. He sed he wos a Amatoor Arkeologist of long standing and he felt tired. I inquired if he thote the parst ought tu be restored. He sed he wuddent tutch it so long as it kud hang tugether. We air the kustodians of the parst, he sed. We've no workmen good enuff tu replace it nor klever enuff tu repare it, and as fur kolour – luk at St. Marks front which they wunted to do sumthin tu, tu give futur ages a chance of lukking at it. Restore it? Bah! John Ruskin's the man fur my money. He sez, 'Dont alter a stun. Keep on drawin till it falls.' He's right. 'How wud yu like to hav yure front restored if yu wur St. Marks?' he suddenly demanded turnin tu me abrupt on his axis.

'Elijer Goff' (William Dawes), quoted in *The Building News*, Dec. 5, 1879.

In the nineteenth century, finally, the cold touch of the restorer's hand destroyed much of the charm of one of the most picturesque monuments of Europe.

Otto Demus, *The Church of San Marco in Venice*, 1960, p. 105.

FULL discussion of the restorations undertaken at St. Mark's during the half-century of Ruskin's involvement with the building would require a lengthy study.[1] One fact, however, is apparent to the most casual observer today. The north and much of the south sides are remarkable for a monochromatic drabness which contrasts strikingly with the rich remains of colour that still manage – especially on a rainy day – to escape from the erosion, soot and sulphate deposits of the west front. The preservation of that contrast was accomplished by the campaign which, beginning in 1877, stopped the rebuilding of the west front by the architect mainly responsible for the present look of the other façades.

The extent to which G.B. Meduna, who had assumed responsibility for the fabric in 1853, altered the disposition of columns, plinths, mouldings and sculptured details of the north and south façades, in programs of 1860–64 and 1865–75 respectively, can be inferred by inspecting what he called the 'scrupulous conformity and identity with the original'[2] of his work on the southwest portico and fifth porch. All the evidence supports F. Forlati's charge that p. 110 'Everything was straightened, the columns and the capitals were scraped, the old decorations were made anew, and the old marble slabs were replaced by new ones of a different kind'.[3]

The north façade had required attention. Ruskin's complaints of 1845 about painted stucco indicate some incrustation was missing. But even the most unsightly exposure of brick can scarcely have been 127 as ugly as Meduna's replacement. The lowliest weekend carpenter, 128 covering a shed with bits of castoff plywood, would be ashamed of the fitting of much of the new marble. It will never be known how much colour was lost in the substitution of 'a facing of unpicturesque smooth-veined Tino marble . . . for the precious ancient one' (24.lix). Rich grounds for speculation are provided, however, by a remnant of the old marble, conveniently framed by Meduna's innovation, on the wall terminating the north external gallery. A Newcastle mason described the 'raw, cold appearance of the new work' in 1880 in terms that could not be improved today:

> I had to make a nearer examination of the upper part of the north side to satisfy myself that it was marble. The appearance is just what would be produced by using a dirty lime wash on a white plastered wall, care being taken to move the brush nearly vertically.[4]

Meduna's work on the north side was applauded, and this 'fatal praise'[5] encouraged a similar assault on the south façade.

By 1877 the leprous growth extended to the southern flank of the fifth western porch. Ruskin, who had the previous year displayed at a lecture 'portions of the alabaster of St. Mark's torn away for recent restorations' (26.192–93), was in despair. In April 1877 he tells an English correspondent:

> It is impossible for any one to know the horror and contempt with which I regard modern restoration – but it is so great that it simply paralyses me in despair, – and in the sense of such difference in all thought and feeling between me and the people I live in the midst of, almost makes it useless for me to talk to them. Of course all restoration is accursed architect's jobbery, and will go on as long as they can get their filthy bread by such business. . . . I am obliged to hide my face from it all, and work at other things, or I should die of mere indignation and disgust. (34.531)

He had not been as passive as this suggests. When Count A.P. Zorzi (1846–1922) had approached him in January with a protest he was writing, Ruskin offered to help.[6] Two days after being wakened by 'a horrid dream about restoration of a Gothic pinnacle and bracket' (D3.937)[7] he begins a preface to Zorzi's *Osservazioni intorno ai ristauri interni ed esterni della Basilica di S. Marco*, 'the best thing I ever saw written on architecture but by myself: and it is more furious than *me*!'[8] Zorzi's thunderous attack on the 'ignorance, carelessness and venality' of the restorers,[9] his caustic wonder at the fact that ancient marbles, declared worthless by the authorities, could nonetheless command good English *denari*,[10] must have delighted his foreign mentor.

In his preface, addressed to Zorzi, Ruskin exercises a flair for public relations which his compatriots would always do well to emulate in

128 Marble incrustation on the north façade of St. Mark's, 1982

such circumstances. He sets aside his own negative feelings about the nineteenth-century Venetians ('a horde of banditti')[11] in order to establish a diplomatic counterpoint to Zorzi's frontal attack. Having determined to be 'courteous in general terms – waiving discussion of petty sales or abstractions of marble by the workmen as beneath contempt in relation to the real points at issue',[12] he proceeds with the most shameless flattery:

In my own country, now given up wholly to the love of money, I do not wonder when I prevail little. But here in Venice your hearts are not yet hardened . . . . The Venetian has still all the genius, the conscience, the ingenuity of his race (24.406).

This famous writer, described in Zorzi's dedication as '*inglese per nascita, veneziano per cuore*' and praised (with a list of eight honorific titles) as '*Autore delle Gemme letterario-artistico-archeologiche LE PIETRE DI VENEZIA*', now humbly – in 'my rough English' – lays all his achievements at the feet of the Serenissima. He is 'in truth a foster-child of Venice. She has taught me all that I have rightly learned of the arts which are my joy' (24.405). His credentials thus impeccably established, Ruskin proceeds to the south side of St. Mark's:

101

of all the happy and ardent days which, in my earlier life, it was granted me
to spend in this Holy land of Italy, none were so precious as those which I
used to pass in the bright recess of your Piazzetta . . . . No such scene
existed elsewhere in Europe, – in the world; so bright, so magically
visionary . . . . I pass the same place now with averted eyes. There is only
the ghost, – nay, the corpse, – of all that I so loved. (24.405–6)

More detailed focus brings tougher language. The mosaics of the
upper façade

100 were of such exquisite intricacy of deep golden glow between the courses
of small pillars, that those two upper arches had an effect as of peacock's
feathers in the sun, when their green and purple glitters through and
through with light. But now they have the look of a peacock's feather that
has been dipped in white paint. . . . this I know, that in old time I looked
every day at this side of St. Mark's, wondering whether I ever should be
able to paint anything so lovely; and that now, not only would any good
colourist refuse to paint it as a principal subject, but he would feel that he
could not introduce that portion of the building into any picture without
spoiling it. (24.407–8)

Even if the restorations had improved the building,

the fact would remain the same that it was *not* the old church, but a model
of it. Is this, to the people of the lagoons, no loss? To us foreigners, it is *total*
loss. We can build models of St. Mark's for ourselves, in England, or in
America. (24.410)

After declaring that he 'must be mute, for shame, knowing as I do
that English influence and example are at the root of many of these
mischiefs', Ruskin slips in the hard advice which, as a meddling
foreigner, he must deliver with utmost caution:

I venture partly to answer the question which will occur to readers whom
you [Zorzi] convince, – what means of preservation ought to be used for a
building which it is impossible to restore. The single principle is, that after
any operation whatsoever necessary for the safety of the building, every
external stone should be set back in its actual place (24.410).

His message delivered, Ruskin resumes the flowery style, humbly
entrusting 'this stranger's testimony' to 'your hands, dear Count'.
The preface ends with a flourish worthy of Dostoyevsky's Lebedev,
in which phrases such as 'sincerity so fearless and so earnest', 'never-
ending gratitude', 'unblemished honour', 'your ancient name' (Zorzi
came from a famous Venetian family), and even a resounding 'Once
more, farewell' (Ruskin was not to leave Venice until a month after
publication), set the tone. Translated into Italian by the Count's
fiancée, Ruskin's words provided a perfect verbal anaesthetic for the
surgery with which Zorzi followed.

While many of his arguments echo Ruskin – especially 'The Lamp of Memory'[13] – the most impressive of Zorzi's *Osservazioni* outline technical factors affecting the colour and durability of marbles. Ruskin's claim that this 'analysis of the value of colours produced by age . . . cannot possibly be better done' (24.409) has recently received support from a writer who finds these 'extremely precise technical contents . . . still valid'.[14]

Zorzi describes a threefold process through which the marbles had originally received a surface which, while permitting richest expression of colour, also protected them from atmospheric damage.[15] After cutting to shape, they were smoothed by vigorous application of a special 'sawing sand' (*sabbia da segati*). This sanding, productive of great heat, causes the surface crystals to fuse and, Zorzi points out, without the thin transparent film thus produced no subsequent polishing can bring out the full colours of the marble. The next operation consists of repeated application of pumice powder. While smoothing the marble, the pumice grinds together tiny particles of its surface to form a coating of whitish opacity. Thirdly, polishing with a very fine sand (*sabbia finissima*) removes this deposit while producing a second transparent film over the first to provide fullest colour and a relatively tough safeguard against the elements.

Meduna had scraped through both films[16] and then, after hasty pumicing, left the unprotected marble with a whitish, water-absorbent surface.[17] Several shafts of the fifth porch, their lower portions reduced to this condition and standing unprotected from the weather, can be seen in an 1870s photograph (the shafts to their right exhibit the full treatment). Besides obscuring the true colours, Meduna's porous surface absorbs dirt-bearing moisture which rapidly stains the marbles. Thus, in 1877, the verd antique shafts of the new south side already look 'like fake marbles painted with distemper, and many of the other marbles look tarnished and wan'.[18] With the protective films, as well as the patina produced by time ('a varnish of the centuries'), removed, 'the progress of corrosion is terrible, especially if the marbles are exposed to a salt-filled atmosphere' such as that of Venice.[19] 79

Zorzi attacks other aspects of Meduna's work. The old marbles are notable for the 'stupendous quality' and variety of their markings. They were usually disposed in fairly narrow vertical strips (many slabs were cut from shafts brought from Constantinople in 1204), with their veins set more or less horizontally. Meduna had substituted large panels with straight parallel veins, set vertically or 128, x near-vertically. Whereas the old horizontal patterns provide a contrast to the vertical lines of the shafts, the modern replacements encourage the eye to confuse the veins of the wall marbles with the column edges. Such violation of the 'physiognomy' of the building, caused by the 'ignorance or indifference' of the restorers, is especially obnoxious when seen beside the original incrustation.[20]

Meduna's treatment of mouldings and carved ornament is just as offensive. While the old dentils are large and dominant, their tiny successors substitute 'the contemptible for the weighty, the shabby for the grand'.[21] The replacement of capitals by copies is equally abominable.[22] A copy is inevitably a caricature, because of the 'pedantry of the copyist'. Echoing countless passages in Ruskin, Zorzi argues that no amount of mere *diligenza volgare* can replace the 'free creativity' of the originals. Where capitals are hopelessly damaged, replacements should be purchased after a careful survey of ancient capitals in the collections of antiquaries.[23] Zorzi concludes that while the stability of Meduna's engineering is not in doubt, it has inflicted intolerable aesthetic damage.[24] The fabric of St. Mark's should be preserved and secured rather than restored.

The publication on St. Mark's Day (25 April) of 'this terrible book of Count Zorzi's and mine' (37.221) produced '*una vasta eco nell' opinione pubblica*'.[25] About 8 May, Ruskin writes Joan Severn: 'Immense fuss and laudation of our book . . . . I believe it . . . will do its work – copies being sent to all members of the government by the most influential people.'[26] However, the momentum established by Meduna's earlier campaigns was not – such are the monetary dependencies inherent in large building projects – easily arrested. Though the authorities halted restoration while awaiting a committee report, it appeared in the autumn of 1879 that rebuilding might continue.

The pressure being exerted in Venice by Zorzi and his supporters was now augmented by a powerful British campaign led by William Morris and his new Society for the Protection of Ancient Buildings (SPAB). Between 1 November and Christmas 1879 at least thirty articles on the subject appeared in the British press, and many were immediately quoted in Italy.[27] In his opening salvo, Morris wrote that St. Mark's,

to the eye of any one not an expert in building looks safe enough from anything but malice or ignorance; but anyhow, if it be in any way unstable, it is impossible to believe that a very moderate exercise of engineering skill would not make it as sound as any building of its age can be. Whatever pretexts may be put forward therefore, the proposal to rebuild it can only come from those that suppose that they can renew and better (by imitation) the workmanship of its details, hitherto supposed to be unrivalled.[28]

A flurry of public meetings during the following weeks produced a Memorial with more than a thousand signatures which made its way to the Italian Ministry of Public Instruction.[29] 'On all grounds', it stated, 'we believe that any re-building of the façade of St. Mark's Church, any renewal of its beautiful and venerable surface, will be an irreparable misfortune to art'.[30] *Punch* put it more briefly on 29 November: 'THE WAY ST. MARK'S IS GOING. – From the Dog(e)s to the Dogs!'

There was criticism of the SPAB campaign in England. *The Architect*, pompously dissociating itself from Morris because it considered it held 'a general retainer' for 'the higher orders of the architectural artists of England', opposed the rebuilding on anti-quarian grounds, but insisted:

we cannot hesitate for a moment to say that the resources of modern design are equal to the composition of any number of substitutes which, aesthetically considered, could not but be deemed vastly superior.

St. Mark's was 'a barbaric Byzantine work, which, if modern, would be scarcely worthy of a London engineer, and by no means of a Paris carpenter'.[31] A writer in *Truth* dismissed Morris as 'a fretful poet with the tooth-ache': modern Italians could easily replace the mosaics and carvings:

It is notorious that there are plenty of art workmen in Florence whose counterfeits of the old works of the finest time have deceived the best judges.[32]

The Globe, commenting on a large meeting held in Oxford on 15 November, warns that the 'deplorable inferiority' of English art would cause the protest to 'excite some little laughter in the art circles of more favoured countries' and that Italians 'may find it awkward to be told that they are vandals'.[33]

That this was the case is confirmed in a telegram sent by the Rome correspondent of *The Standard* on 28 November. While admitting the 'artistic ignorance, technical incapacity, and incredibly gross carelessness' of Meduna's work, the Italian authorities were amused at the indignant tone emanating from Oxford, 'for Italians interested in such matters are perfectly well aware of all that has recently been done at Oxford of the same kind'.[34] The Director of the Ministry of Public Instruction scoffed at the 'recently awakened tenderness of the English for our Monuments', stating that his Ministry, 'seeing how badly the works of the two lateral façades had been carried out, ordered last May that the Commission of Monuments should study the most rational method of restoring not of rebuilding the façade', but conceding: 'in this cold weather, which must be still colder in England, a little excitement can do no harm'.[35]

The mood in Venice was less jocular. John Bunney, to whom Morris had sent a copy of the Memorial, replied on 16 November:

I shall be very glad to sign it and to do all in my power to further such a worthy object – But what do you wish me to do? obtain Signatures from any English artists who may be in Venice? It will scarcely do to make known the contents of the memorial among Italians . . . .[36]

A correspondent to the *Daily News* reports as a 'poor pleasantry' a suggestion that a society be founded 'at Venice for organising resistance to those foreigners who thrust their noses into other peoples' affairs',[37] and Bunney warns Newman Marks of the SPAB on 2 December: 'Public opinion is at present very adverse to the movement made in England. so far as I can ascertain throughout Italy – Here it is very strong'.[38]

The role played during this campaign by Pietro Saccardo (b. 1830), who, as Meduna's churchwarden since 1861, had helped direct the rebuilding of the north and south façades,[39] is difficult to interpret. His pamphlet *S. Marco: gl'inglesi e noi* (Venice, late 1879) is a strange mixture of support for objections raised by Zorzi, Ruskin and the SPAB, justification for the work already done, and thinly veiled resentment at foreign interference. He echoes Zorzi's attack on the scraping of marbles and maintains that the raising of the southwest corner by some 12 cm in the reconstruction indicates an intention to continue the old methods across the west front.[40] At the same time, he seems to justify the previous campaigns, assuring readers that the north façade had not been of much aesthetic consequence to begin with,[41] and that in any case the rebuilding had enjoyed unanimous official approval.[42] The SPAB campaign is described as a 'comedy',[43] and a proposed international investigation as 'excessive', 'strange', and insulting to the 'honour of Italy'.[44] A letter by his fellow guardians (*Fabbricieri*) of the church fabric, appended to the pamphlet, insists they should not be sacrificed to the 'indignations of John Bull', that they have merely been following orders, and that the Italian ambassador in London should demand cessation of the 'meetings, agitations and manifestoes'.[45] By adopting much of the *Inglesi's* position as his own, while simultaneously appealing to the xenophobia which the SPAB protest had aroused locally, Saccardo appears to have been trying to stabilize the shaky position he must have been in after eighteen years of collaboration with Meduna.[46]

At the same time, Saccardo was busily sending plans of the

foundations of St. Mark's to Morris in an attempt to justify the rebuilding. Morris's reply must have seemed anything but 'comedy'. While thanking Saccardo for his 'courteous letters', and professing his inability to 'argue on a matter of technical detail with a person of your experience', Morris is sure that

the renowned engineers of Italy will not find it impossible under any circumstances to devise some scheme for keeping the Basilica standing for ages to come without any change in its external aspect . . . . Meantime, my dear Sir, will you allow me to trespass further on your courtesy by presenting to you my friend Mr. J.J. Stevenson, a distinguished English Architect & a member of our Committee, who has been deputed by that Committee to report to us the present state of S. Mark's Basilica: We believe that your intimate knowledge of the building will be of great use to him in his survey of it, & that you will not grudge him that help as we cannot doubt that you fully understand the good-will which our Society bears both to the Italian people & to Venice, & permit me to add, since you have made us acquainted with you by your letters, to yourself also. . . .[47]

In the meantime, Saccardo's boss was trying to disarm the enemy at St. Mark's itself. In a long letter from Venice dated 13 December 1879, a correspondent tells readers of *The Times* that Meduna had 'not only courteously, but with great satisfaction', taken him around the church and demonstrated the need for each change he had made. Meduna convinced this simpleton that the new incrustation on the north side was 'of the same stone as the original'. On the south side,

the portion which strikes the eye of the visitor is the new veneer of grey marble identical with that which was originally used, but the new surface of which jars on the sense of colour. Time will harmonize it, *but meanwhile a wash of sulphate of iron would remove the rawness without injury* [my italics].

Meduna was apparently unconcerned about the porosity of his scraped marbles. There was, he further reassured his visitor, no plan 'for a demolition and reconstruction of the front of the church' unless, in removing the incrustation as work proceeded, 'the brickwork should be found [as had, it seems, been the case across the entire north and south façades] to be more gravely compromised than is now suspected'. Even the northwest portico 'will not be disturbed, though much disfigured by the iron bars necessary to keep it from falling'.[48] The correspondent – but surely not Meduna? – was ignorant of their presence in Bellini's painting of 1496.

Meanwhile, not one, but three, reports were being prepared by English architects who visited Venice between December 1879 and March 1880. *The Architect* published two on 7 February 1880. Stevenson found the west front 'perfectly stable'. The worst defect was the condition of two pillars at the south end, where the restoration of the south front . . . joins the old work. These have been deprived of their support in the old wall by its removal, and they have not been fixed into the new work, I believe, because this was considered an unnecessary trouble, as it was expected that the whole of the west front was to be taken down.

He reports that £100,000 are to be spent on the west front over the following twenty years, though 'all the repairs necessary to put the building in a sound condition could be executed at a small cost, and without appreciably altering its appearance'.[49]

The second report, by William Scott, states that

After careful and repeated examination of the façade, one is struck by the entire absence of the least evidence to indicate a recent settlement . . . . It is . . . astonishing that men of acknowledged skill and experience should profess to discern amidst so much massive firmness and strength the elements of a dangerous decay.

Scott, working independently of Stevenson and the SPAB,[50] also pointed to the fifth porch as proof of 'local anticipations of the continuance of the work':

the levels of the new portion are higher than those of the old, the necessary 'returns' are omitted, and the wall behind some of the decorative columns . . . has been cut away and rebuilt without renewing their connection with it.[51]

Meduna had meanwhile been invited by the *Building News* to give his side of the story. His reply, published 13 February 1880, can only have increased the suspicions of his critics. It would require 'a treatise of several hundred pages' to explain the need for the works which 'are about to be undertaken', and he 'could not do it at so short a notice'. 'Nothing can be more inexact' than the charge that he proposes 'the *total destruction* and rebuilding of the west front'. All his previous restorations have been 'effected with scrupulous conformity and identity with the original'. To G.E. Street's observation (made at Oxford, 15 November) that the west front was in good condition and the proposed works would be aesthetically damaging, he 'might oppose contrary consideration, but I abstain . . . because I wish to avoid a polemic on such a delicate subject'. He considers it unnecessary to respond to charges made in the SPAB Memorial, but reserves 'the right of answering them when called upon by my Government'. Anyone who knows the true condition of St. Mark's 'must admit that what has been done is exactly what ought to have been done'.[52]

Meduna clearly underestimated the British challenge. The report of 19 March to the SPAB by G.E. Street, published in *The Times* on

18 May, must have ended his illusions:

Neither on plan nor in elevation does the new work already executed on the western front for a few feet in length from the south-west angle agree with the old plan or the old elevation. This is specially to be noticed in the plan. The whole façade has at its base a marble seat or step. In its former state this was continuous throughout. Signor Meduna's seat or base is already built for several feet, and at the point at which it stops it is 12 centimetres higher than the old step on which it abuts, and 15 centimetres in advance westward of it. [Ruskin's measurements corroborate this.] . . . p. 110 What was evidently intended was to make the base straight on plan and level from the south-west to the north-west angle of the front. No other explanation of the work already executed for several feet on the western front is possible. . . . As to the ground plan of this front it is most important to observe that it was originally built and planned on a curved line, the centre being recessed about 25 centimetres from a line drawn from angle to angle. Mr. Ruskin many years ago drew attention to the way in which all the apparently corresponding dimensions of the archways and piers in this façade were varied with, as he said, 'a true artistic instinct.' I do not recollect whether he noticed the curvature of the plan [he does not seem to have]. I had never before done so. But on trying to make out why Signor Meduna could have made his base project 15 centimetres in front of the old base I became aware of the fact. The line adopted by him was intended to be carried in a straight line from the south-west angle to the north-west angle. In not one inch of its whole extent would it have stood where the old base ever stood, and in the centre it would have been 33 centimetres (1 ft 1 in.) in advance westward of the old work. If, however, this step, seat, or base is brought forward it must be assumed that the whole of the rest of the work must be brought forward also. This, of course, means that the west front must be rebuilt, in the same way as the north and south fronts, with the same hard straight lines everywhere. I turn now to what has been proposed as to the elevation. Here the base or plinth as far as the jamb of the first archway of the front has been built 12 centimetres above its old level, and the first columns of the front are placed so much higher than they used to be. The capitals of the new columns are about three inches higher than the old, the capitals of the second order of columns are about level with the old, while finally the parapet at the top is 15 centimetres (6 in.) higher than the old. If the intention was not to rebuild the whole front according to the corrected and exact dimensions of the new work, I can only say that one of the most strange blunders of which I ever heard has been perpetrated. Assuming that it was necessary to rebuild the south front, it would have been most easy to accommodate the new work to the old, both in plan and elevation. Whereas now the columns with their bases and caps of the southern archway must all be taken down and rebuilt at a new level, then the next arch will be declared to be out of the level, and so on all along the front. In the same way the arcaded parapet already built must be taken down again or the whole of the old balustrade or parapet will have to be rebuilt on the new level. It seems to me, I must say, to be less damaging to Signor Meduna as an engineer to assume that it was his intention to rebuild the whole front than to suppose that he went on year by year with the work of renewing the southern façade and south-west angle without observing that he was getting both his plan and his levels different from those of the old work which he had to effect a junction with.[53]

This analysis effectively completed the discrediting of Meduna begun by Zorzi and Ruskin three years earlier.

Many more meetings and reports were aired in the British press during the following months and years. While some of this discussion was well informed,[54] a good deal was pompous and silly. A few verses from the 'CHANT ROYAL, On the Proposed Restoration of St. Mark's, Venice', published in *The Builder* on 6 December 1880 —

> Shall Art's forget-me-not down-trodden be?
> . . . .
> Fling out the banner, let its blazonry,
> 'Saint Mark and Venice' (for sweet memory
> Enwreathen with blue petals) be display'd!
> No stone of Art's carved pray'r shall cloven be! . . . .
> Arm ye, my brothers, for the new crusade!

— should help explain the contempt felt by Venetians for some of their foreign interlocutors. Nor should it be overlooked that Meduna's severest critic was guilty of the very sin he condemned in the Commendatore. At the meeting of the SPAB (28 June 1880) during which Stevenson's report was read to great acclaim, the Chairman, Stanley Leighton, lamented:

Some few years ago the church of Oswestry was restored at great cost: within the church there were no less than 170 monumental stones . . . from the time of Elizabeth to the time of Queen Victoria. Mr. Street, the architect, buried every one of those 170 monumental stones in order that new encaustic tiles might be put in their place. . . . There was only one solitary person in the whole parish who protested against this spoliation; that man was looked upon as a fanatic.[55]

It was partly because of Ruskin's awareness of such double standards within the architectural profession[56] that he avoided the protest meetings of 1879. His absence was attributed — with encouragement from Ruskin — to the pain caused him by the subject. 'Unfortunately Mr. Ruskin was not present,' the *Athenaeum* reports of the Oxford meeting of 15 November 1879, 'because on such occasions a profound despair seizes the author of "The Stones of Venice".'[57] The protesters nonetheless unanimously proclaimed their debt to Ruskin. Feelings about restoration were stronger in England than in Italy, wrote Morris in the *Manchester Guardian* on 29 November 1879, because

we have had the advantage of reading Mr. Ruskin's words in our mother tongue – words which, published so many years ago, in the 'Seven Lamps,' can never be bettered. To his insight we doubtless owe the fact that at this juncture we have been able to excite such a wide-spread interest in this matter. Ten years ago I doubt if a hundred names could have been got to such a memorial as we have set on foot, and to-day, in spite of many disadvantages, it has been signed by a thousand or more, including the very flower of the country in art, literature, and science.

Even those who doubted the seriousness of the threat to St. Mark's appealed to Ruskin's judgment,[58] while one lachrymose admirer must have provided the Master with positively Swiftian delight in his lament that it was impossible to

measure the loss to the past of art, nor to its future, which comes of the circumstance, that when the temple which for centuries has given joy to East and West alike is threatened with partial demolition, silence must lie on the lips of him whose distinguished gift, a supreme birth-possession above all or most of the men of his time, is a wonderfully subtle apprehension of all beauty of form wrought by the hand of the architect.[59]

The silence which sealed Ruskin's lips did not affect his pen. The *Circular Respecting Memorial Studies of St. Mark's, Venice*, published in late 1879 and early 1880, contains some of his most vigorous writing on the building. While doubtful of the usefulness of public protests (he refers readers to the Zorzi pamphlet for his own efforts in that line), he is determined to 'use what time may be yet granted for such record as hand and heart can make of the most precious building in Europe' (24.412–13), and has

entirely honest and able draughtsmen at my command . . . . and all that I   XI, XXIX
want from the antiquarian sympathy of England is so much instant help as may permit me . . . to get the records made under my own overseership . . . . All subscriptions to be sent to Mr. G. ALLEN, Sunnyside, Orpington, Kent. (24.416)

Meanwhile he had placed before the public – including the zealous if inaccurate Ruskinian quoted by Elijer Goff at the head of this chapter – examples of the kinds of record he had in mind. His 1877   XXXI
watercolour of the northwest portico, eight large photographs of the   30, 56
west front, and one of the south side before restoration, were   70, 79, 101
displayed at the 1879–80 exhibition of the Society of Painters in Water-colours (24.413; 416–17). At the same time, a new painting of the so-called Pillars of Acre (probably the watercolour based on the   XXXV

reversed image of a daguerreotype)[60] was hung at the Fine Art Society (24.418). These 'sixth century' pillars[61] exhibit carving still 'as sharp as a fresh-growing thistle', and illustrate Ruskin's contention (how sadly this reads a century later) that

the Greek and Istrian marbles used at Venice are absolutely defiant of hypaethral influences, and the edges of their delicatest sculpture remain to this day more sharp than if they had been cut in steel . . . . Throughout the whole façade of St. Mark's, the capitals have only here and there by casualty lost so much as a volute or acanthus leaf, and whatever remains is perfect as on the day it was set in its place, mellowed and subdued only in colour by time, but white still, clearly white; and grey still, softly grey; its porphyry purple as an Orleans plum, and the serpentine as green as a greengage. (24.418–19)

The 'only possible pretence for restoration', the 'alleged insecurity of the masses of inner wall', is 'really too gross to be answered',[62] while the photograph shows the

79

savage and brutal carelessness with which the restored parts are joined to the old . . . [and] bears deadly and perpetual witness against the system of 'making work,' too well known now among English as well as Italian operatives (24.421).

p. 9   Bitingly ironical about his famous description of the west front, quoted repeatedly during Morris's campaign – 'The words have been occasionally read for the sound of them; and perhaps, when the building is destroyed, may be some day, with amazement, perceived to have been true' (24.413) – Ruskin was irritated when the SPAB Memorial, together with flattering comments, arrived at Brantwood;[63] he was no longer hopeful that the protest would succeed. To a correspondent in Manchester he wrote:

Nothing would be effectual, but the appointment of a Procurator of St. Mark's, with an enormous salary, dependent on the church's being let alone. What you can do by a meeting at Manchester, I have no notion. . . . I don't believe we can save it by any protests. (24.424)

Ruskin's pessimism was a little excessive. New regulations were approved in 1882 confirming that preservation must henceforth prevail over restoration, with all work to be done by the 'Opera' of St. Mark's instead of commercial firms.[64] Under Saccardo, and F. Berchet (already guilty of what is perhaps the most brutal of all nineteenth-century restorations at the Fondaco dei Turchi),[65] the implementation of the new rules was, to put it mildly, 'not always above reproach'.[66] Between 1883 and 1887 some attempt to undo Meduna's work on the south façade and southwest corner was made (it was, as Ruskin's measurements and old photographs prove, by no means as successful as suggested by Berchet),[67] and – under the eye of a more watchful public – the destruction and re-setting of the mosaics was perhaps somewhat slowed.[68]

Ruskin's demand that the old sculpture and incrustation be preserved at all costs has been more consistently honoured in the twentieth century, and he would have applauded the techniques adopted after the Second World War by F. Forlati and his successors for the internal consolidation of piers and vaults.[69] It remains to be seen if the major works begun on the west front in 1981 continue the tradition inaugurated by Zorzi and Ruskin in 1877.

9 CONCLUSION

When Ruskin learned in January 1879 that Zorzi was planning to see him in England, he protested:

Have you not been told, or don't you believe that I was raving mad for two months? – held down in my bed some times by three men? – Do you suppose I can after such warning – allow myself to be excited or grieved, when I *cannot* help.[1]

If Ruskin's alarm was caused by painful thoughts of St. Mark's,[2] it is remarkable that the next year was to see some of his most excited work on the building since 1852.

He had decided to copy his 1877 drawing of the northwest portico for an exhibition in Boston. On 27 February he writes to Norton, who was arranging the event: 'the St. Marks copy appals me a little as I think over *it* today';[3] and on 16 March: 'I could do *so much* more, if you would wait – I *can't* do the St Marks . . . before April'.[4] In fact, Ruskin had plunged headlong into his 1877 notes and was writing the eighth chapter, with accounts of the carved central arch and mosaics, of *St. Mark's Rest*. On 17 March he records:

p. 104
p. 174

Yesterday very dismal, working on St Marks mosaics, but I think something will come of it today. Ive got my pretty drawing beside me [possibly C.F. Murray's drawing of the Doge and his People], – but my hand trembles with the excitement of the thoughts I have to deal with   Must do a little geology first to cool me down. (BD.165)

He is 'kept in' all that day by snow and not only does 'grand work on St Marks' (BD.165) but revises part of the *Stones* for the new Travellers' Edition:

One's thirty years of added knowledge – a mere cumbrous inexpressible heap – hanging over one's head like a pile of useless bricks, make it weary work (30.303).

On the 18th he is 'giddy with work on St Marks' (BD.165). Further work is noted on 23 March and 25 June (BD.166; 177), and on 12 July he pronounces: 'mosaics from St. Marks, good' (BD.181).[5] A letter to Mrs. Burne-Jones in July announces:

I'm just painting a bit of St Marks for Norton – and I think its very nice! – though I *have* been crazy. I don't feel my hand shaky yet.[6]

xxxviii
xxxv During the next six months he finishes this drawing, undertakes at least two more of the southwest portico and Pillars of Acre, exhibits

his photographs and two drawings as evidence against the need for restoration, writes his *Circular Respecting Memorial Studies of St. Mark's* (appealing meanwhile in the Travellers' Edition for financial contributions to the project; 10.463), corresponds at length with several artists concerning paintings he wants of mosaics visible from the southeastern gallery (30.lvii–lviii),[7] and launches a direct attack on Meduna in a second portion of the *Circular*, probably published early in 1880.

After this year of heightened activity, Ruskin's involvement with St. Mark's slackened. But his interest in the building during his last decade of often interrupted working remained strong. In 1882 he corresponds with a friend about the supposed 'sea waves' of the unrestored portions of the floor, agreeing they may have been caused by subsidence due to the activity of sand worms – he has never 'held hard by the symbolic notion' (37.385).[8] The same year he meets Francesca Alexander (1837–1917) and probably soon thereafter gives her a copy or early variant[9] of his old drawing of the inner archivolt of the fifth porch. In 1883 he writes to Venice to ask Quartus Talbot p. 113 (whose mother was an old friend) for details to aid in another drawing:

I just happen to want the colour of the southern vault of St Marks front. dilapidate . . . from restorations I am making a finished drawing from an old photo of it, and I want you to send me the colour, with as much of the form as you find *necessary* but only a sketch – or you would never have done and I want the colour rather quickly. I think the best way would be to take a good photograph and force it into colour with body colours over its shadows.[10]

Since 1881 Ruskin had corresponded with Giacomo Boni (1859–1925), Director of Works at the Doge's Palace, and an opponent of the Meduna/Saccardo tradition at St. Mark's.[11] Boni sends a long account in 1883 of experiments he has done on internal strengthening of weakened marbles.[12] Ruskin requests more records of mosaics which, as partial ruins at the time, were due for restoration.[13] Dissatisfied with his own and Murray's efforts, he asks on 20 April 1883: 'Could you, with Alessandri . . . make me a drawing of the mosaic of the Venetian Clergy, people, and Doge in south upper Gallery of St. Marks, inside?'[14]

Ruskin's evaluation of his copyists' work tells us much about his colour responses to St. Mark's. On 20 July 1879 he had written to T.M. Rooke, who was drawing mosaics:[15] '*Your* work is to give the facts point blank of each figure, as fully as you can' (30.lvii). After receiving samples of Rooke's work, he writes on 23 November:

I am entirely pleased with them as documentary work: but they still – and even more than hitherto, disappoint me in colour, possessing none of the *charm*, to my own eyes, of the originals; but only their dignity and sobriety. I think this may be partly owing to the state of your health ['when you are fatigued or ill you will not see colours well, and when you are ill-tempered you will not choose them well' (15.156)] – and partly to your reading always on the sober – as I do on the gaudy, side of colour . . . .[16]

xxix
xxviii
p. 179 Comparison of Rooke's drawing of the eastern dome with a modern photograph suggests grounds for this dissatisfaction. The 'decorative power' of the blues and purples is not absent from Rooke's attempt, but their infinite tonal ranges (from blackish blue through vivid blue to bluish white; from darkest violet to lilac grey) defeat him utterly. He is even further from justifying Ruskin's claim, made in another letter of 13 December 1879, that

all Byzantine mosaic . . . has splendour for its first object – and its type is the peacock's tail. If your drawings glow and melt like that you are right. Peacock's tail in shade or light it may be – and much sober brown in *any* light may mix with its violet and gold – but *that* is what the mosaicist wanted to do, and for the most part, did. (30.lviii)

The photograph itself (a four-minute exposure on slow film under white February light) is a mere shadow of the original. Ruskin is seeking the impossible. He nonetheless requests yet another copy of 'the mosaic of Doge and people . . . with the scroll ornament below xxvii & in the shadow so [a sketch, based on his drawing]. Then I shall see exactly how we respectively feel'. He has

also desired Mr Bunney with whom on points of colour I am very nearly at one, to make a sketch for me of the David and Solomon, of the apse cupola. You will I hope understand this as it is truly meant, not as putting Mr Bunney in any competition with, or opposition to you – but only that I may obtain by his assistant agency facts of which I think he is more habitually cognizant.[17]

But John Bunney (1828–82) had been set a greater challenge. In January 1877 Ruskin commissioned for £500 the large oil painting of the west front which – after six hundred morning sessions – was xi left unfinished on the artist's death in 1882. Bunney's work is a stupendous memorial. Yet its colour disappointed Ruskin. His xxxvi comments on another Bunney painting, of the northwest portico, are revealing. Though Ruskin describes it in 1879 as 'superb' (26.193n), he qualifies this praise in introducing it to visitors at the Museum of St. George:

The varieties of colour represented in this painting as existing in the ancient

208

marbles, are slightly, though unintentionally exaggerated by the earnest-
ness of the artist's attention to them (30.202).

This exaggeration troubled Ruskin in the same way that overemphatic reading of his favourite poetry did. His comparison between 'a
bad reader of poetry, laying regular emphasis on every required
syllable of every foot' and the 'inimitable cadence of the voice of a
person of sense and feeling reciting the same lines, – not incognizant
of the rhythm, but delicately bending it to the expression of passion'
(6.332–33) suggests why the overemphatic tones of Bunney's oil
painting of the façade made it, finally, not a mere disappointment,
but an irritant to him. In 1883 he sends it to the Whitelands Training
College for Girls in Chelsea, hoping it will prove 'useful as a room-
termination – though it can't stand against Newmans lovely
colour',[18] and in 1885 writes to 'relieve' the College 'of the burden of
St. Marks, which I have never liked leaving to the criticism of
London. At Sheffield its use will be seen' (37.537).

    Henry R. Newman (*c.* 1833–1917), a New Yorker living in Italy
since 1869, possessed a sense of architectural colour which delighted
Ruskin. When shown a painting of Santa Maria Novella (Florence)
in 1877, he wrote: 'I have not for many and many a day seen the sense
of tenderness and depth of colour so united' (30.lxxiii),[19] and several
years later a large oil of San Giorgio Maggiore and the Salute is
described as 'my own Venice – as only you've seen it' (30.lxxiv).[20]
There is no painting of St. Mark's among the Newmans bought for
the Guild of St. George,[21] but a watercolour, now in the U.S.A., of   xxxvii
the horses should demonstrate why Ruskin was so fond of his work.

    Ruskin returned to Venice for a muddled and unhappy visit
between 6 and 17 October 1888.[22] Before leaving, he wrote Angelo
Alessandri, one of his artist-copyists:

there have been symptoms of illness threatening me now for some time
which I cannot conquer – but by getting away from the elements of
imagination which haunt me here (37.608).

St. Mark's figured in certain erotic phantasies indulged in by Ruskin
at this time.[23] More troubling, in all likelihood, was his anguish over
the restorations. He met Saccardo during this visit,[24] and though no
doubt he was gratified to see the grey vertically-veined marbles of   xi
the upper walls of Meduna's southwest portico replaced by incrust-   9
ation set in the ancient manner, this limited restitution did not dispel
Ruskin's gloom. Indeed, if he was as disturbed by the restoration of
the mosaics as the SPAB was at this time,[25] it is not difficult to
understand why, as he left Venice for the last time, he was 'as
unhappy at all I've seen – as anybody well can be'.[26]

xxxviii In 1886 he had asked Norton to return his 1879 copy of the *Northwest Portico*, 'not for myself' but 'for my scholars and lovers', explaining that among all his drawings there are 'few of the church I love best – so good as that arch of St. Mark's'.[27] It is interesting to xxxi speculate why Ruskin, who had the original with him, felt so strongly about this drawing. It has been described as 'Careful and somewhat stiff, the impression it gives is that of a record of a drawing, rather than even a record of a building'.[28] But there are passages of colour here – especially in the shadows shimmering behind the two right porphyry shafts and under the Ice Plinth above – that justify Ruskin's assessment. The original is a lovely rendering of colours seen on the spring mornings of 1877 (24.413). The copy, though less optically factual (even in Ruskin's youth the portico cannot have seemed quite so ethereal), expresses something more, something written indelibly also between every line of the arduous yet loving analysis of 1849–52:

There is something in it besides the facts – a greater fact than any of them – a human soul. (LV.297)

Not far from Ruskin's eloquent shadows stand the mosaic figures of the 'great kings and queens' who once visited St. Mark's and remain, 'always looking on in their hearts' (24.286). It is pleasant to imagine, as one enters the church under their thoughtful gaze today, that John Ruskin is standing among them.

NOTES · BIBLIOGRAPHY

LIST OF ILLUSTRATIONS · INDEX

NOTES

PREFACE pages 7–8

1 Sir Arthur Helps (1813–75) was Clerk of the Privy Council and adviser to Queen Victoria. She entrusted him with the revision of Prince Albert's speeches, published in 1862.

I TRUTH IN MOSAIC pages 9–50

1 MS. of *Stones of Venice*, 11. Pierpont Morgan Library.

2 *Ibid.*, 12.

3 For the stone of each shaft, see Deichmann 1981, plan 7.

4 In modern usage, 'alabaster' designates a crystallized gypsum (calcium sulphate) which is waxy in texture, too soft to take high polish like marble, and easily marked by the fingernail. *Marmor alabastrum* (Italian *alabastro antico*), a true marble composed mainly of calcium carbonate, was considered in antiquity the most valuable of marbles (Pieri n.d., 24). It is formed by stalactitic action and, depending on impurities present, may have veins of every conceivable form and colour. The bluish-grey veins in the golden alabaster of many façade shafts at St. Mark's are caused by carbonaceous matter; yellows, pinks and reds (as in the nave spandrels) by iron oxides; greens by iron and copper sulphides, mica and talc. H.W. Pullen (1894, 103–11) describes 86 varieties, but since alabaster may change hue under various lighting (see pp. 168–70), his classification by colour seems rather arbitrary. Ironically, sulphur dioxide from the refineries at Mestre, which attacks St. Mark's as dilute sulphurous and sulphuric acids, is producing gypsum in its reaction with the marble.

5 Ruskin's influential fantasy about the 'liberty' of the mediaeval worker in 'The Nature of Gothic' (*Stones II*) is a prime instance (see my 'Ruskin, the Workman, and the Savageness of Gothic' in Hewison [ed.] 1981, 33ff). Another blunder is his notion (it forms the backbone of the historical thesis of the *Stones*) that twelfth-to-fourteenth-century Venice, which produced many of his favourite buildings, was notable for high ethical and religious standards. In fact, the Venetian-led Fourth Crusade 'surpassed even its predecessors in faithlessness and duplicity, brutality and greed' (Norwich 1977, 166). Ruskin's belief that the Venice which sacked its ally Constantinople in 1204 – stealing in the process the marbles which enrich much of St. Mark's – was upright and holy, while that of Albinoni and Vivaldi was a cesspool of depravity ('Grotesque Renaissance', *Stones III*), typifies the nonsense to be found on every other page of the *Stones*.

6 He recalls receiving the book 'as soon as it was published' (1830) and 'on my thirteenth (?) birthday' (1832), but adds sensibly: 'if it was a year later, no matter' (35.28, 79).

7 A draft preface for *St. Mark's Rest* dates the first visit 1833, the second 1835 (MS.3915.1.3795.q.1, vol. 1, Princeton University Library). John James Ruskin's itinerary of the 1833 tour (MS. 18, Bembridge) does not list Venice. *Praeterita* dates the first visit 1835 (35.156).

8 For an amusing account by Ruskin of producing one 1835 Venetian drawing 'elaborately out of my head' from 'hasty memoranda', see 35.182.

9 See Alvise Zorzi 1977, 1, 145ff, esp. 179–83. J. Clegg writes: 'The Austrians had begun restoring on St. Mark's in 1818. This was the first time Ruskin had noticed' (1981, 56).

10 Boito (ed.) 1889 translation, 11, 468.

11 Demus 1960, 207. When Longhena was chief architect in the seventeenth century 'frequent tickets' were given to various persons 'to wash or rub [*fregare*] the marbles in the church, and even the columns of the front'. The last official act of the Venetian Republic was 'the appointment of a certain Francesco Vedovelli' in April 1797 as 'Cleaner and Polisher of the Marbles' (Boito [ed.] 1889 translation, 11, 465, 473). For nineteenth-century 'rubbing', see p. 195, and chapter 8, note 16.

12 Ruskin notes a house near St. Mark's 'stuccoed over and painted with calico stripes to imitate alabaster' (RI.202). The Hotel Danieli had received similar treatment (RI.198 and Clegg 1981, plate 2).

13 See DI.340 and Cat. 1939 (38.297). Drawing untraced.

14 See Hanson 1981 for Ruskin's use of the daguerreotype in architectural drawing.

15 Distortions in Bellini's painting suggest the need for caution in doing so. Whereas the second-storey columns (top of capital to bottom of base) are roughly three-quarters the height of the lower, Bellini's are about three-fifths. His central arch is too wide in relation to height: the actual ratio (measuring from inside edge of face carving) is just over three-quarters; Bellini's exceeds four-fifths. His four lateral arches are much too narrow in relation to the central arch (the fourth porch by almost 20 per cent), and also too narrow in relation to their height (the fourth and fifth by some 10 per cent).

16 Canaletto's upper range (top of capital to bottom of base) is half the height of the lower (top of capital to pavement). A view camera photograph from the same position gives the ratio as three-fifths. It is shocking to read that in 1914 a Canaletto of the interior was requested by 'the authorities of St. Mark's, for reference during restoration', but one is relieved that 'the outbreak of World War I prevented this' (Constable 1965, 116).

17 In 1848 Ruskin notes in the Louvre: 'Canaletti; tumbles before Doges Palace Crowd in variously coloured rags – A Bit of St Marks in cold stone grey . . . another St Marks in brown . . . physically impossible perspective daubed mosaics & no colour' ('Sketch and Notebooks for the Seven Lamps', III, 48. Princeton University Library).

18 R. Hewison speculates that Ruskin 'invented a base to the pillar of the arcade of the Ducal Palace' at bottom right (1978, 53). While Ruskin's 1835 pen drawing (ill. 7) does not show a base, his preliminary sketch does (ill. 8). See also illustrations 101, XI, and Ruskin's reference to the base at 9.342.

19 E.T. Cook claims Ruskin made 'elaborate measurements' of Venetian buildings in

1846 (8.xx), but Ruskin refers to pacing of distances at St. Mark's (DI.340).

20 For a related response in the late 1870s see p. 182.

21 Lindsay 1847, I, 68.

22 This included Hope 1835, apparently the first English book to treat Byzantine architecture as a separate style with unique structural and decorative traits; Parker 1836, fourth edition by 1845; Woods 1828, frequently cited in the 1846 diary; Willis 1835.

23 Links 1968; Leon 1949, 119.

24 In the MS. for *Seven Lamps* (Huntington Library), Ruskin had written 'Byzantine capital'. The change to 'ornaments' was made at proof stage, which suggests that, in his hurried preparation of etchings for the book (8.xlv), Ruskin found that his sketches and daguerreotypes did not include a suitable Byzantine capital.

25 Ruskin's catalogue lists two 'Full View' daguerreotypes dated 1845 and 1852 (MS. 27, 620, Bembridge).

26 For an excellent account of Ruskin's 1849–50 working method, see Hewison 1978, 54–60.

27 Lutyens (ed.) 1965, 77.

28 Hewison 1978, 60.

29 'When I go to a church and get my ladders into a chapel I am of course obliged to do all the tombs in it at once' (LV.174). For Ruskin's coolness as a climber, see Dearden (ed.) 1967, 54.

30 Lutyens (ed.) 1965, 146.

31 Some of the materials on the west front collected in 1849–50 are squeezed into an appendix to *Stones II* (10.448–50).

32 Besides the sketch plan given in ill. 103, Ruskin mentions a 'great plan' (M.198l, 199) which has not been traced.

33 Cook and Wedderburn seem unaware of the large drawings reproduced in ills. v and VIII.

34 As Ruskin sent home drafts of *Stones II* in 1851–52, he received in return a persistent murmur from John James Ruskin about the amount of architectural analysis they contained. While working on the chapter on St. Mark's, Ruskin promises ironically that 'every chapter will contain some opening and closing passages of *interest*, and the dryer or bony parts, in which the strength of the book consists, will never be

so long as to be unmanageable' (LV.119; my italics). The conflict between Ruskin's scholarly instincts and John James's desire for a popular success is captured in a letter of January 1852. Ruskin feels he should give 'mere accounts of buildings in the most complete terms I can use . . . and the facts that columns are so high – and so far apart – and that a triangle is not a square – cannot be made very piquant . . . . You may say that other people than *I* could do this – Yes, but other people *won't* with the requisite care' (LV.136). On 18 February 1852 Ruskin laments – in terms often reiterated later in his denunciations of the *Seven Lamps* and *Stones* – 'I am sorry you are not at all interested in my antiquarianism . . . . all my power, such as it is, would be lost the moment I tried to catch people by fine writing' (LV.184–5). Nonetheless, a week later, conceding that the drafts hitherto sent contain 'rather more of the homely facts of Venice than I am afraid you would like', he promises more of the 'adornment' so dear to his father: 'the whole book . . . is a good deal like a house just built – full of dust and damp plaster . . . I must let it dry before I paint or paper it' (LV.197). The cynicism of this image – coming from the author of the recently published 'Lamp of Truth' – cannot, surely, have escaped even John James Ruskin. Even after jettisoning half the material in which he rightly considered the 'strength' of his work to lie, Ruskin felt apologetic about such 'anatomical analysis' as *Stones* still contains (10.78). What would he have thought of the recent claim that his relationship with John James Ruskin was 'never less than inspiring' (Hilton 1982, 1153)? John James was, of course, paying for Ruskin's Venetian studies: one estimate gives the cost of *Stones* as £12,000 (9.xxxviiin). Ruskin's sensitivity to the money his father was losing on *Examples* is often expressed during the 1851–52 visit (LV.97, 142, 177).

35 MS. 'Proof Plates for Stones of Venice/John Ruskin/R. P. Cuff'. Beinecke Library.

36 Undated letter, B.VII (first letter), Bembridge. Ruskin writes in detail of plate 2 of *Stones II* (attributed there to J.H. Le Keux), but refers to 'your workmens

fault'. The second letter in B.VII, dated only 'Monday', refers to engravings which became illustrations 9 and 11 of *Stones II* (also attributed to J.H. Le Keux). The striking difference in quality between these plates confirms that Le Keux contracted some work for Ruskin to others.

37 B.VII, Bembridge (second letter). For Le Keux's comment on Ruskin's generosity in such matters, see 6.xxvii.

38 Comparison between illustrations 47 and v suggests the engraving was based on the latter, though another drawing by Ruskin (Cat. 1949) may have intervened.

39 For example at 11.271 (twice).

40 Letter of 9 August 1876 to A. Wedderburn, Humanities Research Centre, University of Texas, Austin; Ward (ed.) 1922, 161.

2 THE GREAT CADENCE pages 51–60

1 *The Architect*, 3 January 1850. The anonymous author of *Something on Ruskinism . . . . By An Architect* (1851) describes the façade as 'a heterogeneous medley of monstrosities' (44).

2 See Unrau 1978, 54–62.

3 The pier between the fifth porch and the southwest portico was widened by over 16 inches. See p. 114.

4 Interestingly, the figures thus arrived at agree rather well with fine measurements made on large prints of two photographs (ill. 2, and plate 4 in Clegg 1981), taken from the end of the Piazza before the first and fifth porches were restored. Both agree with Ruskin that the arch of the second porch is the narrowest, the fifth much the widest, of the four lateral porches; and the first and fourth as close to identical as his two-inch difference suggests.

5 In 1871 Thomas Adolphus Trollope (1810–92), brother of the well-known novelist, 'spent several mornings in carefully hunting out all the specimens of Byzantine architecture which Ruskin registers as still existing in Venice, and can testify to the absolute exactitude of his topographical and architectural statements. I carefully examined also the examples which he cites as indications of subtle design on the part of the old

architects in cases where abnormality and carelessness might be suspected. His facts and measurements I found invariably correct' (1889, III, 217–18).

6 Ruskin's thought in these matters is echoed by R. Arnheim (1967, 47–49, 403; 1977, 190–91).

7 Pugin 1841, 1.

8 In December 1851 Ruskin asks his father to ascertain whether 'Greek' alabasters are still obtainable, 'their price . . . per cubic foot', and 'how the price rises for *large* pieces' (LV.94–5).

9 Deichmann thinks some external shafts, especially those of the central porch, were gathered in accordance with specific instructions, though he agrees that most were spoils from the sack of Constantinople in 1204 (1981, 13). Ruskin's measurements indicate that some attempt to set the spoils in axially symmetrical pairs was made (see Chapter 4). Deichmann believes the architects tried to hide anomalies; Ruskin thinks these were sometimes exploited to create certain optical effects.

10 Ruskin means the arcaded façades of such churches as the Duomo of Pisa and San Michele in Lucca (8.203–6; 9.245). Demus agrees: 'The colonnaded façades of San Marco are the Venetian counterpart of the protorenaissance façades of the churches of Pisa and Lucca' (1960, 101).

11 See note 6.

12 For the chiaroscuro, see Demus 1960, 100, 103. Ruskin would, however, object to Demus's reference to the 'indiscriminate use of columns' (1960, 101).

13 MS. of *Stones of Venice*, 12 (cancelled by Ruskin). Pierpont Morgan Library.

14 Parts of the façade still hint at what Ruskin saw. The lower shafts of the second porch, for example, appeared yellow and grey in bright afternoon light in June 1980. Under cloud, however, and especially when the columns were wet, the yellow became a tawny gold and the grey a delicate flax-blue.

15 Ruskin did most of this work in February, a damp, cold season in Venice. Anyone who has tried measuring (which involves embracing) a shaft of $4\frac{1}{2}$ feet girth will appreciate the fortitude – and obliviousness to public curiosity – this required. Ruskin avoids mention of the pigeons, but

their manners cannot have changed much since 1850.

3 BOUND WITH ALABASTER pages 61–74

1 Plans, with measurements, of the Basic and Second Plinths are preserved at Bembridge (WS.128 and 129; M.189l–190, and WS.133; M.196l).

2 MS. 'Stones of Venice II. St. Mark's and the Ducal Palace. Additional', headed by Ruskin 'St Marks Façade. 1.' Pierpont Morgan Library.

3 *Ibid.*

4 *The Builder*, 30 January 1869, 79.

5 The Gothic capitals referred to are at the Casa Falier.

6 Deichmann 1981 analyses more than 600 and illustrates over 300 capitals.

7 Profiles not clearly convex or concave are designated 'transitional' at 10.159.

8 Capitals with four eagles decorating the full height of the bell, for example, are 'a favourite early Lombardic form' (10.160).

9 For good illustrations of the relationship between incrustation and underlying flat and rounded brick surfaces see Marangoni 1933 'L'architetto', figs. 26, 30.

10 See Unrau 1978, 65ff.

11 Wolters (ed.) 1979, 54–55 and Cat. 197, 198.

4 A CONFUSION OF DELIGHT pages 75–119

1 MS. 'St. Mark's. Topical.', loose sheet in 'Stones of Venice II. St. Mark's and the Ducal Palace. Additional.' Pierpont Morgan Library.

2 Note the coincidence of the pigeon on the second tier of the angle with the daguerreotype's (reversed) image. The drawing's chief oddity is its subdivision by joints in the paper or placement of one layer over another. Slight imprecisions in fitting one segment to the next, staining by glue, imperfect pasting down of some joints, are evident. One strip at the right is unaccountably given a deep red wash. Ruskin had trouble with this drawing (LV.258–59), and similar problems in copying part of Veronese's *Solomon and the Queen of Sheba* in 1858 resulted in the same patchwork technique: 'Solomon has just this morning had an inch added all up him . . . . I took care to have a piece to begin

on large enough for anything, but it is impossible to hide joints even in colour' (Hayman [ed.] 1982, 146). Ruskin never exhibited his 'pale drawing' of the north-west angle, but valued it sufficiently to order a frame to await its arrival from Italy (LV.299–300).

3 The sagging of the angle (ill. 38) must owe something to the foundation. See drawing of 1912 in Marangoni 1933 'L'architetto', fig. 21. The corner column was until then supported by poplar piles 9 cm in diameter, and only 25 to 75 cm long. See also Zuliani 1975, 52–55 and ills.

4 F. Forlati in Demus 1960, 197; Zuliani 1975, 52. Photographs taken between 1909 and 1913 during restorations are given in Marangoni 1933 'L'architetto', figs. 17, 22, 23. Fig. 9 in Perocco (ed.) 1979 shows the corner column removed during restoration.

5 See Chapter 8. Changes were made in the first porch, however (see pp. 84–87).

6 Deichmann 1981, Cat. 304, 372, 373.

7 Ibid., Cat. 167, 172 (the sixth-century capitals); Cat. 436 (the mediaeval capital singled out by Ruskin).

8 Wolters 1979, Cat. 68. Demus considers it Lombardo-Emilian (1960, 118).

9 Wolters 1979, Cat. 75. Demus regards it as a good example of Islamic influence in thirteenth-century Venetian sculpture (1960, 148).

10 While the chain is reversed in the engraving, its asymmetrical apex remains unreversed; top of plant between upper peacocks missing; feet of lower birds wrongly placed; double dentils between birds and chain too narrow. A letter to Le Keux indicates that this plate had low priority during hasty preparation of plates for *Stones II* (MS.B.VII, Bembridge).

11 'St Marks. First Porch continued'. Cat. 1639. Bembridge.

12 Ruskin's figures (ibid.) are: 'proximate angle of 8' to 'outer angle of 9', 1 ft 3 in. (1 ft 3¾ in. in 1980); between 'proximate outer angles' of 9 and 10, 1 ft 3 in. (same in 1980); between 'proximate outer angles' of 10 and 11, 1 ft 3 in. (same in 1980).

13 Wolters 1979, Cat. 80. Demus believes the two end pieces were made for their present place c. 1250–70, with the other sections taken from another work: some 'were

originally attached to a curved surface, since the larger scenic reliefs are unmistakably convex' (1960, 169).

14 Compare Wolters 1979, ill. for Cat. 86.

15 Deichmann 1981, Cat. 440.

16 The largest variant found in 1980 was that the badly worn 'white plinth . . . between I and K', given by Ruskin as 2 ft 2 in. ('St. Marks. 2nd Porch'. Cat. 1642. Bembridge), ranges from 2 ft 0½ in. at north edge of column 18 to almost 2 ft 2¾ in. at south edge of column 19.

17 'St Marks. 2nd Porch'. Cat. 1642. Bembridge.

18 Daguerreotypes 136, 137, in Ruskin's catalogue. MS. 27, p. 622. Bembridge.

19 Wrongly identified as part of fourth porch at 11.350.

20 In the MS. Ruskin had written: 'The mere arrangement of the colour is given in the next plate'. Pierpont Morgan Library.

21 Wolters 1979, Cat. 89–91.

22 Ruskin's figures vary between 4 ft 7 in. and 4 ft 9 in. ('Third Porch. Plate III' and '4th Porch'. Cat. 1642. Bembridge). This near-uniformity supports Deichmann's thesis (1981, 13) that the shafts framing the central doorway were specially gathered.

23 'Plate III. Upper Story' and 'Plate IV. Upper Story' in Cat. 1641, 1642. Bembridge.

24 The curve is 'parabolic or hyperbolic' (M.189).

25 'Plate III. Upper Story'. Cat. 1641. Bembridge.

26 Deichmann 1981, Cat. 339.

27 Deichmann dates these ten capitals fifth-century (1981, Cat. 333–342).

28 As noted by Ruskin (SMB.71).

29 In 'earlier monastic thought . . . women were an occasion of stumbling rather than of veneration, as the frequent reliefs of Luxuria in the form of a naked woman bitten by serpents indicate' (Crichton 1954, xiv).

30 For detailed plates, see Wolters 1979, Cat. 99–106.

31 Eight casts were made for St. George's Museum (30.188). Ruskin queries the provenance of these figures in a letter of 1877 to Rawdon Brown (MS.36.304.f.140. British Library). He did not notice their close resemblance to the Virtues lining the rim of the Ascension dome inside.

32 'The one I drew is January' (SMB.44). Drawing untraced.

33 Demus considers the iconography of the Months cycle 'a typical instance of Venetian eclecticism, freely compounded from Byzantine and western (Italian) traditions'. His comparison of the framing acanthus scrolls with carvings at Saint-Denis (Paris) invites speculation about Gothic influence (1960, 153–54). For comparison with Ruskin's interpretation of individual figures see also Wolters 1979, Cat. 118–130.

34 Demus 1960, 155.

35 Crichton 1954, 89.

36 Crichton dates completion of the 'outermost arch' 1275 (1954, 90). For Demus's evaluation of its carving, see p. 107.

37 MS.36.304.f.152. British Library.

38 Demus agrees: 'It must be assumed that it begins . . . at the right, as do all the other cycles of the façade' (1960, 162). Surely, however, the Months on the second carved arch begin with January on the left.

39 Demus speculates 'a merchant?' (1960, 162). The figure was traditionally considered a portrait of the architect.

40 MS.36.304.f.152. British Library.

41 Demus 1960, 161, 165. See also Wolters 1979, Cat. 146–160.

42 Crichton (1954, 91) and Demus (1960, 163) also see classical influence in the carvings of this arch.

43 Demus 1960, 164.

44 Wolters 1979, Cat. 164.

45 A cast of the ball etched by Ruskin in ill. 18 formed part of the 1983 Arts Council exhibition, 'John Ruskin' (Clegg 1983, Cat. 130). For a good photograph of the cast see 30.188.

46 '4th Porch'. Cat. 1642. Bembridge.

47 'Plate IV. Upper Story'. Cat. 1642. Bembridge.

48 'The work in style just like the former one' (SMB.34). Ruskin, working from south to north, had just studied the fifth porch.

49 'St Marks. Plate 5th. 5th Porch'. Cat. 1642; also SMB.25l (ill. 81, top).

50 Distance between angles of bases (1980 measurements in italics): 61/60, 1 ft 9 in. (*1 ft 9 in.*); 60/59, 1 ft 8½ in. (*1 ft 8½ in.*); 59/58, 2 ft 4 in. (*2 ft 4⅛ in.*). Ruskin's figures are at SMB.25l (ill. 81, top).

51 'St Marks. Plate 5th. 5th Porch'. Cat.

1642. Bembridge.

52 The plate, probably prepared *c.* 1852, was published in Collingwood (ed.) 1895. A drawing for the engraving (Cat. 1940) is privately owned. A pale blue wash, heightened on the projecting bosses and capitals with Chinese white, sets the columns and plinths into lovely contrast with the delicate gold of the spandrels of, and little arches and roundels under, the main arch.

53 Inscription on the copy made for Francesca Alexander. Fogg Art Museum, Harvard.

54 No statue appears in Ruskin's daguerreotype, illustration 12. See Wolters 1979, Cat. 79, for 'this modern copy'.

55 On 20 November 1849 Ruskin describes the 'Byzantine or Lombard double arch, so often found in St. Mark's – as on the left in my elaborate drawing' (D2.451). The same day he is 'drawing in the arcade of Doge's palace' (D2.450).

56 The daguerreotype connection was suggested by J.G. Links (Hewison 1978, 70). Ruskin's drawing is actually taken from a point to the left of, and higher than, the daguerreotypes. (Note the greater exposure of the top of the pillar in the drawing, and the different position of its top left edge against the corner of the building; also the 'wider gap in the drawing between the abacus heads over the lily columns.)

57 Girths of columns 68–70 and dimensions of their bases still tally with Ruskin's figures.

58 Meduna raised the entire corner (see p. 198).

5 PEACOCK'S FEATHERS IN THE SUN
pages 121–127

1 Deichmann 1981, Cat. 419–22.

2 Demus 1960, 186.

3 The panels referred to are Cat. 18–26 in Wolters 1979.

4 See Wolters 1979, 22–26, for synopsis.

5 Ruskin's remarks are consonant with Demus's opinion that the panel is a thirteenth-century imitation of an Early Christian original, showing 'a curious mixture of archaisms and Gothicisms' (Demus 1960, 174). Others date it sixth-century Roman, Syrian Early Christian,

and fourteenth-century. See Wolters 1979, Cat. 56.

6 Belting 1972. For a bewildering array of theories see Wolters 1979, Cat. 61.

7 Wolters 1976, Cat. 175 and ills 605–632; also Goldner 1977.

8 Goldner (1977, 45) dates the sculpture of the upper north side 1385–1415, claims it was finished before that of the south and west façades, and that the 'sculpture of the lateral sides is little more than prologue to the statuary of the West façade' (for the comparison with Milan, see *ibid.*, 42–43).

9 E.g., Goldner 1977, figs. 18, 19. For the contrast between the later (equal-foiled) cusp profiles and Ruskin's favourites, compare with ills 97, 98 in this book.

10 See Wolters 1976, I, 247–48 and ills 635–44. The figures are usually dated fifteenth-century.

11 Deichmann 1981, Cat. 538. His plate for Cat. 476 shows similar pine cones.

12 A plan for Ruskin's 'Educational Series' of drawings (Viljoen Bequest, Pierpont Morgan Library) lists as item 89, 'St Mark – South side – before restoration – Grand old colour', but this was probably his 1846 study (ill. II) of a lower arch, eventually numbered 209 in the series (21.93).

13 The central rectangular panel half in shadow under the left upper arch in ill. 100, and the central panel lower down under the right upper arch – both made of a striking white and purple veined marble (see surviving examples on west Treasury wall in ill. XII) – have been replaced by a virtually colourless, and a green and white marble, respectively (ill. x). While the archivolts of the upper and lower right arches are still faced with the purple veined marble, that of the upper left arch – which appears in ill. 100 to be the same marble – is now a pinkish Verona (ill. x). Fragments of 'white and purple veined alabasters, more than a foot square, bought . . . in Venice out of the wrecks of restoration' were, with 'bitter sorrow', displayed by Ruskin in a lecture of 1876 (24.408).

14 Deichmann 1981, Cat. 639, 640.

6 CHAPTERS TO BE WRITTEN pages 128–170

1 MS. for *Stones of Venice*, cancelled passage, back of p. 18. Pierpont Morgan Library.

2 Some of these fragments, which are divided between Bembridge and Pierpont Morgan Library, are passages written for the *Stones* or *Examples*; others are notes and worksheets of 1849–50. They are arbitrarily arranged here for systematic presentation.

3 Some piers are cut back to permit passage at angles of the galleries. In several cases the attenuation – measured at the gallery floor – exceeds 1 ft.

4 So also Crichton 1954, 92.

5 'Mosaics. p. 2'. Cat. 1638. Bembridge.

6 'In the first place, it is intensely vulgar, and vulgarity inside a church is more than commonly offensive. In the second place, it is false, for everybody knows . . . that the marble does not shape itself into set patterns in its quarry. And, in the third place, it utterly destroys all impression of solidity. . . . the aim of the builder should be . . . so to clothe his plinths and pedestals as to make them appear like solid cubes' (Pullen 1894, 28). His sense of 'falsity' seems curiously inconsistent.

7 In this and following references, Ruskin uses 'decorative' and 'ornamental' in a sense which must be recognized if his meaning is to be grasped. See 9.284–309, 451–52. For Ruskin's concept of architectural ornament, see Unrau 1978, 65–139.

8 'Mosaics. p. 2'. Cat. 1638. Bembridge.

9 *Ibid.*

10 Described as 'a rough sketch of their effect from the nave. in about true proportion: all but diameter of shafts, which it is easy to correct from the measures' (M.44l).

11 MS. 76, p. x–5. Bembridge.

12 Ruskin drew a careful outline of the third arch of north arcade on the back of the worksheet given in illustration XXII. This arch, and two others over the nave columns, conform closely to Ruskin's description. Two of the arches linking the end nave columns with the square piers are badly distorted: the most easterly of the south arcade is dramatically flattened on its pier side, though the side falling on the column has the horseshoe shape. The slope of the galleries as they meet the piers (ill. XXI) shows the latter have settled. In 1850 Ruskin suggests to Rawdon Brown that many Venetian horseshoe doorheads were

'originally nothing more than common stilted arches' which have been deformed by 'pressure from above and yielding from below' (MS. 36304. British Library). It seems likely that the arches of the nave and transepts of St. Mark's were, however, intended to have the slight horseshoe form. Those of the Duomo of Torcello have shapes similar to the arches of illustration XV.

13 MS. 76, p. X-5. Bembridge.

14 *Ibid.* (unnumbered page, bound in after p. X-5).

15 *Ibid.*, p. X-8.

16 *Ibid.*, p. X-9.

17 WS.22. Pierpont Morgan Library.

18 *Ibid.*

19 *Ibid.*

20 The galleries, originally covering the full width of the aisles, were given their present form in the late twelfth or early thirteenth century (Demus 1960, 83–4, 206).

21 Zuliani n.d., 44 and plate 3. See also Grabar 1975.

22 This quotation bridges MS. 76, p. X-10 (Bembridge) and Add. X-11 (Pierpont Morgan Library).

23 MS. 76, p. X-10. Bembridge.

24 Deichmann 1981, Cat. 256. Traces of blue are still visible.

25 Deichmann 1981, Cat. 17–20, 51, 52.

26 The transparent effect is visible only from certain angles.

27 Ruskin's quotation from Dante (*Inferno* 22.129) may thus be even more apt than he realized. C.H. Sisson translates: 'The devil, swooping, threw out his chest and rose' (*Divine Comedy*, 1980). Alichino, angry at missing his prey, then grapples with a fellow fiend, 'and both of them went down/Into the middle of the boiling pond'. Interestingly, the partner of the figure shown in ill. 114 has had his head buried in the flame-coloured Verona marble of the backing wall.

28 Demus considers the lunette a copy (*c.* 1270–80) of Byzantine models (1960, 146–47). For Ruskin's analysis of restorations of the lunette, see D2.459.

29 Ruskin wanted to trace the evolution of Venetian sarcophagi in *Stones*, but his father expressed 'repugnance' at this idea in February 1852 (Clegg 1981, 101). Part of the MS., dealing with sixteen tombs, is given at 11.289–307. A sheet of moulding profiles ('Tombs. Plate 2'. Fogg Art Museum) relates to that discussion.

30 See Wolters 1976, I, 156, and plates 48, 51.

31 Wolters echoes Ruskin on the tomb's Venetian character (1976, I, 189).

32 The consistency of this light intrigued Ruskin. In the MS. of *Stones* he first wrote: 'On that tomb it shines always – from the time when the sun first rises over the long sweep of the Lido – through its daily course – whatever else it looks upon, or leaves, the dim ray is never wanting that touches that headstone' (p. 14, Pierpont Morgan Library). Wolters, 1976, gives five photographs of the tomb, all taken under artificial light. One showing the Doge's face (plate 311) gives him a white-lipped, leprous look, and calls to mind Wölfflin's claim that 'it is absolutely futile to try to understand monumental art on the basis of what we can learn from photographs' (Freitag 1979, 120).

33 MS. 8, p. 22. Bembridge. Omitted at D2.475, as part of materials described as 'reading notes'.

34 Date and hour of photography are noted in the captions. Exposure varied from 5 seconds (ill. XV) to $6\frac{1}{2}$ minutes (ill. XVI) on film with effective speed, depending on filters used, of between 8 and 40 A.S.A.

35 Kornerup 1978, 7.

36 Pieri n.d., 24.

37 Quoting Pullen's useful book of 1894, 103–116.

38 Pieri n.d., 24.

39 Hayman (ed.) 1982, 81.

40 Letter of 1860 in Surtees (ed.) 1972, 40. F. Birren claims it is possible that 'one particular color (red) might appear filmy like a patch of sunset sky; that it might be hard and structural; that it might be three-dimensional; and further that it might be luminous, lustrous, iridescent, transparent, metallic, plain, thickly textured, etc. Although a scientific instrument might record one and the same red energy in all instances, there would be a world of difference in human experience' (1961, 42).

41 Similarly, it is no accident that the mosaic of Christ's Temptation is positioned so that it is always in shadow relative to the Entry into Jerusalem below (ill. XXV).

Photographs showing mosaics as evenly lit 'pictures' have hindered understanding of their visual – and, as here, even their iconographical – role in buildings such as St. Mark's.

42 It should be noted that Ruskin, in the 1850s, preferred the colour of the exterior. On 28 June 1854 he writes G.P. Boyce: 'I am very glad to hear you like St Marks, inside or outside. but I believe on the whole, the outside is the finer study – the inside is too Rembrandtesque. – too much dependent on flashing of gold out of gloom – which is always effective – but comparatively vulgar – and for the rest – exhausted in idea by many painters before now. while the white pure, veined marbles, & dark porphyries of the exterior afford *genuine* colour of the highest quality' (Beinecke Library). In assessing these comments, the reader should bear in mind that he sees the interior free of the film of lampblack which dimmed it in Ruskin's day. An article in the *Builder* (16 January 1869) warned: 'besmirched . . . as the entire surface appears high and low wherever not brightened here and there by attrition of heads or shoulders of worshippers, the original tint may easily be misinterpreted through adventitious dinginess'.

7 ONE GREEK SCHOOL pages 171–189

1 Norton (ed.) 1904, I, 32–36.

2 Report in the *Builder*, 19 February 1859.

3 Diary entry for 23 July 1867. MS. 14. Bembridge.

4 Bradley (ed.) 1964, 290.

5 Clegg 1981, 133–50; Hewison 1978, 25–27.

6 Norton (ed.) 1904, II, 137 (letter of 2 August 1876).

7 Clegg 1981, 161.

8 Norton (ed.) 1904, II, 84 (letter of 12 August 1874).

9 G. Mathew writes that the Byzantine church evolved into 'a single great ikon', and by the tenth century was thought of as 'a microcosm representing all earth and sky' (1963, 105–06).

10 Demus 1935, 79.

11 Lord Lindsay claimed study of the mosaics would not 'repay the trouble' (1847, I,

122). A.F. Rio, whose *De la poésie chrétienne* (1836) is said by P. Conner to have affected Ruskin 'more deeply' than 'any other work on the subject of art' (1979, 56), considered Byzantine art a 'miserable school' which 'always exercised a most pernicious influence on art in Italy' (1854, 13, 15).

12 Wavering between reverence for, and suspicion of, the interior atmosphere is apparent in paragraphs 16–21 of Chapter 4 of *Stones II*. Within a few lines of the description quoted on pp. 128–45, the 'darkness and mystery', 'confused recesses of building' and 'preciousness of material' have become 'stage properties of superstition' (10.90). Ruskin seems unwilling even to concede genuine religious experience to worshippers in St. Mark's: 'hardly a moment passes . . . in which we may not see some half-veiled figure enter . . . cast itself into long abasement on the floor of the temple, and then . . . leave the church, *as if* comforted' (10.89, my italics). A nasty demonstration of bigotry coincides with Ruskin's work in November 1851 on early drafts of the St. Mark's chapter for *Stones*. He is shocked, on meeting an Englishman and his invalid wife, to find they are Catholics ('"Mass!" I said, "What were you doing at Mass?"'), but assures his father: 'They are to stay here for the winter and I am very glad of it for through them I shall get a good deal of information which would otherwise have been inaccessible to me, and they are too far off – and too sickly to require any rudeness in keeping them out of my way' (LV.48–9). When the woman died several weeks later Ruskin told his parents she had 'gone where she will find out which is the right side' (LV.62). In the 1870s Ruskin was appalled by the 'sectarian puppyism and insolence' of the *Stones* (10.76n; 24.277–78). See also Clegg 1981, 115–16.

13 Norton (ed.) 1904, II, 143 (letter of 7 February 1877).

14 For the essentially Byzantine conception of the dome, see Demus 1935, 24ff. Recently be has stated that its Venetian creators were, after a period of westernization in the earlier twelfth century, 'again *au courant*' with developments in Constantinople. (1979 'Venetian Mosaics', 342).

15 'The puerility of a superannuated art and the insufficiencies of an infantile art have on all sides multiplied manikins whose enamel eyes no longer see . . . . The extraordinary feet of the angels must be seen' (Taine 1869, 240–41).

16 For Ruskin's divisions of Venetian history in *St. Mark's Rest*, see Clegg 1981, 178–81. For a corrective to Ruskin's notion of the city's 'unsacrificed honour', see Norwich 1977, esp. 146–67 ('The Shameful Glory').

17 See C.F. Murray's painting at 24.296. Plate 21 in Kreutz 1843 shows the same gap.

18 In August 1877 Ruskin announced a change of name from 'St. George's Company' to 'St. George's Guild' (29.182). For details about the organization, which received a legal constitution in 1878, see Spence 1957 and Hewison 1979.

19 Ref. Series 170, Ashmolean Museum. The label attributes it to T.M. Rooke, with 'Ruskin?' added in pencil. At 21.43 it is attributed to Rooke, but a footnote shows the editors are confusing it with C.F. Murray's drawing. To complete the confusion, the Catalogue suggests the drawing is 'possibly by R.', then refers the reader to a reproduction of Murray's work (38.298). It is clearly by Ruskin, who made a sketch from it in a letter to Rooke of 1879 (see p. 208).

20 Demus agrees, 'to the extent that they remain in their original state' (1935, 23).

21 In 1877 Ruskin describes himself as 'much of a Turk, more of a Jew; alas, most of all, – an infidel; but not an atom of a heretic: Catholic, I, of the Catholics' (29.92).

22 In notes omitted at D3.953, Ruskin becomes badly muddled about the number of windows in the dome (MS. 21, p. 109. Bembridge. Entry for 20 May 1877).

23 'Madonna in dark purple robe with lines of gold lovely, and around, more or less divided into white and dark by their falling robes or purple square masses of kingly dress., the old Test.ͭ prophets' (*ibid.*).

24 D.F. Strauss's *Leben Jesu* (1835–36), translated by George Eliot (*The Life of Jesus*, 1846), and *Der alte und der neue Glaube* (1872, translated by M. Blind, 1873), and Ernest Renan's *Vie de Jésus* (1863, trans-lated as *Life of Jesus*, 1864) had caused much controversy.

25 Ruskin's first extended study of the Greek mythic imagination occurs in chapter thirteen of *Modern Painters III* (1856). D. Birch's excellent D.Phil. thesis traces the growth in Ruskin's thought of 'the concept of Greek religion as a standard of faith with which to measure and condemn the modern spirit' (1980, 179–80). See also Fitch 1982; Landow 1971, 399–418; Drake 1974; Helsinger 1982, 260–65.

26 For the Chest of Cypselus at Olympia, see Pausanias, *Description of Greece*, 5.17.5. Ruskin studied fragments of the Erech-theum in the British Museum in February 1876 (28.527).

27 Demus 1970, 10, 239.

28 A diary containing notes on Egyptian myths is preserved at Bembridge (MS. 17). For Ruskin's study of the subject, see Birch 1980, chapter 5. Ruskin's most explicit claim of Cimabue's 'Greekness' occurs in *The Laws of Fésole*, where he states that Giotto's principles of drawing were de-rived 'from the Attic Greeks through Cimabue, the last of their disciples' (15.345).

29 For a corroborative view of the influence of the mosaics on Bellini, Titian and Tintoretto, see Demus 1970, 235–36.

30 Taine 1869, 241.

31 For Ruskin's study of illuminated MSS. of Montecassino, see 21.50; 33.208n, 309.

32 Diary entry for 20 May 1877 (omitted at D3.953). MS. 21. Bembridge. The Pantoc-rator was remade *c.* 1506 after fires of 1419 and 1489 (Demus 1977, 639).

33 'Mosaics. Baptistry. St Marks.' Filed with 'Original Drawings for the Stones of Venice'. Pierpont Morgan Library.

34 Wolters 1979, Cat. 62. Demus suggests it is eleventh-century with thirteenth-century reworking. Surprisingly, he com-plains of the 'hardness of the forms and the dryness of the composition' (1960, 173).

35 See especially Demus 1960, 132–35.

36 Wolters 1979, Cat. 70–73.

37 Demus: 1954, 93ff; 1960, 127; 1966, 145. On 29 April 1877 Ruskin writes to R. St. John Tyrwhitt: 'please I want the name of the pig . . . that Hercules killed among his twelve labours . . . . he's carved on St Mark's bringing a big pig on his shoulders

to some tiny Lilliputian people – in a sack or a well' (MS. letter, Humanities Research Centre, University of Texas, Austin). The reference is to the Erymanthian Boar. The 'Lilliputian' is Eurystheus, retreating into a large vessel to hide.

38 E.g., Venturi thinks the St. George is Byzantine, the St. Demetrius a Venetian copy (1902, II, 529ff.). Demus argues the reverse (1960, 129–30).

39 Ruskin again anticipates modern study. Demus, who agrees the carving is of 'very good quality' (1960, 132), first thought it a thirteenth-century Greek work (1954, 100), but has since stressed the sculptor's receptivity to 'new Gothic motifs and forms' (1960, 132).

40 Wrongly dated early 1850s at 10.lxiv. A photograph of a nearly identical drawing, showing the four right columns only, is preserved at Bembridge. Both drawings untraced.

41 Letter to J. Severn of 7 May 1877. L41. Bembridge.

42 Letter of 3 October 1877 to Norton. Houghton Library.

43 The editors of Diaries suggest the reference might be to Cat. 1945, which was, however, engraved and published in Stones in 1853.

44 Demus 1948, 4.

45 Letter to Rawdon Brown of 30 April 1877. British Library.

46 The story is told in V.A. Burd's book of 1979.

47 Ruskin's notes on the mosaics in the south transept of the finding of St. Mark's body include a special sketch of the Doge's cap ('Details for the Stones of Venice'. Pierpont Morgan Library). His 1877 drawing (ill. XXVII) of the Doge and his People studies the ducal headgear separately: 'not the contracted shell-like cap, but the imperial crown' (24.295). In 1879 he again insists upon this 'king's diadem, not the republican cap' (14.428).

48 'Mr. Ruskin's Illness Described by Himself', published a week after Ruskin's death in the British Medical Journal for 27 January 1900, partially quoted at 38.172, and cited by Viljoen as if it were authoritative (BD.64, 135), must be treated with scepticism. Apart from its hilariously contrived introduction – with Ruskin's smile 'ever playing prettily about his mouth' as he serves breakfast to his visitor – the words attributed to Ruskin (they are triggered by 'the sudden crowing of a bantam cook [sic?]') are notable for a crude rhetoric of the kind Ruskin had abandoned by his late teens: 'No malignant spectre arose which I pantingly looked for – nothing happened. – I had triumphed! Then, worn out with bodily fatigue, with walking and waiting and watching, my mind racked with ecstasy and anguish, my body benumbed with the bitter cold of a freezing February night, I threw myself upon the bed, all unconscious, and there I was found later on in the morning in a state of prostration, and bereft of my senses.' Ruskin's editors suggest the anonymous 'H' who wrote this drivel was 'possibly Dr. Harley' (38.172). It is not easy to believe that George Harley might have supposed a person who was 'all unconscious' capable of throwing himself upon a bed and recalling the action afterward. Stylistic considerations support a Harley connection, however. His Simplification of Spelling (1877), a lengthy diatribe against double consonants, ends: 'Having now fairly launched our little bark on the restless and endless ocean of thought, we leave it to the tender mercies of the winds and waves of Public Opinion'; and no degree of bathos could be beyond the capacities of the physician who warned readers of The Urine and its Derangements (1872, 353) that 'as one swallow does not make a summer, neither does one tubecast in kidney disease at any time suffice to establish an exact diagnosis'. Harley had, however, died in 1896. The biography George Harley, F.R.S., published in 1899 by his daughter Mrs. Alec Tweedie, contains a number of stories – attributed to Harley – similar in tone to 'Mr. Ruskin's Illness'. Mrs. Tweedie's own narrative style is rather harrowing ('Blind, blind, blind! All his hopes in life suddenly blasted. . . . Alas! when that morrow dawned he was in bed shrieking with agony!'; 182, 193), and it is possible that a fair proportion of 'Mr. Ruskin's Illness' might be ascribed to the tender sensibility which, recalling Charlotte Cushman's singing, enthused: 'every heart was stirred

when she repeated Kingsley's well-known song "Call the Cattle Home". It was most thrilling' (*ibid.*, 145–46).

49 The date seems actually to have been 23 February (BD.102n).

50 But see Viljoen's useful commentary (BD.114–32).

51 This aspect of Ruskin's mind is forcefully presented by C. Wragge-Morley. She claims Ruskin was 'a materialist; he found the material world trustworthy' (1975, 22). See also her article (1982).

8 SERVILE AND HORRIBLE RIGIDITY
pages 191–205

1 Especially difficult because documentation on the rebuilding of the north and south sides between 1860–75 is lacking. F. Berchet's account of the attempt to correct Meduna's rebuilding of the southwest portico in 1886 states that no record had been kept of the old dimensions (Boito [ed.] 1888 'Testo', 434). F. Zuliani's praise of the records kept by Berchet and Saccardo during their control of the works after 1882 (1975, 58) may be optimistic. Unless Berchet experienced a total conversion after his brutalization of the Fondaco dei Turchi (Clegg 1981, plates 9, 10), his account of any restoration must be viewed with suspicion. Certainly his suggestion that the southwest portico was 'restored to just proportions in correspondence with the two façades' (Boito [ed.] 1888 translation, I, 35) overlooks the fact that those proportions are altered from the old, and his claim that the arch of the fifth porch was returned to its original measures (Boito [ed.] 1888 'Testo', 433) skirts the fact that the columns and plinths of the south side of the porch and of the adjoining pier were not returned to their previous positions. Saccardo does admit that a mere compromise was made in respect of the latter changes (1890, 9). For reasons mentioned later in this chapter (see p. 198 and notes 46, 66, 68), however, it seems likely that Saccardo's testimony may often be biased.

2 Letter to *The Building News*, 13 February 1880.

3 F. Forlati, in Demus 1960, 196–97. An earlier phase of similar activity seems to have been in progress during Ruskin's 1845 visit (see p. 19).

4 S. Burton, in *The Architect*, 19 June 1880.

5 Berchet, in Boito (ed.) 'Testo', 1888, 432. One of those who praised Meduna was Viollet-le-Duc (Clegg 1981, 184, 222).

6 Between 27 January and 24 February 1877 there are nine references in Ruskin's diary to meetings with, or work for, Zorzi. Ruskin subsidized Zorzi's publication.

7 Ruskin describes a pinnacle, in need of repair in 1876, at 24.421–22.

8 Letter to Joan Severn of 16 February 1877. L.41. Bembridge.

9 Zorzi 1877, 54.

10 *Ibid.*, 57. Zorzi claims marbles from the south side were shipped to England through the agency of a 'signor Malcolm' (*ibid.*, 56).

11 Letter to Norton of 15 April 1877. Houghton Library.

12 Undated letter to Rawdon Brown, *c.* February 1877. MS. 36.304.f.162. British Library.

13 Zorzi wrote later: 'my head was full of the *Seven Lamps*' (29.xvi).

14 Robotti 1976, quoted from author's summary in *R.I.L.A.*

15 Zorzi 1877, 73–75.

16 *The Builder*, citing C. Yriarte, stated on 1 May 1880 that on the north façade 'It was thought proper, for the sake of uniformity, to reduce the ancient columns . . . to the diameter of the capitals with which they had been surmounted. Thus the chisel and the rasp destroyed the graceful entasis of the columns, and the brilliancy of which their rich material is susceptible'. For similar vandalism at the Fondaco dei Turchi in the 1860s, see Alvise Zorzi 1977, I, 208.

17 An experiment comparing rapid absorption of water by the scraped marbles with the resistance to water of the unrestored is outlined in Zorzi 1877, 72–73.

18 *Ibid.*, 72.

19 *Ibid.*, 73.

20 *Ibid.*, 84–86.

21 *Ibid.*, 95.

22 U. Peschlow lists 80 'modern' capitals in Deichmann 1981, 148–53.

23 Zorzi 1877, 97–100.

24 *Ibid.*, 101.

25 Robotti 1976, 116. See also Alvise Zorzi 1977, I, 206.

26 Letter dated in pencil '8? May 77'. L41. Bembridge. On 30 June, 61 signatories pledged support for Ruskin and Zorzi in the *Gazzetta di Venezia* (Clegg 1981, 186).

27 Articles and letters relating to the protest are preserved in the archives of the Society for the Protection of Ancient Buildings (SPAB) in London.

28 *Daily News*, 1 November 1879.

29 It was sent first to the Italian 'Minister of Public Works' (*The Builder*, 15 November 1879, 1253).

30 Quoted from *The Times*, 19 November 1879.

31 *The Architect*, 8 November 1879. The writer exposes his ignorance by applying Ruskin's description of the 'great mouldering wall' of an English cathedral (10.79) to St. Mark's.

32 *Truth*, 13 November 1879.

33 *The Globe*, 17 November 1879.

34 *The Standard*, 29 November 1879.

35 MS. translation of a letter of 19 November 1879 to the Secretary of the Superior Council of Instruction. SPAB archives.

36 MS. letter to Morris. SPAB archives.

37 *Daily News*, 2 December 1879.

38 MS. letter to Newman Marks. SPAB archives.

39 F. Forlati, in Demus 1960, 196.

40 Saccardo 1879, 32–33.

41 *Ibid.*, 3.

42 *Ibid.*, 7, 13–14.

43 *Ibid.*, 24.

44 *Ibid.*, 35.

45 *Ibid.*, 40–46.

46 It is significant that in 1883, with Saccardo secure in his post as director of restorations, the *Fabbricieri* felt free to describe Zorzi's criticisms as 'invective' (*filippiche*). The pamphlet in which this term is used, *La Basilica di S. Marco in Venezia nel suo passato e nel suo avvenire* (7), may well have been written with Saccardo's help. It is full of the kind of praise of his 'ingenious and patient labour' (29) which, later, he did not scruple to write under his own name. In 1896 he recalls that when in the early 1860s the Patriarch, a man of 'rare good sense', had sought 'wise direction of the affairs of the Basilica', he had discovered 'l'ingénieur Pierre Saccardo, homme qu'il connoissait [*sic*] pour aimer les arts et les monuments du pays' (1896, 113). Indign-

ation at the scrutiny of restorations by outsiders is expressed in the same work (119). In 1887 he had accused foreigners of 'rousing fanciful apprehensions and doubts' through interference in 'our affairs' (1890, 27). Note 68 suggests one probable cause of this outburst.

47 MS. copy of a letter to Saccardo of 13 December 1879. SPAB archives.

48 *The Times*, 24 December 1879.

49 *The Architect*, 7 February 1880.

50 He was Pugin Travelling Student of the Royal Academy.

51 *The Architect*, 7 February 1880.

52 *Building News*, 13 February 1880.

53 *The Times*, 18 May 1880.

54 See especially Scott 1880 and Burton 1880.

55 Third annual *Report* of the SPAB, 1880, 8–9.

56 See his contemptuous refusal of the Royal Gold Medal of the RIBA in 1874 (34.513–16).

57 *Athenaeum*, 22 November 1879.

58 'If any real Vandalism is apprehended, let Mr. Ruskin speak out' (*Building News*, 14 November 1879).

59 T. Hall Caine 1879.

60 R. Hewison (1978, 90) suggests the reversal may be due to 'mental confusion'. Ruskin attempted, using the same purple paper and daguerreotype, to get the image right, but abandoned the drawing (Suppl. Series 174, Ashmolean Museum) before rendering the carved detail it is meant to demonstrate. He was very busy at the time (see note 63 and pp. 206–07), and may have copied the reversed image simply to save time.

61 The pillars come from the church of St. Polyeuktos in Constantinople (AD 524–27), where seven similar ones have been excavated. The tradition that they were brought from Acre dates from the late middle ages or early Renaissance (Deichmann 1981, 141).

62 The campanile's fall in 1902 proved the insecurity of one nearby brick structure, but an enquiry found it had been systematically weakened from within. On the ground floor a '*cucina economica*, possibly a hot plate or perhaps a gas stove, had been installed in the thickness of the external wall; in the centre of the tower the brickwork had been cut away in order

to form cupboards, recesses and lastly a small aquarium. Another face of the tower had been cut into as far as the middle of the thickness of the wall, to increase the size of the caretaker's lodge and in the wall thus reduced in thickness, openings had been formed for ventilation'. G. Boni likened the tower to 'a man who had had both his legs amputated' (translation, in unknown hand, of a French article of 18 October 1902. SPAB archives). See also Alvise Zorzi 1977, I, 232–35.

63 'This morning I am quietly working on my translation of the Laws of Plato, and enjoying myself; in comes the post, with a lot of letters and your parcel. I take a quarter of an hour to unfold the pink paper – growling and swearing all the time at the supposed young lady who has sent me her drawings to look at. I find the Memorial, which brings me instantly back out of the Laws of Plato into the entirely accursed tumult of Modern Venice, and her idiocies. I read your letter, and find I've got to write one of senti-mental thanks in return (so here it is!), and to transfer the Memorial to the Society! – and I don't know where "the Society" is! any more than the Pope (perhaps he *does*). And so – with a few more growls and oaths – I roll up the document again . . . . And here's my breakfast coming, and all my letters unanswered – and my friends won't understand that the one thing they can do for me is to let me rest, and mind my own business – while they look after what is, if they understand it, wholly *theirs*' (Letter to John Morgan of 19 December 1879; 37.304).

64 F. Forlati, in Demus 1960, 197n.

65 Clegg 1981, plates 9 and 10.

66 Forlati, in Demus 1960, 197n. According to Henry Wallis (a member of the SPAB), Meduna and Saccardo were still colla-borating in April 1883 on the west front: 'Mr Wallis with much difficulty got behind the screens' and noted that 'Meduna (the architect?) supported by Saccardi [*sic*] the Engineer seems deter-mined to persevere'. Wallis reports the discovery during work on the fifth porch of '4 niches with marble capitals. These were 12 century covered with 13 century facing. . . . The present restorers removed

these even destroying the caps & have replaced the whole with new brick-work'. Wallis suggests a meeting be convened in London, but warns: 'Do not mention source of information or I shall be shut out of works' (MS. synopsis of letters sent by Wallis to the SPAB, dated 24 and 27 April 1883. SPAB archives).

67 See note 1 above and pp. 110–19.

68 Saccardo's treatment of the mosaics in-duced the SPAB to commission a report by J.H. Middleton and G. Wardle, who stated on 24 May 1887 that it showed 'an impatience of accidental imperfections very dangerous in the guardians of an ancient work of art'. The report cites 'The most recent restorations of mosaic in the Church . . . in the Chapels of S. Isidore and S. Zeno. The mosaics here appear to be almost wholly new. . . . Dr. Saccardo is merely accurate when he says, "immense quantities of new cubes have been used." As all the mosaics of the Church are about to be "examined," the system on which repairs are done is a matter of the gravest importance. They appear to have two methods at St. Mark's: the temporary expedient of driving clamps through the tesserae to hold loose parts to the backing, and the more thorough way of bringing all loose or condemned work down with a pick and re-making the mosaic *de novo*. Members of the Society will remember seeing the pickaxe at work in the Baptis-tery. We have now seen the mosaics "restored." *The Times*' correspondent boasts, July 27th, 1886, that one subject, not in the Baptistery, "has been entirely renewed on the slight indications of the old one." It is difficult to offer suggestions to experts who are capable of such a feat, but we would submit that the influence of the Society . . . be exerted towards *the adoption of some method which would leave the* original mosaics in their places.' (Printed report, headed 'PRIVATE, NOT FOR PUBLICATION.' SPAB archives.) For F. Forlati's ingenious technique of achieving the last-mentioned aim, see Demus 1960, 198–99 and plates 116–18.

69 For a survey of work done between 1882 and the late 1950s see F. Forlati in Demus 1960, 197–201. Berchet's account for 1882–87, and an additional report dated,

1893, appear in Boito (ed.) 'Testo' 1888, 433–36 (the publication in 1888 of a report dated 1893 is the least of the mysteries surrounding this era). For reports by Saccardo, see the works listed under his name for 1890, 1892 and 1896 in the bibliography. Manfredi 1904, and Manfredi and Marangoni 1908, carry the story into the twentieth century. Next come three works by Marangoni (1933, 1933, 1946). Forlati 1975 traces developments between about 1948 and the early 1970s. Wolters 1979 and Deichmann 1981 record the recent condition of the external sculpture, and of the capitals, respectively. L. Marchesini and B. Badan ('Corrosion phenomena on the Horses of San Marco') in Perocco (ed.) 1979 are useful on pollutants in the Venetian atmosphere. An anonymous article, 'Preventing Death in Venice' (*Building Research and Practice*, Jan./Feb. 1980, 38–45), describes new techniques for consolidating Venetian walls and foundations.

9 CONCLUSION pages 206–210

1 Quoted in Clegg 1981, 186–87.

2 He may simply have wished to get on with his work unimpeded. See chapter 8, note 63.

3 Letter to Norton of 27 February 1879. Houghton Library.

4 Letter to Norton of 16 March 1879. Houghton Library.

5 This could refer either to his own account of the mosaics in *St. Mark's Rest* or to paintings sent from Venice by one of his copyists (see pp. 207–09).

6 Letter dated in another hand 'July 9. '79'. MS. 'Burne-Jones Papers'. Fitzwilliam Museum.

7 See pp. 207–08.

8 The simplest explanation is that the floor settled unevenly over the vaulting cells of the crypt. For Ruskin on the 'sea waves' theory in 1851, see LV. 69.

9 Hewison 1978, Cat. 44. The left vine cap is more carefully rendered in Francesca's copy than in the engraving (ill. 82). The engraving, however, shows one more leaf boss on the left side of the arch, and is generally more painstaking.

10 MS. letter of 4 April 1883. John Rylands Library. On 9 April he writes Mrs. Talbot: 'I've given Quarry rather a problem . . . nothing less than the colour of one of St Marks Porches' (Spence [ed.] 1966, 116).

11 Clegg 1981, 222, n.178.

12 MS. Am.1088–6216. Houghton Library.

13 Kreutz 1843 records the ruinous state of many mosaics in the 1840s. See also chapter 8, note 68.

14 Transcript of letter to Boni of 20 April 1883. T34. Bembridge. Alessandri's painting is reproduced in Clegg 1983, 55.

15 Hewison 1978, 101, 106.

16 MS. letter to Rooke of 23 November 1879. Humanities Research Centre, University of Texas, Austin.

17 *Ibid.*

18 MS. letter to J.P. Faunthorpe dated Candlemas 1883. Wellesley College Library.

19 Two Newman paintings of S. Maria Novella are listed in the *Inventory of American Paintings*. Another is at Randolph-Macon College, Lynchburg, Virginia.

20 A Newman drawing of San Giorgio and the Salute, and a watercolour, *Venice*, are reproduced in Forman 1884.

21 See catalogue in Williams (later Wragge-Morley) 1972.

22 Ruskin's journey may be traced in letters to Joan Severn at the Illinois University Library.

23 Another Hibernian, Kathleen Olander, is involved. Ruskin had written from Milan on 25 September 1888: 'I wanted you at Paris, – to give yourself to me there – I want you *now* in St. Mark's, quicker, if I can get you anyhow . . . and meantime I'll write you *such* love letters!' (Unwin [ed.] 1953, 77).

24 Zorzi 1906, 377.

25 See chapter 8, note 68.

26 MS. letter to J. Severn of 18 October 1888. Illinois University Library.

27 Letter of 16 May 1886 to Norton. Houghton Library.

28 Weinberg 1979, 31.

BIBLIOGRAPHY

Place of publication of books is London unless otherwise specified.

I MANUSCRIPTS

British Library, London. Letters of JR to Rawdon Brown. MS.36.304.

Fitzwilliam Museum, Cambridge. Letters of JR to Mrs. E. Burne-Jones. MS. 'Burne-Jones Papers'.

Houghton Library, Harvard University. Letters of JR to C.E. Norton. MS. Am 1088. Letter of G. Boni to JR of 27 June 1883. MS. Am 1088.6216.

Humanities Research Centre, University of Texas (Austin). Letter of JR to T.M. Rooke of 23 Nov. 1879. Letters of JR to R. St. John Tyrwhitt of 31 Jan. and 29 April 1877.

Huntington Library, San Marino, Calif. MS. of *The Seven Lamps of Architecture*.

University of Illinois Library, Urbana, Ill. Letters of JR to Joan Severn during 1888 journey on the Continent.

Pierpont Morgan Library, New York. MS. for *The Stones of Venice*. 'Stones of Venice II. Chapter 4. Additional'. 'Details for the Stones of Venice'.

Princeton University Library. Draft of preface for *St. Mark's Rest*. 'Sketch and Note-books for *Seven Lamps of Architecture*'.

Ruskin Galleries, Bembridge School, Isle of Wight. St. M. Book. Bem. 1621. *Bit Book*. Bem. 1614. *Gothic Book*. Bem. 1616. Notebook M (Diary for 1849–50). Bem. MS. 10. Worksheets for 1849–50 in 'Ruskin. Stones of Venice. Notes.' Vols 1–3 Bem. 1636–38. 'Ruskin. Original Notes and Sketches for *Stones of Venice*.' Vols 1–4. Bem. 1639–42. 'Ruskin. MS. *Stones of Venice*'. Bem. MS. 76. Catalogue of daguerreotypes. In Bem. MS. 27. Letters from JR to the firm of Le Keux, engravers. Bem B. VII. Typed transcripts of JR's letters to G. Boni. Bem. T34. JR's letters to Joan Severn. Esp Bem. L41. Diary of JR for 1867 and 1877. Bem. MSS. 14 and 21.

John Rylands University Library of Manchester. Letters of JR to Quartus Talbot. MS. 1163.

Archives of the Society for the Protection of Ancient Buildings, London. Letters of J.W. Bunney to Wm. Morris and Newman Marks (Nov./Dec. 1879). Copy of letter of Wm. Morris to P. Saccardo of 13 Dec. 1879. Summaries of letters from H. Wallis to the SPAB of 24 and 27 April 1883.

Wellesley College Library, Wellesley, Mass. Letters of JR to the Rev. J.P. Faunthorpe.

Yale University: Beinecke Rare Book and Manuscript Library. Notebook M2 (1849–50). 'Proof Plates for *Stones of Venice*. John Ruskin/R.P. Cuff'. Letter from JR to G.P. Boyce of 28 June 1854. Letters from John James Ruskin to JR.

2 PUBLISHED TEXTS OF RUSKIN'S WRITINGS

Bradley, J.L. (ed.), *Ruskin's Letters from Venice: 1851–52*, New Haven, 1955.

Bradley, J.L. (ed.), *The Letters of John Ruskin to Lord and Lady Mount-Temple*, Ohio, 1964.

Cook, E.T., and A. Wedderburn (ed.), *The Works of John Ruskin*, 39 vols, 1903–12.

Evans, J., and J.H. Whitehouse (ed.), *The Diaries of John Ruskin*, 3 vols, Oxford, 1956–59.

Hayman, J. (ed.), *John Ruskin: Letters from the Continent: 1858*, Toronto, 1982.

Norton, C.E. (ed.), *Letters of John Ruskin to Charles Eliot Norton*, 2 vols, Boston, 1904.

Shapiro, H.I. (ed.), *Ruskin in Italy: Letters to His Parents: 1845*, Oxford, 1972.

Spence, M. (ed.), *Dearest Mama Talbot: A Selection of Letters Written by John Ruskin to Mrs Fanny Talbot*, 1966.

Surtees, V. (ed.), *Sublime & Instructive:
Letters from John Ruskin to Louisa,
Marchioness of Waterford, Anna
Blunden and Ellen Heaton*, 1972.

Unwin, R. (ed.), *The Gulf of Years:
Letters from John Ruskin to Kathleen
Olander*, 1953.

Viljoen, H.G. (ed.), *The Brantwood Diary
of John Ruskin*, New Haven, 1971.

Ward, W.C. (ed.), *John Ruskin's Letters to
William Ward*, Boston, 1922.

3 WORKS DEALING WITH RUSKIN

Birch, D., 'Ruskin and the Greeks',
unpublished D. Phil. dissertation,
Oxford, 1980.

Burd, V.A., *Ruskin and Rose La Touche:
Her Unpublished Diaries of 1861 and
1867*, Oxford, 1979.

Caine, T.H. Hall, 'Mr. Ruskin and St.
Mark's, Venice', *Building News*, 5
Dec. 1879.

Clegg, J., *Ruskin and Venice*, 1981.
'John Ruskin's Correspondence with
Angelo Alessandri', *Bulletin of the
John Rylands Library*, 1977–78,
404–433.
John Ruskin (Arts Council exhibition
catalogue), 1983.

Collingwood, W.G. (ed.), *Studies in Both
Arts: Being Ten Subjects Drawn and
Described by John Ruskin*, Orpington,
1895.

Conner, P., *Savage Ruskin*, 1979.

Dearden, J.S. (ed.), *The Professor: Arthur
Severn's Memoir of John Ruskin*, 1967.

Drake, G., 'Ruskin's Athena, Queen of
the Air', *Classical Bulletin*, 1974,
17–24.

Feltes, N., 'The Stones of Ruskin's
"Venice": a Materialist Analysis',
Prose Studies, May 1980, 54–68.

Fitch, R.E., *The Poison Sky: Myth and
Apocalypse in Ruskin*, Athens, Ohio,
1982.

Forssman, E., *Venedig in der Kunst und im
Kunsturteil des 19. Jahrhunderts*,
Stockholm, 1971, 58–74.

Garrigan, K.O., *Ruskin on Architecture:
His Thought and Influence*, Madison,
1973.

Hanson, B., 'Carrying off the Grand
Canal', *Architectural Review*, Feb.
1981, 104–09.

Hayman, J., 'Ruskin's Foundations for
The Stones of Venice', *Bulletin of the
New York Public Library*, 1976–77,
345–54.

Helsinger, E.K., *Ruskin and the Art of the
Beholder*, Cambridge, Mass., 1982.

Hewison, R., *John Ruskin: the Argument
of the Eye*, 1976.
Ruskin and Venice, 1978.
*Art and Society: Ruskin in Sheffield
1876* (Guild of St. George Ruskin
Lecture), 1979.
(ed.), *New Approaches to Ruskin:
Thirteen Essays*, 1981.

Hilton, T., 'The way of the
unconverted', *Times Literary
Supplement*, 22 Oct. 1982.

Hunt, J.D., *The Wider Sea: A Life of John
Ruskin*, 1982.
(ed., with F. Holland), *The Ruskin
Polygon: Essays on the Imagination of
John Ruskin*, Manchester, 1982.

Landow, G., *The Aesthetic and Critical
Theories of John Ruskin*, Princeton,
1971.

Leon, D., *Ruskin: The Great Victorian*,
1949.

Links, J.G., *The Ruskins in Normandy*,
1968.

Lutyens, M. (ed.), *Effie in Venice:
Unpublished Letters of Mrs John Ruskin
written from Venice between 1849–1852*,
1965.

Parker, J.C., 'An Architectural
Notebook of John Ruskin,
1849–1850', *Yale University Library
Gazette*, Oct. 1975, 77–90.

Rhodes, R., and D.I. Janik (ed.), *Studies
in Ruskin: Essays in Honor of Van Akin
Burd*, Athens, Ohio, 1982.

Robotti, C., 'Le idee di Ruskin ed i
restauri della Basilica di S. Marco
attraverso le "Osservazioni" di A.P.
Zorzi', *Bollettino d'arte*, Jan./June
1976, 115–21.

Spence, M., *The Guild of St. George:
Ruskin's Attempt to Translate his Ideas
into Practice*, Manchester, 1957.

Rosenberg, J.D., *The Darkening Glass: A
Portrait of Ruskin's Genius*, New
York, 1961.

Unrau, J., *Looking at Architecture with
Ruskin*, 1978.

Walton, P., *The Drawings of John Ruskin*,

228

Oxford, 1972.

Weinberg, G.S., *Drawings of John Ruskin (1819–1900)*, exhibition catalogue (Fogg Art Museum), Cambridge, Mass., 1979.

Whittick, A., *Ruskin's Venice*, 1976.

Williams, *see* Wragge-Morley.

Wragge-Morley, C. (formerly Williams), 'Ruskin's Late Works, c. 1870–1890, with Particular Reference to the Collection Made for the Guild of St. George', unpublished Ph.D. dissertation, London University, 1972.
Ruskin's Philosophy, Penzance, 1975.
'Ruskin's Critical Method and Intentions: Towards a Materialist Epistemology', *Journal of Pre-Raphaelite Studies*, Nov. 1982, 105–20.

Zorzi, A.P., 'Ruskin in Venice', *Cornhill Magazine*, Aug./Sept. 1906, 250–65; 366–80.

4 OTHER WORKS CONSULTED

Arnheim, R., *Art and Visual Perception*, 1967 (1st ed. Berkeley, 1954).
The Dynamics of Architectural Form, Berkeley, 1977.

Bacchion, E., *The Basilica of St. Mark*, Venice, 1972.

Basilica di S. Marco in Venezia nel suo passato e nel suo avvenire, La, Venice, 1883.

Belting, H., 'Eine Gruppe Konstantinopler Reliefs', *Pantheon*, 1972, 263ff.

Bettini, S., *Mosaici antichi di San Marco a Venezia*, Bergamo, 1944.
L'architettura di San Marco; origine e significato, Padua, 1946.

Birren, F., *Color, Form, and Space*, New York, 1961.

Boito, C. (ed., with F. Ongania), *La Basilica di San Marco in Venezia*, Venice 1880–93. The text of this work, translated by W. Scott and F.H. Rosenberg, was published as *The Basilica of S. Mark in Venice* (Venice, 1888–89).

Boni, G., 'Il colore sui monumenti', extract from *Archivio Veneto*, 1883.

Burton, S.B., 'St. Mark's, Venice', *The Architect*, 19 June 1880, 430–31.

Constable, W.G., *Canaletto*, Toronto and Montreal, 1965.

Crichton, G., *Romanesque Sculpture in Italy*, 1954.

Deichmann, F.W., *Corpus der Kapitelle der Kirche von San Marco zu Venedig*, Wiesbaden, 1981.

Demus, O., *Die Mosaiken von San Marco in Venedig: 1100–1300*, Baden bei Wien, 1935.
Byzantine Mosaic Decoration, 1948.
'Die Reliefikonen der Westfassade von San Marco', *Jahrbuch der Österreichischen Byzantinischen Gesellschaft*, III (1954), 88ff.
The Church of San Marco in Venice, Washington, 1960.
'Bisanzio e la scultura del Duecento a Venezia', in *Venezia e l'Oriente fra Medioevo e Renascimento*, Florence, 1966 (Civiltà europea e civiltà veneziana. Aspetti e problemi 4).
Byzantine Art and the West, New York, 1970.
'Probleme der Restaurierung der Mosaiken von San Marco im XV. und XVI. Jahrhundert', in *Venezia: centro di mediazione tra oriente e occidente (secoli XV–XVI): aspetti e problemi*, ed. H.-G. Beck *et al.*, Florence, 1977, II, 633–53.
'Venetian Mosaics and their Byzantine Sources', *Dumbarton Oaks Papers*, 1979, 337–43.
'Der skulpturale Fassadenschmuck des 13. Jahrhunderts', in Wolters (ed.) 1979, 1–15.

Forlati, F., 'The Work of Restoration in San Marco', in Demus 1960, 193–201.
La Basilica di San Marco attraverso i suoi restauri, Trieste, 1975.

Forman, H.B., 'An American Studio in Florence', *The Manhattan*, June 1884.

Freitag, W.M., 'Early Uses of Photography in the History of Art', *Art Journal*, Winter 1979–80, 117–23.

Goldner, G., 'Niccolò Lamberti and the Gothic Sculpture of San Marco in Venice', *Gazette des Beaux-Arts*, Feb. 1977, 41ff.

Grabar, A., 'Les Reliefs des chancels des tribunes de Saint-Marc', *Arte Veneta*, 1975, 43ff.

Hempel, G. (with J. Julier), 'Katalog der

Skulpturen', in Wolters (ed.) 1979, 17–55.

Hope, T., *An Historical Essay on Architecture*, 2 vols, 1835.

Howe, J., *The Geology of Building Stones*, 1910.

Julier, J., *see* Hempel.

Kornerup, A. (with J. Wanscher), *Methuen Handbook of Colour*, 3rd ed., 1978.

Kramer, J., 'Zur Herkunft der Spolienkapitelle', in Deichmann 1981, 1–7.

Kreutz, J. and L., *Der Dom des Heil. Markus in Venedig*, Venice, 1843.

Lazzarini, L., 'I rilievi degli arconi dei portali della Basilica di San Marco a Venezia: ricerche tecnico-scientifiche', in Wolters (ed.) 1979, 58–64.

Lee, A., *Marble and Marble Workers*, 1888.

Lindsay, A., *Sketches of the History of Christian Art*, 3 vols, 1847.

Manfredi, M., *Basilica di S. Marco in Venezia: direzione dei restauri e dello studio di mosaico. Le condizioni statiche della Basilica*, Venice, 1904.
and L. Marangoni, *Le opere di restauro nella basilica*, Venice, 1908.

Marangoni, L., 'L'architetto ignoto di San Marco', *Archivio Veneto*, 1933, 1–78.
'Conservazione della scultura ornamentale in San Marco', *Rivista di Venezia*, Feb. 1933, 51ff.
La Basilica di S. Marco a Venezia. Urgenza di provvedimenti per la sua conservazione, Venice, 1946.

Mariacher, G., 'Capitelli veneziani del XII e XIII secolo', *Arte Veneta*, 1954, 43ff.

Mathew, G., *Byzantine Aesthetics*, 1963.

Meduna, G.B., 'The Restoration of St. Mark's, Venice', *Building News*, 13 Feb. 1880.

Middleton, J. (with G. Wardle), 'Restoration at St. Mark's, Venice', printed but unpublished report, 24 May 1887 (Archives of the SPAB).

Morris, Wm., 'The "Restoration" of St. Mark's at Venice', *Daily News*, 1 Nov. 1879.

Norwich, J.J., *Venice: The Rise to Empire*, 1977.

Parker, J.H., *Glossary of Terms Used in Grecian, Roman, Italian, and Gothic Architecture*, 1836 (4th ed. by 1845).

Perocco, G. (ed.), *The Horses of San Marco* (translated by V. and J. Wilton-Ely), 1979 (Italian ed. 1977).

Peschlow, U., 'Systematische Übersicht der Kapitelle nach Typen und Entstehungszeit', in Deichmann 1981, 148–53.

Pieri, M., *I marmi d'Italia*, Milan, n.d. (2nd ed. late 1950s or early 1960s).

Pugin, A.W., *The True Principles of Pointed or Christian Architecture*, 1841.

Pullen, H.W., *Handbook of Ancient Roman Marbles*, 1894.

Renwick, W., *Marble and Marble Working*, 1909.

Rice, D.T., *Byzantine Art*, Oxford, 1935.

Rio, A.F., *De la poésie chrétienne dans son principe, dans sa matière, et dans ses formes*, Paris, 1836. Translated as *The Poetry of Christian Art*, 1854.

Saccardo, P., *S. Marco: gl'inglesi e noi*, Venice, 1879.
I restauri della Basilica di San Marco nell'ultimo decennio, Venice, 1890.
Relazione sui restauri eseguiti nella Basilica di S. Marco in Venezia dall'agosto del 1890 a tutto l'anno 1891, Venice, 1892.
Les Mosaïques de Saint-Marc à Venise, Venice, 1896.

Scott, W., 'St. Mark's, Venice. – Notes on the Proposed Rebuilding and Restoration', *The Architect*, 7 Feb. 1880.
A Glance at the Historical Documents Relating to the Church of Saint Mark in Venice, Venice, 1887.

Taine, H., *Italy: Florence and Venice* (translated by J. Durand), New York, 1869.

Trollope, T.A., *What I Remember*, 3 vols, 1889.

Venturi, A., *Storia dell'arte italiana*, II, Milan, 1902.

Wanscher, J., *see* Kornerup.

Wardle, G., *see* Middleton.

Willis, R., *Remarks on the Architecture of the Middle Ages, Especially of Italy*, Cambridge, 1835.

Wolters, W., *La scultura veneziana gotica (1300–1460)*, 2 vols, Venice, 1976.

230

(ed.), *Die Skulpturen von San Marco in Venedig: Die figürlichen Skulpturen der Aussenfassaden bis zum 14. Jahrhundert*, Munich, 1979.

Woods, J., *Letters of an Architect, from France, Italy, and Greece*, 2 vols, 1828.

Yriarte, C., 'Les restaurations de Saint-Marc de Venise', *Revue des deux mondes*, 1880, 827ff.

Zannier, I., *Venice: The Naya Collection*, Venice, 1981.

Zorzi, A.P., *Osservazioni intorno ai ristauri interni ed esterni della Basilica di San Marco*, Venice, 1877. Preface by John Ruskin.

Zorzi, Alvise, *Venezia scomparsa*, 2nd ed., 2 vols, Milan, 1977.

Zuliani, F., 'Considerazioni sul lessico architettonico della San Marco contariniana', *Arte Veneta*, 1975, 50–59.

I marmi di San Marco, n.p., n.d.

LIST OF ILLUSTRATIONS

Measurements are given in inches and centimetres, height before width.

COLOUR

I Mosaic of the Flood in the atrium of St. Mark's, 1982. Photo: author.

II John Ruskin. *South side of St. Mark's after rain*, 1846. Pencil, ink and watercolour. 16 × 11½ (40.6 × 29.2). Ashmolean Museum, Oxford.

III John Ruskin. *Detail of the south side of St. Mark's*, 1846. Pencil, ink and watercolour. 4½ × 4½ (11.4 × 11.4). Ruskin Galleries, Bembridge. Photo: John Webb.

IV Gentile Bellini. *Procession of the Cross in St. Mark's Square* (detail), 1496. Oil painting. Original image reproduced approx. 6½ ft × 12¾ ft (approx. 2 m × 4 m). Accademia, Venice.

V John Ruskin. *Northwest angle of the façade of St. Mark's*, 1852. Pencil and watercolour heightened with white. 37 × 24 (94 × 61). Tate Gallery, London.

VI First porch of St. Mark's from the west, 1982. Photo: author.

VII Window and spandrel of the second porch of St. Mark's, 1982. Photo: author.

VIII John Ruskin. *Southwest portico of St. Mark's from the loggia of the Doge's Palace*, probably 1849. Pencil and watercolour heightened with white. 37¾ × 17⅞ (95.9 × 45.4). Mr and Mrs Evelyn Joll.

IX John Ruskin. *Study of a zigzag capital of the southwest portico (St. M. Book)*, 1850. Pencil, ink and watercolour. 4½ × 6 (11.4 × 15.2). Ruskin Galleries,

Bembridge. Photo: John Webb.

X South façade of St. Mark's, 1982. Photo: author.

XI J.W. Bunney. *The west front of St. Mark's*, 1877–82. Oil on canvas. 57 × 89 (144.8 × 226.1). The Guild of St. George. Photo: John Webb.

XII West and south walls of the Treasury of St. Mark's, 1982. Photo: author.

XIII Old marbles framed by nineteenth-century replacements on the north side of St. Mark's, 1982. Photo: author.

XIV Looking east from the south nave aisle, beside the Baptistery door, 1982. Photo: author.

XV North arcade of the nave from the south nave aisle near the Baptistery door, 1982. Photo: author.

XVI Mosaic of King David in the south nave aisle, 1982. Photo: author.

XVII Looking over the screen into the eastern dome, 1982. Photo: author.

XVIII The central dome and part of the eastern dome, 1982. Photo: author.

XIX The interior from south of the west central door, 1982. Photo: author.

XX Mosaic of the martyrdom of St. James, 1982. Photo: author.

XXI Parapet of the north nave gallery and mosaic of Paradise from the south nave gallery, 1982. Photo: author.

XXII John Ruskin. *Study of part of the north arcade of the nave* (Worksheet 21), 1849. Pencil, ink and watercolour. 12 × 7⅜ (30.5 × 18.7). Ruskin Galleries, Bembridge. Photo: John Webb.

XXIII John Ruskin. *Study of a ram capital in the north arcade of the nave*, 1849–52. Pencil, ink and wash on paper, mounted on cardboard. $4\frac{1}{4} \times 3$ (10.8 × 7.6). Ruskin Galleries, Bembridge. Photo: John Webb.

XXIV John Ruskin. *Details of the lunette over the Porta di San Giovanni* (*Gothic Book*), 1850. Pencil, ink and watercolour. $7\frac{3}{4} \times 4\frac{3}{4}$ (19.7 × 12.1). Ruskin Galleries, Bembridge. Photo: John Webb.

XXV Mosaic of Christ's Temptation and Entry into Jerusalem, 1982. Photo: author.

XXVI Mosaic of the Doge and his People, 1982. Photo: author.

XXVII John Ruskin. *Study of mosaic of the Doge and his People*, 1877. Pencil, ink and watercolour. $14\frac{1}{8} \times 19\frac{5}{8}$ (35.9 × 49.8). Ashmolean Museum, Oxford.

XXVIII Mosaics of the eastern dome, 1982. Photo: author.

XXIX T.M. Rooke. *Mosaics of the eastern dome of St. Mark's*, 1879. Watercolour. $14\frac{7}{8} \times 19\frac{5}{8}$ (37.8 × 49.8). The Guild of St. George. Photo: John Webb.

XXX Detail of mosaic of the eastern cupola of the Baptistery, 1982. Photo: author.

XXXI John Ruskin. *Northwest portico and part of the first porch of St. Mark's*, 1877. Pencil and watercolour heightened with white. $25\frac{1}{2} \times 30\frac{1}{4}$ (64.8 × 76.8). The Education Trust, Brantwood. Photo: Graham Edwards.

XXXII Mosaic of Salomé in the Baptistery, 1982. Photo: author.

XXXIII Mosaic, spandrel and columns of the first porch, 1982. Photo: author.

XXXIV John Ruskin. *Carved boss from the face of the outer central arch of St. Mark's*, 1877. Pencil and watercolour heightened with white. 6×5 (15.2 × 12.7). The Guild of St. George. On long-term loan to the Sheffield City Art Galleries.

XXXV John Ruskin. *The Pillars of Acre and southwest portico of St. Mark's* (reversed image), 1879. Pencil and watercolour heightened with white on purple paper. $6 \times 3\frac{1}{2}$ (15.2 × 8.9). British Museum, London.

XXXVI J.W. Bunney. *The northwest portico of St. Mark's*, 1870. Watercolour. $46\frac{1}{2} \times 27\frac{1}{2}$ (118.1 × 69.9). The Guild of St. George. Photo: John Webb.

XXXVII H.R. Newman. *The horses of St. Mark's from the north*, 1890. Watercolour. $26\frac{1}{8} \times 17\frac{1}{8}$ (66.4 × 43.5). Hirschl and

Adler Galleries (New York), courtesy of Stuart Feld.

XXXVIII John Ruskin. *Copy of part of the drawing of the northwest portico of St. Mark's made in 1877*, 1879. Pencil and watercolour heightened with white. $15 \times 10\frac{1}{8}$ (38.1 × 25.7). Fogg Art Museum, Harvard University.

MONOCHROME

1 The northwest angle of St. Mark's (reversed image), probably 1852. Daguerreotype probably by John Ruskin and/or John Hobbs. $6 \times 4\frac{3}{8}$ (15.2 × 11.1). Ruskin Galleries, Bembridge. Photo: W.L.C. Baker.

2 St. Mark's from the west during the rebuilding of the north side, 1860–64. Photo: C. Ponti. Gernsheim Collection, University of Texas (Austin).

3 Sculpture of the upper arches of St. Mark's. Photo: Böhm.

4 Central doorway of St. Mark's. Photo: Courtauld Institute of Art.

5 Two of the horses of St. Mark's, c. 1880. From Boito (ed.), *La basilica di San Marco*, 'Dettagli di altari, monumenti, scultura ecc.', 1883. Photo: John Webb.

6 Unknown artist. *The west front of St. Mark's* (detail of engraving in Samuel Rogers' *Italy*), c. 1830. Original image reproduced approx. $\frac{3}{4} \times \frac{3}{4}$ (1.9 × 1.9). Photo: author.

7 John Ruskin. *St. Mark's from the southwest*, 1835. Ink and pencil, $6\frac{1}{2} \times 9\frac{1}{2}$ (16.5 × 24.1). The Education Trust, Brantwood.

8 John Ruskin. *St Mark's from the southwest*, 1835. Pencil. $11\frac{3}{16} \times 13\frac{1}{8}$ (28.4 × 33.3). Smith College Museum of Art.

9 St. Mark's from the southwest, 1982. Photo: author.

10 After J.M.W. Turner (engraved by G. Hollis). *St. Mark's Place, Venice – Juliet and her nurse* (detail), 1842. Original image reproduced approx. 4×5 (10.2 × 12.7). Yale Centre for British Art.

11 John Ruskin. *Courtyard of the Doge's Palace*, 1841. Pencil, ink and watercolour. $13\frac{3}{4} \times 18\frac{1}{2}$ (34.9 × 47.0). Ashmolean Museum, Oxford.

12 Southwest portico of St. Mark's from

the west, 1845–52. Daguerreotype possibly by Ruskin and/or John Hobbs. 6 × 4⅜ (15.2 × 11.1). Ruskin Galleries, Bembridge. Photo: W.L.C. Baker.

13 South wall of the Treasury of St. Mark's (reversed image), 1845–52. Daguerreotype possibly by Ruskin and/or John Hobbs. 4⅜ × 6 (11.1 × 15.2). Ruskin Galleries, Bembridge. Photo: W.L.C. Baker.

14 Antonio Canaletto. *Piazza San Marco from the Piazzetta* (detail), 1726–28. Oil on canvas. Original image reproduced approx. 67 × 30 (170.2 × 76.2). Reproduced by Gracious Permission of Her Majesty the Queen.

15 John Ruskin. *Details of south side of St. Mark's* (fig. 6 is from one of the Pillars of Acre), 1846. Pencil, ink and watercolour. 5½ × 7 (14.0 × 17.8). Ruskin Galleries, Bembridge. Photo: John Webb.

16 Southwest portico of St. Mark's from the loggia of the Doge's Palace (reversed image), 1845–49. Daguerreotype possibly by Ruskin and/or John Hobbs. 6 × 4⅜ (15.2 × 11.1). Ruskin Galleries, Bembridge. Photo: A.C. Cooper.

17 Mosaic of the Drunkenness of Noah in the atrium of St. Mark's. Photo: author.

18 John Ruskin. *Sculptured ball from the face of the outer central arch of St. Mark's.* Etching from Plate I of *The Seven Lamps of Architecture*, 1849. Photo: author.

19 John Ruskin. *Spandrel from a panel under the pulpit of St. Mark's* (reversed image). Etching from Plate XII of *The Seven Lamps of Architecture*, 1849. Photo: author.

20 The west front of St. Mark's, 1845 or 1852. Daguerreotype possibly by Ruskin and/or John Hobbs. 4⅜ × 6 (11.1 × 15.2). Ruskin Galleries, Bembridge. Photo: W.L.C. Baker.

21 John Ruskin. *Study of bases in the nave of St. Mark's* (Worksheet 20), 1849. Pencil and ink. 13¾ × 9½ (35.0 × 24.1). Ruskin Galleries, Bembridge. Photo: John Webb.

22 John Ruskin. *Study of the moulding of the central door of St. Mark's* (Bit Book), 1850–52. Pencil, with ink inscription. 7½ × 4¾ (19.1 × 12.1). Ruskin Galleries, Bembridge. Photo: John Webb.

23 John Ruskin. *Plan of the moulding of the central door of St. Mark's*, 1852–53. Ink and wash on cardboard. 6¾ × 2 (17.1 × 5.1), irregular. Ruskin Galleries, Bembridge. Photo: John Webb.

24 John Ruskin. *Plan of the moulding of the central door of St. Mark's*. From *The Stones of Venice III*, 1853.

25 St. Mark's from the west, 1860–65. Photo: C. Ponti. Gernsheim Collection, University of Texas (Austin).

26–27 John Ruskin. *Leaf analogies to porches of St. Mark's*, 1851–52. Marginal sketches in MS. 'Stones of Venice II. Ch. 4, Add.' Pierpont Morgan Library, New York.

28 Atrium of St. Mark's, 1860–65. Photo: C. Ponti. Gernsheim Collection, University of Texas (Austin).

29 St. Mark's from the northwest, 1860–65. Photo: C. Ponti. Gernsheim Collection, University of Texas (Austin).

30 The northwest portico and part of first porch of St. Mark's, 1860–75. Photograph owned by Ruskin. Wellesley College Library.

31 John Ruskin. *Profile of the frame moulding of the Second Plinth* (Worksheet 129), 1849–50. Ink. 1½ × 7½ (3.8 × 19). See ill. 87. Ruskin Galleries, Bembridge. Photo: John Webb.

32 John Ruskin. *Profile of the moulding linking the Second Plinth and the wall.* From Plate X of *The Stones of Venice I*, 1851.

33 The Great Plinth in the fifth porch, 1982. Photo: author.

34 The Great Plinth and the Ice Plinth in the fifth porch from below, 1980. Photo: author.

35 John Ruskin. *Floral moulding at the base of the Great Plinth* (St. M. Book), 1850. Pencil and ink. 4¾ × 7⅞ (12.1 × 19.4). Ruskin Galleries, Bembridge. Photo: John Webb.

36 John Ruskin. *Profile and elevation of two mouldings at St. Mark's*. Engraving from *The Stones of Venice I*, 1851.

37 John Ruskin. *Study of a lobed capital at St. Mark's*, 1849–52. Pencil, ink and watercolour. 2¼ × 2¾ (5.7 × 7.0). Victoria and Albert Museum, London. Photo: John Webb.

38 The northwest portico of St. Mark's

from the northeast, 1982. Photo: author.

39 John Ruskin. *Sixth-century capital in the atrium of St. Mark's*, 1849–52. Pencil and watercolour. $5\frac{13}{16} \times 6\frac{1}{2}$ (14.8 × 16.5). Fogg Art Museum, Harvard University.

40–41 John Ruskin. *Studies in archivolt decoration: the dentil*. From *The Stones of Venice I*, 1851.

42 The northwest angle, 1982. Photo: author.

43 John Ruskin. *Plan of the northwest portico and northern side of the first porch*, 1850. Ink and wash. $5 \times 8\frac{1}{4}$ (12.7 × 21.0). Ruskin Galleries, Bembridge. Photo: John Webb.

44 John Ruskin. *Study of the lily capital of the northwest angle* (Worksheet 170), 1850. Pencil, ink and watercolour. $11\frac{1}{2} \times 9\frac{3}{8}$ (29.2 × 23.8). Ruskin Galleries, Bembridge. Photo: John Webb.

45 John Ruskin (engraved by R. P. Cuff). *Details of the lily capitals of St. Mark's*. From *Examples of the Architecture of Venice*, 1851.

46 John Ruskin. *Profile lines of the lily capitals of St. Mark's*. From *The Stones of Venice II*, 1853.

47 John Ruskin (engraved by J.H. Le Keux). *Lily capital of the northwest angle of St. Mark's*. From *The Stones of Venice II*, 1853.

48 Grotesque figure on the northwest angle of St. Mark's, *c.* 1880. From Boito (ed.), *La basilica di San Marco*, 'Dettagli di altari, monumenti, scultura ecc.', 1883. Photo: John Webb.

49 John Ruskin. *Bird capital of St. Mark's*, 1851–52. Ink and pencil drawing for engraving in Plate VIII of *The Stones of Venice II*, 1853. 1×1 (2.5 × 2.5). Ruskin Galleries, Bembridge. Photo: John Webb.

50 Relief of peacocks in the northwest portico of St. Mark's. Photo: C. Naya/Böhm.

51 John Ruskin. *Study of relations of bases, abaci and shafts of the south side of the first porch* (Worksheet 166), 1850. Ink and pencil. $14 \times 10\frac{1}{2}$ (35.6 × 26.7). Ruskin Galleries, Bembridge. Photo: John Webb.

52 John Ruskin. *Prophet in the left spandrel of the inner arch of the first porch*, 1850–52. Pencil. $5\frac{5}{8} \times 4\frac{1}{4}$ (14.3 × 10.8). Ruskin

Galleries, Bembridge. Photo: John Webb.

53 John Ruskin. *Plan of double-spurred capitals*. From *The Stones of Venice I*, 1851.

54 Double-spurred capitals on the south side of the first porch, *c.* 1880. From Boito (ed.), *La basilica di San Marco*, 'Dettagli di altari, monumenti, scultura ecc.', 1883. Photo: John Webb.

55 The northern columns of the first porch, 1980. Photo: author.

56 The first and second porches of St. Mark's, 1860–75. Photograph owned by Ruskin. Wellesley College Library.

57 John Ruskin. *Plan of the first storey of the northern half of the second porch*, 1850. Ink and wash. $4\frac{7}{8} \times 5\frac{3}{8}$ (12.4 × 13.7). Ruskin Galleries, Bembridge. Photo: John Webb.

58 John Ruskin. *Section and details of left side of archivolt/spandrel of the window of the second porch* (St. M. Book), 1850. Ink and pencil. Ruskin Galleries, Bembridge. Photo: John Webb.

59 John Ruskin. *Archivolt/spandrel of the window of the second porch* (reversed image). From *The Stones of Venice II*, 1853.

60 John Ruskin. *Plan of the first storey of the northern half of the third porch*, 1850. Ink and wash with a pencil notation. $5 \times 8\frac{1}{4}$ (12.7 × 21.0). Ruskin Galleries, Bembridge. Photo: John Webb.

61 Second-storey columns between the third and fourth porches, 1980. Photo: author.

62 Third porch of St. Mark's, 1860–65. Photo: C. Ponti. Gernsheim Collection, University of Texas (Austin).

63 Upper columns and soffit of the second sculptured arch of the north side of the third porch, 1860–75. Photograph owned by Ruskin. Wellesley College Library.

64 John Ruskin. *Capital of the third porch*. From *Examples of the Architecture of Venice*, 1851.

65 Carvings on the face of the innermost arch of the third porch. Photo: Alinari.

66 Inner three arches of the third porch, 1860–75. Photograph owned by Ruskin. Wellesley College Library.

67 Capitals and carvings of the inner arches

of the third porch. Photo: Alinari.

68 Carvings on the soffit of the innermost arch of the third porch. Photo: Böhm.

69 Carvings on the face of the second decorated arch of the third porch. Photo: Böhm.

70 Face of the outer carved archivolt of the third porch, 1860–75. Photograph owned by Ruskin. Wellesley College Library.

71 March and April. Soffit of the second decorated arch of the third porch. Photo: Alinari.

72 July, August and the grapes of September. Soffit of the second decorated arch of the third porch. Photo: Alinari.

73 Carvings on the soffits of the innermost and second of the decorated arches of the third porch, 1860–75. Photograph placed by Ruskin in St. George's Museum. The Guild of St. George.

74–76 Details of the Trades Cycle on the soffit of the outer arch of the third porch. Photo: Alinari.

77 Bird and leafage from the face of the outer arch of the third porch. Photo: Böhm.

78 John Ruskin. *Plan of the north half of the fourth porch*, 1850. Ink and wash. 5 × 6 (12.7 × 15.2). Ruskin Galleries, Bembridge. Photo: John Webb.

79 The fourth and fifth porches, *c.* 1875. Photograph owned by Ruskin. Wellesley College Library.

80 Rough plan of the first storey of the fifth porch and southwest portico.

81 John Ruskin. *Superimposition of shafts of the south side of the fifth porch (St. M. Book)*, 1850. Ink and pencil. Entire opening $9\frac{1}{2} \times 7\frac{5}{8}$ (24.1 × 19.4). Ruskin Galleries, Bembridge. Photo: John Webb. Additions to photographic image made by the author.

82 John Ruskin. *Inner arch and columns of the fifth porch*. Probably engraved *c.* 1852. From W.G. Collingwood (ed.), *Studies in Both Arts: Being Ten Subjects Drawn and Described by John Ruskin*, 1895.

83 Inner arch of the fifth porch, 1849–52. Daguerreotype probably by Ruskin and/or John Hobbs. $6 \times 4\frac{3}{8}$ (15.2 × 11.1). Ruskin Galleries, Bembridge. Photo: W. L. C. Baker.

84 John Ruskin. *Study of the inner arch of the fifth porch (Worksheet 162)*, 1850. Ink and pencil. $13\frac{1}{2} \times 9\frac{3}{4}$ (34.3 × 24.8), irregular. Ruskin Galleries, Bembridge. Photo: John Webb.

85 John Ruskin. *Study of the profile of the members (from capital to top of Great Plinth) sustaining the right side of the inner arch of the fifth porch (St. M. Book)*, 1850. Ink and pencil. $7\frac{5}{8} \times 9\frac{1}{2}$ (19.4 × 24.1). Ruskin Galleries, Bembridge. Photo: John Webb.

86 John Ruskin. *Study of the leaf moulding of the inner arch of the fifth porch (St. M. Book)*, 1850. Ink and pencil. Entire opening $7\frac{5}{8} \times 9\frac{1}{2}$ (19.4 × 24.1). Ruskin Galleries, Bembridge. Photo: John Webb.

87 John Ruskin. *Study of the disposition of bases and pavement of the southwest portico before its rebuilding (Worksheet 129)*, 1849–50. Ink, pencil and wash. $3 \times 8\frac{1}{2}$ (7.6 × 21.6). Sheet includes ill. 31. Ruskin Galleries, Bembridge. Photo: John Webb.

88 John Ruskin. *The southwest portico of St. Mark's*. From *Examples of the Architecture of Venice*, 1851.

89 Part of the southwest portico, 1982. Photo: author.

90 John Ruskin. *Study of the southwest portico from the east*, 1849–52. Reproduced from a print at the Ruskin Galleries, Bembridge.

91 The southwest portico from the southeast, 1982. Photo: author.

92 The southwest portico from the east, 1982. Photo: author.

93 St. Christopher; north façade. Photo: Alinari.

94 John Ruskin. *Study of a capital on the north façade of St. Mark's*, 1849–52. Ink and watercolour. $5\frac{1}{4} \times 4\frac{1}{4}$ (13.3 × 10.8). Ruskin Galleries, Bembridge. Photo: John Webb.

95 Alexander the Great; north façade. Photo: Alinari.

96 John Ruskin. *Mouldings of the northeast tabernacle (St. M. Book)*, 1850. Ink and pencil. $4 \times 4\frac{3}{4}$ (10.2 × 12.1). Ruskin Galleries, Bembridge. Photo: John Webb.

97 Northeast tabernacle of the upper storey, 1982. Photo: author.

98 John Ruskin. *Details of the northeast tabernacle* (*St. M. Book*), 1850. Ink and pencil. Entire opening $7\frac{5}{8} \times 9\frac{1}{2}$ (19.4 × 24.1). Ruskin Galleries, Bembridge. Photo: John Webb.

99 The Ship Captain's Companion (see p. 126); north façade, 1982. Photo: author.

100 Upper part of the south façade before restoration, 1860–65. Photo: C. Ponti. Gernsheim Collection, University of Texas (Austin).

101 The south side of St. Mark's before restoration, before 1865. Photograph owned by Ruskin. Wellesley College Library.

102 The Baptistery, looking northwest, 1860–65. Photo: C. Ponti. Gernsheim Collection, University of Texas (Austin).

103 John Ruskin. *Sketch plan of St. Mark's,* 1849–52. $3\frac{1}{2} \times 4$ (8.9 × 10.2), irregular. Ruskin Galleries, Bembridge. Photo: John Webb.

104 Angel at the southeast of the crossing under the Ascension dome. Photo: Böhm.

105 John Ruskin. *Study of vegetation as depicted in several mosaics at St. Mark's,* 1849–52. Ink and watercolour. 12 × 7 (30.5 × 17.8), irregular. Fogg Art Museum, Harvard University.

106 Capital (a modern copy) of the Loggetta at the base of the campanile of St. Mark, Venice. Photo: author.

107 John Ruskin. *Ram capital of the nave of St. Mark's,* 1849–52. Pencil and watercolour. $4\frac{1}{2} \times 4$ (11.4 × 10.2). South London Art Gallery.

108 John Ruskin. *Details of a ram capital,* 1849–52 (see colour ill. xxiii). Pencil and watercolour. Top figure $2 \times 2\frac{5}{8}$ (5.1 × 6.7), bottom figure $1\frac{1}{2} \times 2\frac{1}{8}$ (3.8 × 5.4). Ruskin Galleries, Bembridge. Photo: John Webb.

109 John Ruskin. *Study of chiaroscuro of Corinthian capital in the nave: instructions for engraving,* 1850–52. Pencil and wash. $5\frac{1}{2} \times 3$ (14.0 × 7.6), irregular. Ruskin Galleries, Bembridge. Photo: John Webb.

110 Panel on the north gallery of the nave. Photo: Böhm.

111 John Ruskin. *Capital in the Baptistery of St. Mark's,* 1849–52. Pencil, ink and watercolour. $3\frac{1}{4} \times 3\frac{1}{2}$ (8.3 × 8.9). Victoria and Albert Museum, London. Photo: John Webb.

112 John Ruskin. *Study of a capital in the transept of St. Mark's,* 1851–52. Drawing in ink, pencil and watercolour for engraving in Plate VIII of *The Stones of Venice II,* 1853. 1 × 1 (2.5 × 2.5). Ruskin Galleries, Bembridge. Photo: John Webb.

113 Capital of the screen of St. Mark's. Photo: author.

114 Angle spur of a base in the Baptistery. Photo: author.

115 Lunette over the Porta di San Giovanni. Photo: author.

116 John Ruskin. *Angel in the left spandrel of the Porta di San Giovanni* (*Gothic Book*), 1850. Pencil, ink and watercolour. Image reproduced $7\frac{3}{4} \times 5\frac{3}{4}$ (19.7 × 14.6). Ruskin Galleries, Bembridge. Photo: John Webb.

117 John Ruskin. *Apex of the lunette over the Porta di San Giovanni* (fragment of Worksheet 118), 1850. Pencil and watercolour. $8\frac{1}{4} \times 8$ (21.0 × 20.3). Ruskin Galleries, Bembridge. Photo: John Webb.

118 Tomb of Doge Soranzo in the Baptistery: John the Baptist. Photo: Böhm.

119 Tomb of Doge Soranzo in the Baptistery: a Bishop. Photo: author.

120 Tomb of St. Isidore. Photo: Alinari.

121 Tomb of St. Isidore: the Martyrdom of the Saint. Photo: Böhm.

122 Doge Andrea Dandolo, detail of his Tomb. Photo: author.

123 Tomb of Doge Andrea Dandolo. Photo: Böhm.

124 Bas-reliefs on the north façade of St. Mark's. Photo: author.

125 Bas-relief on the west front: St. George. Photo: Böhm.

126 John Ruskin. *Shafts, capitals and Ice Plinth between the second and third porches,* 1876. Watercolour. $5\frac{1}{4} \times 8\frac{3}{4}$ (13.3 × 22.2). From a plate in vol. 10 of *The Works of John Ruskin,* ed. Cook and Wedderburn. Photo: John Webb.

127 The Porta dei Fiori (north façade) before restoration, before 1864. Photo: C. Ponti. Gernsheim Collection, University of Texas (Austin).

128 Marble incrustation on the north façade of St. Mark's, 1982. Photo: author.

INDEX

Notes are listed by chapter and number
(n6.27,30,31). Illustration numbers are
given in *italic* (for monochrome) and
ROMAN NUMERALS (for colour).

AESCHYLUS 58
Albinoni, T. n1.5
Alessandri, A. 207, 209, n9.14
Alexander, F. 207, n4.53, n9.9
Allen, G. 203
Arnheim, R. n2.6
Arona 169
Athens: Erechtheum 180, n7.26;
  Parthenon 93, 185

BAYEUX: cathedral 122
Beauvais: cathedral 148
Bellini, Gentile IV, 14, 20, 21, 72, 97,
  101, 199, n1.15
Berchet, F. 205, n8.1,5,69
Birch, D. n7.25,28
Birren, F. n6.40
Boni, G. 207, n8.62
Boyce, G.P. n6.42
Bozza, B. 152
Brown, Rawdon 104, n4.31, n6.12, n8.12
Bunney, J.W. XI, XXXVI, 8, 68, 114, 198,
  208, 209
Burd, V.A. n7.46
Burne-Jones, G. 206
Burton, S. n8.4,54
Byron, G.G. 14

CAINE, T.H. n8.59
Canaletto, A. 14, 20, 21, 66, n1.16,17
Carpaccio, V. 72, 181
Chartres: cathedral 171
Cimabue 171, 180, n7.28
Clegg, J. n1.9,12, n2.4, n4.45, n7.5,7,16,
  n8.5, n9.1,11,14
Conner, P. n7.11
Constantinople 70, 122, n7.14; marbles
  from 195, n1.5; St Polyeuktos 82, 87,
  n8.61.
Cook, E.T. 187, n1.19
Crichton, G.H. 103, n4.29,35,36,42, n6.4
Cuff, R.P. 32

DAGUERREOTYPE 1, 12, 13, 16, 20, 83,
  20–1, 25, 28, 29, 75, 82, 86, 91, 113,

114, 116, 203–4, n1.14,25, n4.54,56,
n8.60
Dandolo, Doge A. 189; tomb of 122,
  123, 166; n6.32
Dante Alighieri n6.27
Dawes, W. ('Elijer Goff') 191, 203
Dearden, J.S. 8, n1.29
Deichmann, F.W. 82, 87, 149, 159, n1.3,
  n2.9, n3.6, n4.6,7,15,22,26,27,
  n5.1,11,14, n6.24,25, n8.61,69
Demus, O. 13, 59, 103–5, 107, 121, 173,
  185, 188, 191, n1.11, n2.10,12,
  n4.8,9,13,33,34,38,39,41,43, n5.2,5,
  n6.20,28, n7.10,14,20,27,29,32,34,
  35,37–9,44
Dostoyevsky, F.M. 194
Drake, G. n7.25

EZEKIEL 178

FAUNTHORPE, J.P. n9.18
Fitch, R.E. n7.25
Forlati, F. 191, n4.4, n8.3,39,68,69

GIOTTO 180
Goldner, G. 124, n5.8,9
Grabar, A. n6.21

HANSON, B. n1.14
Harley, G. n7.48
Hayman, J. n4.2, n6.39
Helps, A. 7, n.pref. 1
Helsinger, E. n7.25
Hewison, R. n1.18,26, n7.5,18, n8.60,
  n9.15
Hilton, T. n1.34
Homer 180
Hope, T. n1.22

JUNG, C.G. 179

KINGSLEY, C. n7.48
Knight, H.G. 16
Kreutz, J. n7.17, n9.13

LAMBERTI, N. 125
Landow, G. n7.25
Landseer, E. 156
La Touche, Rose 188–9
Leighton, S. 202

Le Keux, J.H. 32, 49, n1.36,37
Lindsay, A. 26, n7.11
Links, J.G. n1.23, n4.56
London: Bermondsey 126; Whitelands
    Training College 209
Longhena, B. n1.11
Lucca: San Michele n2.10

MARANGONI, L. n3.9, n4.3,4, n8.69
Marks, N. 198
Mathew, G. n7.9
Meduna, G.B. (and his 'restorations') 51,
    110–12, 114–19, 126, 191–202, 209,
    n4.58, n8.1,5,66
Mestre n1.4
Milan: cathedral 122, n5.8
Montecassino (illum. MSS. from) 182,
    n7.31
Morris, William 196–9, 203–4
Murano: San Donato 70, 146, 155
Murray, C.F. 177, 206, n7.17,19

NEWMAN, H.R. XXXVII; 8, 209, n9.19,20
Norton, C.E. 174, 206, 210
Norwich, J.J. n1.5, n7.16

OLANDER, K. n9.23
Oswestry: church 202
Oxford: meeting at 197, 200, 202

PARIS: Saint-Denis n4.33
Peschlow, U. n8.22
Phidias 181
Pieri, M. n1.4, n6.38
Pindar 58
Pisa: cathedral n2.10
Pope, A. 58
Proust, M. 60
Pullen, H.W. n1.4, n6.6,37

REMBRANDT 59
Renan, E. n7.24
Rio, A.F. n7.11
Robotti, C. n8.14,25
Rogers, S. 14
Rooke, T.M. XXIX, 207–8; n7.19
Royal Institute of British Architects 171,
    n8.56
Ruskin, Effie 29
RUSKIN, JOHN: care in observing,
    measuring 7, 19–25, 30–32, 55, 60,
    113–14, n2.5; anticipates later
    scholarship 58, 59, 70, 103–5, 122,
    173, 180, 185, n2.6, 10, n4.33, n5.5,8,

n7.9,20,29; careless in youth 14–16,
n1.8; and later when preaching
instead of looking 13, 30, 149, n1.5;
scholarly bent troubles his father 25;
n1.34; abandons many data on St.
Mark's 30, 50, 145, 152–3; at work
29, 60, 186–87; n1.26,29, n2.15;
attachment to material things 60,189,
n7.51; delights in mediaeval
irregularity, asymmetry 51–9, 66,
95–6, 159; hates 'pontifical rigidities'
of engineering mind 51, 55; and
hence 19th-c. restoration of St.
Mark's 119, 176, 182, 192, 194, n5.13;
which he helps stop 7, 78, 191–4,
202–5; despite 'jobbery' of architects
192, 202, 204, n8.56. Bigoted in 1850s
174, n7.12; religious longing,
uncertainty of 1870s 171, 174,
178–80, n7.21; develops mythological
approach to mosaics 179–82,
n7.25,28; asserts spiritual oneness of
ancient Greek, Byzantine art 180–1.
Has fantasies of power in St. Mark's
176–7; symbolic bond with St.
Mark's during 1878 breakdown 189;
'Mr. Ruskin's Illness Described by
Himself' a hoax? n7.48; erotic fantasy
of 1888 209, n9.23. Bullies his readers
in 1870s 174–9; easily irritated 204,
n8.63; yet capable of oily diplomacy
193–4.
Drawings: 1835 beginnings 7, *8*, n1.8; of
1841 visit *11*; detailed studies begin
1845, aided by daguerreotypes 19–20;
'truth in mosaic' of 1846 studies II, III,
15, 23–5; 1849 etchings for *Seven
Lamps 18, 19, 27*; large drawings of
1849–52 aided by daguerreotypes V/*1*
& 75, n4.2, *82/83* & 113, VIII/*16* & 116,
n4.56; 1849–52 drawings reproduced
V, VIII, IX, XXII, XXIII, XXIV, *35, 37, 39,
45, 47, 49, 52, 59, 64, 82, 88, 90, 94,
105, 107–9, 111–12, 116–17*; drawings
of 1876–77 XXVII & 177, *126*, XXXI,
XXXIV & 186–88; 1879 Pillars of Acre
XXXV, 203–4; 1879 copy of NW
Portico XXXVIII, 206, 210.
Publications: *Modern Painters I* (3rd ed.
1846), on architectural drawing 20–1;
review of Ld Lindsay's *Sketches*
(1847) 26–7; *Seven Lamps* (1849)
27–8, 52–3, n1.24; *Examples of the
Architecture of Venice* (1851) 30, 32, 50,

238

75, 78, 113, n1.34; *Stones of Venice*
(1851–3): brilliant, also silly 13, 149,
n1.5; architectural matter sacrificed to
popular treatment 30, n1.34;
problems with engravings for 30–2,
49–50, 83, 92, n1.36, n4.10; R's later
dissatisfaction with 171, 178, 206,
n7.12; Preface to Zorzi's *Osservazioni*
(1877) 192–4; *St. Mark's Rest*
(1877–84) 104–7, 171, 174–86;
Circular Respecting Memorial Studies
(1879–80) 203, 207
Ruskin, John James 25, 30, 32, n1.7,34,
n2.8
'Ruskinian' approach to Ruskin 13

SACCARDO, P. 198–99, 207, 209,
n8.1,46,66,68
St. George, Company (later Guild) and
Museum of 101, 107, 176–7, 209,
n4.31, n7.18
ST. MARK'S, Venice (*see table of contents
for subjects with specific locations*):
Chiaroscuro: of offset shafts 12, 59, 186,
210, n2.12, *126*, XXXI; of caps from
distance 66–8; of base moulding 63;
of Great Plinth 64; of cornice 66; of
dentils 72; of sculpture/gold mosaic in
bas-reliefs 74; of caps and plinth
116–17, 186; interior 'labyrinthine
darkness' 145; of aisle/gallery scheme
147; interior, 'Rembrandtesque'
n6.42; disregard of, in mosaics 173;
extremes in, defeat photography 170;
of bas-reliefs 26, 72–3; of bosses, caps
27, 97, 117, 156, 159.
Colour: & greatness of St. Mark's 51, 150,
168; cannot be reproduced 84, 93,
170, 208; of exterior, like Rembrandt
& Veronese united 59; gradation &
mystery of, inside 150, 168–70;
splendour of mosaic 127, 208;
treatment/mistreatment of marble &
195, 199, n8.16; as painted by Bellini
20; Canaletto 20, 21, n1.17; J. W.
Bunney XI, XXXVI, 208–9; H.R.
Newman XXXVII, 209; T.M. Rooke
XXIX, 208; effect of 19th-c.
'restoration' on XI, XIII, 127, 191–2,
194–5, n5.13; effect of 19th-c.
lampblack on interior n6.42; & 20th-
c. pollution 59–60, 93, 97, 107.
Irregularity/asymmetry: In large-scale
composition 51–9, 84, 90, 94, 98, 107,

112, 114, *51, 81*; causes perceptual
binding 55, 59, n2.6; 'corrected' by
Meduna 54, 114, 191, 201, n2.3. *In
detail* 23, 27–8, 69, 73, 83, 150, 159.
Lighting: & present colour of W shafts
93, n2.14; effects of unevenness of,
inside 168–70, n6.41; falseness of
photos taken under artificial 166, 168,
n6.32, 41.
Marble: (1) *Incrustation* 72, 149–50, n3.9;
& character of sculpture 26, 72, 87,
93, 162; ancient setting of veins in
150, 195–6, n6.6; gradation in colour
of alabaster 168; contrast between
ancient & 19th-c. XI, XIII, 128, 191–2,
195, n5.13; faked 19, n1.12; sold to
foreigners 192, n8.10. (2) *Shafts*
dominant consideration in design
56–7; of alabaster 9, 12, 93–4, 153,
168, n1.4; effects of scrape on 195;
effects of pollution on 59–60, 94, 107,
n1.4.
Mosaics: I, XVI–XXI, XXV–XXX, XXXII,
XXXIII, *17*; main refs 150–2, 171–83;
scoffed at by previous writers n7.11;
and by H. Taine 175, 182, n7.15; R's
admiration for 26, 173, 179; as part of
architecture 150–2; and colour of
interior 169–70, 208; part of one vast
ikon 172–3; images of timeless
spiritual presence 173, 182; & ancient
Greek art 180–2; & Byzantine
'mythic' manner 175, 178; influence
on later Venetian art 181, n7.29;
Renaissance & later 13, 152; foully
restored 176, 182–3, n8.68.
Mouldings: R's care in studying 49–50;
Canaletto's false rendering of 66;
dentil 64, 71–2; base 63; of Gothic
tabernacles 122–3; sensitive
adaptation of interior 158–9; R's
studies reproduced *22–4, 35, 58, 85,
86, 96, 98*.
Pollution & its effects: 7, 8, 59–60, 68, 82,
93, 94, 107, n1.4, n6.42, n8.69.
Rebuilding & restoration: 7, 19, 54, 84,
110–19, 127, 191–205, n4.3,4, n5.13,
n8.1–69.
Sculpture: (1) *Architectural* 73; subordinate
to dominant forms 27; influence of
incrustation on 72; adapted to
viewing distance 66–8, 87, 117,
157–8, 159; asymmetry/irregularity in
28, 64, 66, 69, 73, 83, 97, 159; R's

early attempts to depict *7, 8,* 16;
Canaletto's daubings of *14,* 21; R
dissatisfied with engravers' depiction
of 32, 49; capitals drawn by R IX,
XXIII, *37, 39, 44–7, 49, 64, 94, 107–9,
111, 112, 126*; more distant views in V,
VIII, XXXI, XXXVIII; Byzantine caps
compared with Gothic 68, 159–60;
with Renaissance 154–5; gilding of
caps 97, 155; spandrels/archivolts over
doors/windows 73–4, 86–7, 91–3,
113–14, 160–2; of arches of 3rd porch
98–107; Byzantine, of 3rd porch,
compared with Lombardic 101, 103;
Gothic & classical influence in 3rd
porch 102–7; Gothic, of tabernacles,
upper arches 10, 13, 122–6. (2) *Inlaid
panels* 73, 82–3, 121–2, 183–6. (3)
Gothic tombs 162–6, n6.29–32.
Comparisons: of W front with proto-
Renaissance façades of Pisa, Lucca 58,
n2.10; of interior with extremes of
'ponderous & slender', 'highly
decorated & perfectly plain',
architecture 148
Sansovino, J. 154
Scott, W. 200, n8.54
Selvo, Doge D. 180, 189
Severn, J. 175, 196, n9.22
Sheffield: St. George's Museum 176, 209
Soranzo, Doge G.: tomb of 162–3
Society for the Protection of Ancient
Buildings (SPAB) 196–202, 209,
n8.66
Spence, M. n7.18
Spenser, E. 102
Stevenson, J.J. 199, 200, 202
Strauss, D.F. n7.24
Street, G.E. 110, 171, 200–2

Taine, H. 175, 182, n7.15
Talbot, Mrs. F., & Q. 207, n9.10

Tintoretto, J. 19, 189, n7.29
Titian 19, 189, n7.29
Tolstoy, L. 60
Torcello: cathedral 146, n6.12
Trollope, T.A., on Ruskin's
measurements n2.5
Turner, J.M.W. *10,* 16
Tweedie, Mrs. A. n7.48
Tyrwhitt, R. St. J. n7.37

Venice: 'Fall' of 14, 26; annihilation of,
imminent 128; 'point of pause'
between opposing traditions 148;
Arsenal 188; Campanile 9, 10, n8.62;
Doge's Palace 16, 154, 207, n11.18;
Casa Falier n3.5; Fondaco dei Turchi
204, n8.1, 16; Hotel Danieli n11.12; St.
Mark's *see* St. Mark's
Venturi, A. n7.38
Verona: cathedral carvings 101
Veronese, P. 59, n4.2
Viljoen, H. n7.48,50
Viollet-le-Duc, E. 51, n8.5
Vivaldi, A. n11.5
Vivarini (family of painters) 175

Wallis, H. n8.66
Weinberg, G. n9.28
Wightwick, G. 51
Wölfflin, H. n6.32
Wolters, W. 7, n4.8,9,13,14,21,30,33,44,
n5.3–7,10, n6.30,31, n7.34,36,n8.69
Wragge-Morley, C. n7.51, n9.21

Yeats, W.B. 180
Yriarte, C. n8.16

Zorzi, Count A.P. 78, 110, 192–6, 203,
205, 206, n8.6,10,13,17,26, n9.24
Zorzi, Alvise n11.9, n8.16,25,62
Zuliani, F. n4.3,4, n6.21, n8.1